Ars Celebrandi

SERVING THE MYSTERY OF
CHRIST IN THE EUCHARIST

Reverend Gerald Dennis Gill

Our Sunday Visitor
Huntington, Indiana

Nihil Obstat
Msgr. Michael Heintz, Ph.D.
Censor Librorum

Imprimatur
✠ Kevin C. Rhoades
Bishop of Fort Wayne-South Bend
May 28, 2024

The *Nihil Obstat* and *Imprimatur* are official declarations that a book is free from doctrinal or moral error. It is not implied that those who have granted the *Nihil Obstat* and *Imprimatur* agree with the contents, opinions, or statements expressed.

29 28 27 26 25 24   1 2 3 4 5 6 7 8 9

Our Sunday Visitor Publishing Division
Our Sunday Visitor, Inc.
200 Noll Plaza
Huntington, IN 46750
www.osv.com
1-800-348-2440

ISBN: 978-1-63966-208-1 (Inventory No. T2900)
1. RELIGION—Christian Rituals & Practice—Worship & Liturgy.
2. RELIGION—Christian Rituals & Practice—Sacraments.
3. RELIGION—Christianity—Catholic.
eISBN: 978-1-63966-209-8
LCCN: 2024943362

Cover and interior design: Amanda Falk
Cover art: Pitu Cau / Alamy Stock Photo

Printed in the United States of America

Ars Celebrandi

To Reverend Monsignor John J. Miller,
a priest of the Archdiocese of Philadelphia
(1937–2017)

Contents

Preface

The Lord Jesus instructs his disciples with particular detail as to how they are to prepare to eat his final Passover:

> On the first day of the Feast of Unleavened Bread, when they sacrificed the Passover lamb, his disciples said to him, "Where do you want us to go and prepare for you to eat the Passover?" He sent two of his disciples and said to them, "Go into the city and a man will meet you, carrying a jar of water. Follow him. Wherever he enters, say to the master of the house, 'The Teacher says, "Where is my guest room where I may eat the Passover with my disciples?' Then he will show you a large upper room furnished and ready. Make the preparations for us there." The disciples then went off, entered the city, and found it just as he had told them; and they prepared the Passover. (Mark 14:12–16)

By the time of Jesus, the Jewish Passover knew a structure and form carefully outlined by the Hebrew Scriptures and refined through the previous centuries. Yet the New Testament includes a significant conversation between Jesus and his disciples about the preparations for the meal that would give enduring shape to the divine Passover of his Paschal Mystery in the celebration of the Eucharist. The Lord's final Passover meal was to take place in "a large upper room furnished and ready." In this room, the disciples followed through on the Lord's mandate to make the preparations.

From New Testament times to the present, descriptions and directions abound for how Christians are to celebrate the Eucharist. At different times in the history of the Christian Eucharist, these same descriptions and directions moved between more and less elaborate detail. The current edition of the *General Instruction of the Roman Missal*, the latest in this series of descriptions and directions, aims "to offer general lines for a suitable ordering of the celebration of the Eucharist"[1] for our own time. This book recognizes the historical and practical value of the ordering of the Eucharist for Christians throughout the centuries up to the present day. However, with high regard for the liturgical and theological assistance of such an ordering through descriptions and directions for the celebration of the Eucharist, this book infuses the contemporary preparations for the divine Passover of Christ's Paschal Mystery with *a new focus for a greater purpose*.

This new focus is the *ars celebrandi*: an artful and careful celebration of the Eucharist, which is the best way to ensure the active and fruitful liturgical participation of the ordained and baptized.[2] *Ars celebrandi*, a rather recent term to define such participation, is the fruit of a faithful engagement of the descriptions and directions for the Eucharist that allows for a living encounter with the Mystery of Christ being celebrated. *Ars celebrandi* is a skill. This skill seeks to let Christ be the Artist so that our participation becomes a sharing in what he does in the Eucharist. We become sharers in his action, in his prayer, in his offering. We enter into the eternal self-offering of Jesus, the new Sacrificial Lamb, so long ago prepared for by the disciples in that "large upper room furnished and ready."

The greater purpose of *ars celebrandi* is to carry out all that is required for the celebration of the Eucharist to achieve a genuine communion with Christ and all the members of his Body, to glorify God, and to share in the holiness of God. This communion gives deeper meaning to the structure of the liturgical celebration and its many elements and parts. In this way the artful and careful celebration of the Eucharist promotes a greater correspondence between the celebration of Christ's Mystery and the living of the Christian life.

Who will benefit from this book?

The enduring value of *Sacrosanctum Concilium* (Constitution on the Sacred Liturgy), promulgated on December 4, 1963, which inaugurated the most comprehensive reform of the ordering of the Eucharistic celebration in its history, will not be found in the revisions to the Order of Mass it proposed, or even in the liturgical or theological reasons supporting the revisions. Rather, its enduring value will be an increasingly more mature and true participation in the Eucharist on the part of those in holy orders and the baptized, with a real impact on living out the Mystery celebrated.

This book will not only be informational about the *ars celebrandi* but will also invite and challenge the ordained and all the baptized to a new and important responsibility for it. Many learn how to celebrate the Eucharist by "watching." A studied *ars celebrandi* takes someone inside the actual celebration. Those in holy orders will benefit from this book by gaining a greater understanding of and clarity on how to translate the current descriptions and directions for the Eucharist into an artful and careful celebration. In addition, it will highlight the unique role of the ordained oriented to the baptized through the lens of the *ars celebrandi* for the bishop, the priest, and the Deacon. The baptized will benefit from this book as well: It will explain the gestures and postures, as well as the texts and parts proper to the faithful, to underscore their full meaning and foster a more immediate encounter with the divine event of the Eucharist. The *ars celebrandi* is expected of every member of the Church and thus serves to imbue the ordained and all the baptized more thoroughly with the spirit and power of the Liturgy.

How is this book organized?

The *ars celebrandi* is presented in this book as a complement to the continued reception of the English translation of the third edition of the *Roman Missal* now in use in the United States since Advent 2011. The book consists of two main parts. The first part, "*Ars celebrandi*: Some Necessary Contexts," consists of three chapters, which present the *ars celebrandi* as 1) a type of liturgical theology and 2) a pathway to authentic liturgical participation, with the addition of 3) some general considerations. *Ars celebrandi* as a type of liturgical theology recognizes that the actual celebration of the Sacred Liturgy is a primary form of revelation, of God presently speaking and acting. *Ars celebrandi* as a pathway to authentic liturgical participation leads those celebrating to fully engage in the divine event of our redemption in the Sacred Liturgy. Some general considerations of the *ars celebrandi* include a presentation of the proper place for the celebration of the Eucharist and fitting furniture and items needed for the celebration.

The second part of the book, "*Ars celebrandi*: An Artful and Careful Celebration of the Eucharist," consists of seven chapters. The first looks at the various forms for the celebration of Mass.

The following six chapters look at each part of the Order of Mass in terms of an *ars celebrandi*, against the backdrop of the material in Part One of the book. These chapters present the *ars celebrandi* for the Introductory Rites, the Liturgy of the Word, and the Liturgy of the Eucharist in each of its distinct parts (namely, the Preparation of the Gifts, the Eucharistic Prayer, the Communion Rite), and finally the Concluding Rites. The *General Instruction of the Roman Missal* and the Order of Mass from the *Roman Missal* provide the principal content for the second part of the book, with these current directions given for the celebration of the Eucharist, and as the principal guide for the *ars celebrandi*. Each chapter first presents the elements for the part of the Mass discussed and follows with how these elements are artfully and carefully celebrated with each form of the Mass. These chapters demonstrate how the *ars celebrandi* allows for greater communion with the Mystery unfolding and for a deeper understanding of the meaning of the rite.

The book concludes with a re-echoing of the pastoral need for the *ars celebrandi* in the celebration of the Eucharist and its compelling force to deepen faith in and understanding of the Mystery of Christ.

How can this book be used?

There are three principal ways this book can be used, among many others. First, this book is both a liturgical and theological work. The *ars celebrandi* for the Eucharist displays the relationship of the order for its celebration with the faith of the Church in this Mystery. The structure of the Mass, with its many elements and parts, is presented in terms of the liturgical celebration. This liturgical celebration manifests the Church's understanding of the role of the ordained and the baptized in the Eucharist, the manifold presences of Christ in the Eucharist, and the Eucharist as the font and apex of the Christian life.

Second, this book is a pastoral guide for the ordained to develop the skill of an artful and careful celebration of the Eucharist. A recovered regard for liturgical norms allows those in holy orders to be more consistently in the service of the Mystery celebrated and in the service of the genuine participation of the baptized.

Third, this book is a formative aid to the baptized to ensure that their participation in the celebration of the Eucharist is in concert with the ordained. This guidance for their full participation leads to a more profound encounter with Christ's Paschal action in the Eucharist.

What is unique about this book?

A book like this has not yet been written in English. It provides for and anticipates the need to surround the celebration of the Eucharist, for the ordained and baptized, with a new sense of reverence and prayer, of communion with Christ and his Body. Such a serious, simple, and beautiful celebration occasions a profound conversation with God and God with us, a faith-filled announcement of the Word and the words of the Eucharist, a deeper understanding of its integrated structure, and an openness to the indispensable source of a holy Christian life. This book promises to make more available truly beautiful celebrations of the Mystery of Christ, celebrations that reveal this heavenly reality in an earthly setting.

Introduction

In the first article of the *General Instruction of the Roman Missal* (GIRM), which belongs to the front matter of the third typical edition of the *Roman Missal*, we read:

> As Christ the Lord was about to celebrate with the disciples the paschal supper in which he instituted the Sacrifice of his Body and Blood, he commanded that a large, furnished upper room be prepared (Lk 22:12). Indeed, the Church has always judged that this command also applied to herself whenever she decided about things related to the disposition of people's minds, and of places, rites, and texts for the Celebration of the Most Holy Eucharist. The present norms, too, prescribed in keeping with the will of the Second Vatican Council, together with the new Missal with which the Church of the Roman Rite will henceforth celebrate the Mass, are again a demonstration of this same solicitude of the Church, of her faith and her unaltered love for the supreme mystery

> of the Eucharist, and also attest to her continuous and consistent tradition, even though certain new elements have been introduced. (1)

This recollection of the Lord's instruction to the disciples to prepare in a particular way for his Paschal supper underscores the Church's duty to provide similar instructions for the celebration of Mass — the celebration of the same Paschal supper for every time. These instructions go beyond "a large, furnished upper room" to "the disposition of people's minds ... places, rites and texts for the Celebration of the Most Holy Eucharist." This book, looking at the topic of the *ars celebrandi* and its application to the celebration of Mass, recognizes the value of the present norms found in the *General Instruction* and the liturgical and theological connection with the Lord's own instruction for the first Paschal supper. Likewise, the attentiveness of the Church in directing the celebration of the Eucharist, her abiding faith in the divine event that occurs with the Eucharist, and "her unaltered love for the supreme mystery of the Eucharist," underscore every aspect of the presentation of the *ars celebrandi* in this book.

As the third edition of the *Roman Missal*, which builds on its two antecedent editions following the Second Vatican Council, continues to express and shape the faith and life of the Church, the character, quality, and authenticity of the celebration of the Mass deserve regular attention and reflection on the part of all who celebrate it — the ordained and all the baptized. This is the overarching significance of the *ars celebrandi*: With its focus on the saving Mystery of Christ in the Eucharist, it allows for an unambiguous proclamation of the Faith and a greater communion with this same Mystery.

Discussion of the *ars celebrandi* and published works on the topic will increase in the years ahead. These works bring to a new level the important contribution of the ancient *Ordines Romani* and the more recent ceremonial guides for the Roman Mass over the last century. This work and new works on the *ars celebrandi* require an already firmly established value for the ordo of celebration, as well as the directions, instructions, and rubrics found in the liturgical books. The *ars celebrandi* promotes a celebration funded by the spirit and power of the Liturgy and so fosters in those celebrating a compelling love of Christ with hearts set on fire: "From the liturgy, therefore, and especially from the Eucharist, as from a font, grace is poured forth upon us; and the sanctification of men in Christ and the glorification of God, to which all other activities of the Church are directed as toward their end, is achieved in the most efficacious possible way."[1]

With the *ars celebrandi*, the artful and careful celebration of the Eucharist, every effort is made, even in minor matters, to observe what is required to ensure a "noble simplicity" combined with dignity (see GIRM 351).

PART ONE

Ars Celebrandi: Some Necessary Contexts

Part one presents a necessary context for the *ars celebrandi* and the actual celebration of Mass. A simple and straightforward observance of the rubrics for the Eucharist does not necessarily allow for or promote an artful and careful celebration. A grasp and understanding of several fundamental liturgical, theological, and practical dimensions of the celebration are in order for a more complete application of the *ars celebrandi* to the celebration.

Chapter one provides a clear description of the *ars celebrandi* and the Sacred Liturgy, demonstrating how their relationship offers a type of liturgical theology. This liturgical theology requires the stable relationship in the celebration itself between those ordained and those baptized. Chapter two presents the relationship of the *ars celebrandi* and liturgical participation as well as how those in holy orders and the baptized uniquely participate. Several elements in the celebration of the Eucharist are also discussed as contributing to liturgical participation. Chapter three looks at many of the practical and physical parts of the celebration and how their proper use fosters the *ars celebrandi.*

Every aspect of the Mass, even before the celebration begins, has a role in the promotion of the *ars celebrandi* that accompanies the here and now event of the Mystery of Christ. This is not only in an overall way, for every celebration, but also for every member of the clergy and all the faithful. Understanding what we do, why we do it, how we do it, and what we use to do it, as the Church keeps the Last Supper commandment of the Lord, "Do this in memory of me," forms the prerequisite standard for an effective and serious *ars celebrandi* in the course of the celebration of the Eucharist.

In this first part of the book, which provides the larger context for the *ars celebrandi* during the celebration of Mass, both the bishop and priest are considered equally as the celebrant. In the second part of the book, which makes use of the *General*

Instruction of the Roman Missal and the *Order of Mass* for a presentation of the *ars celebrandi*, the priest is considered as the celebrant. The bishop is referenced as the celebrant only when he is specifically identified in either of these sources.

CHAPTER ONE
A Type of Liturgical Theology

Ars celebrandi has become an often-used slogan with several possible meanings. It does have a precise meaning, however, especially for its use in this book. This meaning moves beyond observable ways to carry out the celebration of the Eucharist. In fact, for its correct application, *ars celebrandi* requires a clear notion of the Sacred Liturgy as articulated in recent magisterial documents as part of its precise meaning. Only with both terms (*ars celebrandi* and *the Liturgy*) clearly described is it possible to present the *ars celebrandi* as a path with theological meaning — a type of liturgical theology. Again, with both terms clearly described and uniquely related, the liturgical and theological importance of stability to the order for celebrating the Eucharist and the relationship between the ordained and the baptized are more apparent.

Ars celebrandi

The term *ars celebrandi*, although only recently noted in magisterial and other texts on the Sacred Liturgy, has an antecedent in the more ancient concept of the *ordo agendi*. This concept implies that the order or directions for carrying out — for doing — the Sacred Liturgy manifests the faith of the Church in the arrangement of the rite. The *Catechism of the Catholic Church* brings forward in more contemporary language this same concept, describing the work of the Holy Spirit in the Liturgy: "By means of the words, actions, and symbols that form the structure of a celebration, the Spirit puts both the faithful and the ministers into a living relationship with Christ, the Word and Image of the Father, so that they can live out the meaning of what they hear, contemplate, and do in the celebration."[1]

The order or arrangement of the various parts of the celebration of the Sacred Liturgy, in this instance the Eucharist, is not arbitrary or only the product of historical development. Rather, its very order or arrangement and how it is observed, the *ordo agendi,* is the inspired and guided work of the Holy Spirit. In some way, it is a participation in how God reveals himself to us in the Liturgy. Likewise, the various parts — "the words, actions, and symbols" — that form the order or arrangement or, as the *Catechism* states, "the structure" of the celebration not only participate in how God makes himself known but also allow those who participate to enter into the Mystery of Christ that the Liturgy celebrates. From this encounter with the Mystery of Christ, those who participate can live out in their Christian lives what occurs in the celebration.

Thus, the *ordo agendi,* which as a concept predates the more modern concept of the *ars celebrandi*, underscores the theological value to the structure of the celebration and grounds the need for the celebration to be carried out in an artful and careful way. The *ars celebrandi* goes further and assists all who celebrate the rites authentically both to engage them properly, as received from the Church and her tradition, and also to live out without ambiguity the Mystery celebrated.

The term *ars celebrandi* is best translated as "the art of celebrating." The translation of the term alone is insufficient to grasp its meaning with reference to the celebration of the Liturgy. The *ars*, the art, is the more important part of the phrase. Art here is more than nuance or style. This is too subjective and horizontal. The starting point in capturing the meaning of *art* in this phrase is to consider the artist. The artist is Christ. The celebration is the divine event, the Mystery of Christ, his Paschal Mystery. Thus, the primary way of understanding *art* in the phrase always has Christ in his saving death and resurrection as its reference point. All those celebrating, then, with due regard for the *ordo agendi* (the structure of the celebration with its various elements), celebrate with a faith-filled focus on the Mystery. This faith-filled focus translates into the manner of celebration — into an artful, careful manner.

This artful way of celebrating is much more than a mere observance of the rubrics in the *Roman Missal*. While the rubrics are necessary guides for the celebration and can assist with an understanding of the rites and how they are carried out, to merely follow the rubrics runs the risk of a robotic or pastorally vacuous celebration. At the center of the celebration of the Eucharist, as with every celebration of the Sacred Liturgy, is the worship of God the Father, through the Paschal Mystery of his Son, with the Holy Spirit, in association with all the members of the Church. It is the Mystery of Christ that worships the Father. The ordained and all the baptized sacramentally belong to the same Mystery in unique ways, uniting them with Christ in this act of worship. The *ars celebrandi*, the artful and careful celebration of the Eucharist, looks at every part of the celebration through the lens of the Mystery of Christ, and how the manner of celebration then points to this same Mystery in the actual celebration for all who celebrate.

The *ars celebrandi* requires three things: a thorough knowledge and grasp of the rites in all their parts, the skill to carry out the rites with practical competence, and a humble faith in the service of the Mystery of Christ. Throughout this book, the rites of the Eucharist will be presented as described and directed by the *General Instruction of the Roman Missal* along with the *Order of Mass*. Again, the aim of the *General Instruction* is to guide the ordering of the celebration of the Eucharist and to establish the norms by which the forms of the celebration are arranged (see GIRM 21). The *General Instruction* becomes a key source for a knowledge and understanding of the rites of the Eucharist. This knowledge and understanding combines with a familiarity with the rites, the experience with their celebrated form, and a truly pastoral approach to the celebration. A truly pastoral approach celebrates the rites in terms of the truth of their meaning as intended by the Church for the celebration of the Mystery of Christ, and not in terms of an imposed or diluted meaning. Finally, knowledge and understanding along with practical competence require a disposition of humble faith. This is a willingness to be a believing servant of the divine event, the unfolding of the saving death and resurrection of the Lord in our midst, which is especially true in the case of the bishop or priest celebrant. At the time of the Second Vatican Council (1962–65), with the advent of the reform of time-honored rites, and again in the current *General Instruction*, the following reminder highlights this humble servant disposition of the celebrant for an authentic *ars celebrandi*: "The Priest will remember that he is the servant of the sacred Liturgy and that he himself is not permitted, on his own initiative, to add, to remove, or to change anything in the celebration of Mass."[2] The *ars celebrandi* demands a thorough knowledge of the *General Instruction*.

The bishop and the priest have an overarching responsibility for the artful and careful celebration of the Eucharist — to be its servant. However, the responsibility belongs as well to all the baptized, to the whole liturgical assembly. As will be seen later in this chapter, in the Mass there are proper duties and ministries that belong specifically to the ordained and to the baptized. The editions of the *Roman Missal* subsequent to the Second Vatican Council differ from their predecessors in both the instructions that prefaced them and the outline of the *Order of Mass*. In those previous editions very little, if any, attention was given to the role the baptized would carry out in the course of the celebration, except perhaps for the reception of Holy Communion. In most instances their role would have been substituted by those serving the Mass. With the *General Instruction* and *Order of Mass* in the modern editions of the *Roman Missal*, there is the expectation that the baptized understand the rites, can carry them out, and enter into the worship of the Father that is taking place with the celebration of the Mystery of his Son. So, the baptized as well should not be overlooked as to their shared responsibility to do what is proper to them in an informed and careful manner. Throughout this book, both the ordained and all the baptized will be considered for their contribution to the *ars celebrandi* with the celebration of the Eucharist.

In the final article of the most recent edition of the *General Instruction*, which introduces the current third edition of the *Roman Missal*, a point is made that suggests an immediate and ongoing significance of the *ars celebrandi*: "And so, the *Roman Missal*, though in a diversity of languages and with some variety of customs, must in the future be safeguarded as an instrument and an outstanding sign of the integrity and unity of the Roman Rite" (GIRM 399). The ritual book itself is indeed an instrument for the *ordo agendi*, the structure with its many elements, of the Eucharist. However, the manner of the doing, a manner rooted in the instructions for the celebration but with a focus on the faith in the Mystery celebrated, is what allows this instrument to be "an outstanding sign of the integrity and unity of the Roman Rite." The *ars celebrandi* gives a universal aspect to the celebration of the Mass as it intentionally expresses the single faith of the Church and allows this same faith to be carried out in a way that is beautiful — that is, in an artful and careful way.

Additionally, a conscious application of the *ars celebrandi* underscores the values of justice and charity with regard to the celebration of the Sacred Liturgy. When the bishop or priest celebrant approaches the Sacred Mysteries along with the baptized as to approach Christ and his action for and with the Church, the generous gift of salvation and redemption for all overrides any personal or particular imposition over the celebration or, and even worse, a capricious rearranging of the very structure. The celebration of the Eucharist with this just approach on the part of all allows for God to continue to accomplish the work of redemption through the rites that we all equally receive from the Church. Such a just approach leads to a remarkable charity where, from the pope to the poorest of the poor, everyone enjoys the same access to an authentic celebration of the Sacred Mysteries.

A clear notion of the Liturgy

At the time of the Second Vatican Council, after decades of serious study of the Liturgy, combined with similar intense studies of the Scriptures and the Church Fathers, *Sacrosanctum concilium* (the Constitution on the Sacred Liturgy) offered a concluding, concise description of the nature and purpose of the Liturgy:

> To accomplish so great a work, Christ is always present in His Church, especially in her liturgical celebrations. He is present in the sacrifice of the Mass, not only in the

> person of His minister, "the same now offering, through the ministry of priests, who formerly offered himself on the cross," but especially under the Eucharistic species. By His power He is present in the sacraments, so that when a man baptizes it is really Christ Himself who baptizes. He is present in His word, since it is He Himself who speaks when the holy scriptures are read in the Church. He is present, lastly, when the Church prays and sings, for He promised: "Where two or three are gathered together in my name, there am I in the midst of them" (Mt 18:20).
>
> Christ indeed always associates the Church with Himself in this great work wherein God is perfectly glorified and men are sanctified. The Church is His beloved Bride who calls to her Lord, and through Him offers worship to the Eternal Father.
>
> Rightly, then, the liturgy is considered as an exercise of the priestly office of Jesus Christ. In the liturgy the sanctification of the man is signified by signs perceptible to the senses, and is effected in a way which corresponds with each of these signs; in the liturgy the whole public worship is performed by the Mystical Body of Jesus Christ, that is, by the Head and His members.
>
> From this it follows that every liturgical celebration, because it is an action of Christ the priest and of His Body which is the Church, is a sacred action surpassing all others; no other action of the Church can equal its efficacy by the same title and to the same degree.[3]

Note that article seven begins by stating, "To accomplish so great a work." This *work* is the Paschal work of Christ, a work that is present in the Church, present in the celebration of the Liturgy — in every liturgical celebration, in all the sacraments. In fact, borrowing from Tradition, article seven recalls the words of Saint Augustine, who identifies Christ as the worker. In this divine work, this Paschal work, this liturgical event, Christ is not working or acting alone. Christ cannot but act with the members of his Body, all those who belong to him as Head of his Body, made so by the Paschal work of his death and resurrection. Jesus' work in offering his life on the cross and rising from the dead perfectly glorifies his Father and shares the holiness of the Father with all who belong to him as members of his Body.

With this prelude description of the work, the text of *Sacrosanctum concilium* continues by defining the Liturgy as an "exercise of the priestly office of Jesus Christ." The Liturgy is the Christ event of the cross and resurrection as the Savior achieves the fullness of his priesthood. Precisely because the Liturgy is an action of Christ, and not an action of Christ alone but acting with his Body, no other act or work of the Church can be its equal.

This clear description of the nature and purpose of the Sacred Liturgy comes forward with the Second Vatican Council, not only as a result of study and reflection characteristic of the liturgical movement that preceded it, but more forcefully from the Church's prayer. The First Eucharistic Prayer, the Roman Canon, for centuries the lone Canon of the Mass, prays and instructs:

> Therefore, O Lord,
> as we celebrate the memorial of the blessed Passion,
> the Resurrection from the dead,
> and the glorious Ascension into heaven
> of Christ, your Son, our Lord,
> we, your servants and your holy people,
> offer to your glorious majesty
> from the gifts that you have given us,

this pure victim,
this holy victim,
this spotless victim,
the holy Bread of eternal life
and the Chalice of everlasting salvation.[4]

The Eucharist is the remembering and making present of the Paschal work of the Lord. The Roman Canon prays in the present tense: The priest and people — "we, your servants and your holy people" — now make the offering that is the "exercise of the priestly office of Jesus Christ." Each of the ten Eucharistic Prayers in the current, third edition of the *Roman Missal*, which includes those published in the first edition of the *Roman Missal* subsequent to the Council and those since added, imitate the Roman Canon with a similar anamnesis — a living memorial — and at times even more precisely (see GIRM 79e). The Sacred Liturgy, and in this instance the Eucharist, is the actual divine event of the saving death and resurrection of Christ.

Earlier in chapter one, in the description of the Liturgy, *Sacrosanctum concilium* quotes a Secret Prayer from the 1570 *Missale Romanum* that has also found its way into the *Roman Missals* published since the Second Vatican Council. The prayer is called "secret" because it was prayed quietly by the priest celebrant. This prayer, now titled "Prayer over the Offerings," is currently prayed on the Second Sunday in Ordinary Time and at the Evening Mass of the Lord's Supper:

Grant us, O Lord, we pray,
that we may participate worthily in these mysteries,
for whenever the memorial of this sacrifice is celebrated
the work of our redemption is accomplished.
Through Christ our Lord.[5]

This oration announces in the moment prior to the Eucharistic Prayer (and like the First Eucharistic Prayer itself) that "the work of our redemption is accomplished," the Paschal work of Christ which is the Liturgy. This oration is one of countless examples in the *Roman Missal* in which the clear notion of the Sacred Liturgy as articulated in *Sacrosanctum concilium* has a foundation in the prayers of the celebration itself, and especially in the divine event that occurs with the Eucharistic Prayer.

The *Catechism* brilliantly summarizes the prayers of the *Roman Missal* and the first paragraphs of *Sacrosanctum concilium* in its succinct presentation of what the Liturgy is:

> In the liturgy of the Church, it is principally his own Paschal mystery that Christ signifies and makes present. During his earthly life Jesus announced his Paschal mystery by his teaching and anticipated it by his actions. When his Hour comes, he lives out the unique event of history which does not pass away: Jesus dies, is buried, rises from the dead, and is seated at the right hand of the Father "once for all." His Paschal mystery is a real event that occurred in our history, but it is unique: all other historical events happen once, and then they pass away, swallowed up in the past. The Paschal mystery of Christ, by contrast, cannot remain only in the past, because by his death he destroyed death, and all that Christ is — all that he did and suffered for all men — participates in the divine eternity, and so transcends all times while being made present in them all. The event of the Cross and Resurrection *abides* and draws everything toward life. (1085)

The *ars celebrandi* derives its purpose and necessary role in the celebration of the Sacred Liturgy precisely because "his Paschal mystery is a real event that ... participates in the divine eternity." This unambiguous understanding of the Liturgy, the Mystery of Christ as it actually occurs in the celebration, this clear notion of the Liturgy, is manifested and communicated with greater clarity and brilliance when the rites are carried out in an artful and careful manner by all who celebrate.

Ars celebrandi as a Type of Liturgical Theology

Liturgical theology takes many forms. Essentially, there are three forms that can be easily described. Perhaps the most common form is to reflect on parts of the liturgical celebration — prayers and rites — and then from these parts disclose what actually takes place in the celebration of the Sacred Liturgy. Another form, more common during the period following the Council of Trent and the presentations on the Faith consequent to that Council, is to look to the celebration — its prayers and rites — to affirm an article of Faith and support a teaching of the Church. Today, the form of liturgical theology that continues to mature in significance, and one more prevalent since the Second Vatican Council, is to come to a knowledge and understanding of the Sacred Liturgy by what actually happens in the celebration. In the celebration of the Sacred Liturgy, the divine event of the Mystery of Christ, God continues to act in our here and now. This action is the source for theology — a primary source. This type of liturgical theology allows for the revelation of God — as God is worshiped — to bring forward from the source itself what God wants us to know about him and us as the Liturgy takes place.

The *ars celebrandi*, with its focus the Mystery of Christ in the actual celebration and the artful and careful celebration of this same Mystery, occasions an engagement of the divine action in the Liturgy. The *ars celebrandi* reflects in the manner of celebration the essential source of theology, the liturgical action. In this way, the *ars celebrandi* is a type of liturgical theology. It likewise brings forward from the celebration of the Mystery itself a grasp and knowledge of it as we participate in it. To consider the *ars celebrandi* a type of liturgical theology, then, requires like all theologies that a discipline be maintained. This discipline includes a clear definition of the *ars celebrandi*, as described above, which is guided by a similarly clear notion of the Liturgy. As a type of liturgical theology, the *ars celebrandi* in the celebration of the Eucharist depends on the established stability of the order of the celebration and in the roles of those celebrating as directed by the *General Instruction* and the *Order of Mass*.

The stable order for the celebration of Mass

The *General Instruction* itself gives a description of the Mass in terms of what occurs as well as the presence of Christ in the celebration:

> At Mass or the Lord's Supper the People of God is called together, with a Priest presiding and acting in the person of Christ, to celebrate the memorial of the Lord or Eucharistic Sacrifice. In an outstanding way there applies to such a local gathering of the holy Church the promise of Christ: "Where two or three are gathered in my name, there am I in their midst" (Mt 18:20). For in the celebration of Mass, in which the Sacrifice of the Cross is perpetuated, Christ is really present in the very assembly gathered in his name, in the person of the minister, in his word, and indeed substantially and uninterruptedly under the Eucharistic species. (27)

This description assembles several key theological points that combine to explain the Eucharist. The first is that the assembly is convoked: "the People of God is called together." The Mystery of

Christ is eternal. As the *Catechism* indicates, in the celebration of the Sacred Liturgy, Christ, seated at the right hand of the Father, pours out the Holy Spirit on his Body and so acts through the signs he instituted (see 1084). This eternal event, this same event at the right hand of the Father, unfolds in the here and now when the priest and the people are assembled for "the memorial of the Lord or Eucharistic Sacrifice." The memorial of the Lord or the Eucharistic Sacrifice is further and more completely described as the event of the Cross actually taking place — it "is perpetuated." In this way, and because the Mass is the eternal event of the Mystery of Christ taking place in the here and now, Christ himself becomes really present in the here and now in the ways specifically outlined in the *General Instruction*, with the additional note that in the Eucharistic species, the presence is substantial and uninterrupted.

In another part of the *General Instruction*, the Mass is further described as "the center of the whole of Christian life for the Church both universal and local, as well as for each of the faithful individually" (GIRM 16). It is precisely "the center" because with the Mystery of Christ "is found the high point both of the action by which God sanctifies the world in Christ and of the worship that the human race offers to the Father, adoring him through Christ, the Son of God, in the Holy Spirit" (16). The Eucharist can be said to be many things, but it is primarily the worship of God.

As the worship of the Father in the saving Mystery of the Son with the Holy Spirit, this divine event requires an ordering with its logic rooted in Tradition and not in any capricious way. This ordering, or as stated above, this structure, ensures that the Father is adored in the Paschal action of Christ, as remembered and made present by the Holy Spirit (see CCC 1101). Thus, the *Order of Mass* consists of two main parts: the Liturgy of the Word and the Liturgy of the Eucharist. These parts are intrinsically connected, so as to combine as a single act of worship of God (see GIRM 28). Additionally, the typical *Order of Mass* includes the Introductory Rites and the Concluding Rites. On occasion either of these rites can be replaced by other liturgical actions.

This stable order for the celebration of Mass, properly observed, allows for the whole liturgical assembly, the ordained and the baptized, to enter into the actual Mystery of Christ as it takes place and to be sharers in the benefits that come from participation in this same Mystery:

> It is, therefore, of the greatest importance that the celebration of the Mass or the Lord's Supper be so ordered that the sacred ministers and the faithful taking part in it, according to the state proper to each, may draw from it more abundantly those fruits, to obtain which, Christ the Lord instituted the Eucharistic Sacrifice of his Body and Blood and entrusted it as the memorial of his Passion and Resurrection to the Church, his beloved Bride. (GIRM 17)

The *ars celebrandi* does not impose an order to the celebration of the Eucharist. Rather, it depends on the stability of this order as described in the *General Instruction* and provided by the *Order of Mass* in the *Roman Missal*. The Mass — its stable order for celebration, for the worship of Almighty God and for the graces that flow from it — receives greater focus and access when it is artfully and carefully celebrated.

The stable relationship among those celebrating Mass

Chapter three of the *General Instruction* outlines the duties and ministries of those celebrating Mass, the ordained and the baptized. The purpose of this outline is not simply to list responsibilities in the course of the celebration. Rather, as it falls between the chapter describing the elements of the celebration and the chapter describing the order of celebration, this chapter presents the theological relationship between the ordained and the baptized as the Eucharist takes place. This relationship in itself is a sacramental relationship, a sacramental arrangement which bespeaks the Eucharist as the action of the whole Christ, Head and members.

This action is deliberately "arrayed hierarchically" (16), from the stable orientation of the ordained to the baptized in their specific roles:

> The Celebration of the Eucharist is the action of Christ and of the Church, namely, of the holy people united and ordered under the Bishop. It therefore pertains to the whole Body of the Church, manifests it, and has its effect upon it. Indeed, it also affects the individual members of the Church in a different way, according to their different orders, functions, and actual participation. In this way, the Christian people, "a chosen race, a royal Priesthood, a holy nation, a people for his own possession," expresses its cohesion and its hierarchical ordering. All, therefore, whether ordained ministers or lay Christian faithful, in fulfilling their function or their duty, should carry out solely but totally that which pertains to them. (91)

Stability is the characteristic that identifies and manifests the relationship between the ordained, especially the bishop and the priest, and the baptized in the celebration of the Eucharist. Understanding who does what in each part of the Mass and its faithful observance ensures this stability so that the action of the Eucharist is rightfully engaged and understood as an action of

Christ and the Church. Inasmuch as the bishop is the sign of the High Priest in the local church with a responsibility to all the members of this church, priests and people, he has both the duty and authority to protect the stability of this relationship. Likewise, the ordained and the baptized must hold in high regard their unique roles in the celebration of the Sacred Liturgy, as it simultaneously manifests the Eucharist as the action of the whole Christ and continually forms the members of the Church in their proper roles.

Those in Holy Orders

In the celebration of the Eucharist, the bishop, priests, and Deacons — those in Holy Orders — are the signs of Christ the Head and carry out their duties in the person of Christ the Head, although in differing ways. The *General Instruction* succinctly presents the duties for each as they relate to one another, beginning with the bishop:

> Every legitimate Celebration of the Eucharist is directed by the Bishop, either in person or through Priests who are his helpers.
>
> When the Bishop is present at a Mass where the people are gathered, it is most fitting that he himself celebrate the Eucharist and associate Priests with himself in the sacred action as concelebrants. This is done not for the sake of adding outward solemnity to the rite, but to signify more vividly the mystery of the Church, "the sacrament of unity."
>
> If, on the other hand, the Bishop does not celebrate the Eucharist but has assigned it to someone else to do this, then it is appropriate that he should preside over the Liturgy of the Word, wearing the pectoral cross, stole, and cope over an alb, and that he should give the

> blessing at the end of Mass.
>
> A Priest, also, who possesses within the Church the sacred power of Orders to offer sacrifice in the person of Christ, presides by this fact over the faithful people gathered here and now, presides over their prayer, proclaims to them the message of salvation, associates the people with himself in the offering of sacrifice through Christ in the Holy Spirit to God the Father, and gives his brothers and sisters the Bread of eternal life and partakes of it with them. Therefore, when he celebrates the Eucharist, he must serve God and the people with dignity and humility, and by his bearing and by the way he pronounces the divine words he must convey to the faithful the living presence of Christ.
>
> After the Priest, the Deacon, in virtue of the sacred Ordination he has received, holds first place among those who minister in the celebration of the Eucharist. For the sacred Order of the Diaconate has been held in high honor in the Church even from the early time of the Apostles. At Mass the Deacon has his own part in proclaiming the Gospel, from time to time in preaching God's Word, in announcing the intentions of the Universal Prayer, in ministering to the Priest, in preparing the altar and in serving the celebration of the Sacrifice, in distributing the Eucharist to the faithful, especially under the species of wine, and from time to time in giving instructions regarding the people's gestures and posture. (92–94)

These three articles from the *General Instruction* should be considered as a single explanation of the duties of those in Holy Orders in the celebration of the Mass. What is said about the bishop leads into what is said about the priest, and what is said about the bishop and the priest leads into what is said about the

Deacon. There is a hierarchical arrangement here of those in Holy Orders, not so much in terms of a ranking, but in terms of relationship to the priesthood of Christ shared with the bishop, priests, and Deacons. The bishop, above all, as the principal icon of Christ, the Priest and head, in the local Church, has the unique responsibility to order and direct the celebration of the Eucharist. The apostolic and ecclesiological dimensions of this ordering and directing are clearly expressed in a fresh way in *Sacrosanctum concilium* and *Lumen gentium* (Dogmatic Constitution on the Church) of the Second Vatican Council.[6] The norms for the celebration of the Eucharist with regard to the bishop always have him in some way as the bishop celebrant or presiding, which manifests his duty to order and direct the celebration. Unfortunately, it is not a common practice for the bishop, when present but not as the bishop celebrant of the Mass, to be vested as described above in the *General Instruction*, but this practice should be given renewed consideration to emphasize his overarching relationship to the celebration of every Eucharist (see GIRM 92).

Additionally, it is the duty of the bishop to order and direct the celebration (whether he is present or not) for an artful and careful carrying out of the rites. This duty is further described in another section of the *General Instruction*:

> The Bishop should therefore be determined that the Priests, the Deacons, and the lay Christian faithful grasp ever more deeply the genuine significance of the rites and liturgical texts, and thereby be led to the active and fruitful celebration of the Eucharist. To that end, he should also be vigilant in ensuring that the dignity of these celebrations be enhanced and, in promoting such dignity, the beauty of the sacred place, of the music, and of art should contribute as greatly as possible. (22)

The "genuine significance of the rites" is revealed most fully when they are carried out with the disposition that allows these same rites — in all their elements — to be received as the Church intends in her instructions and in a manner marked by faith and reverence. Above all, the bishop is charged with ensuring that the significance of the rites is indeed grasped by all in the local Church. Giving priority to the beauty of all things — especially the place, the music, and the art — greatly aids in people's understanding of the rites. The bishop is not only the principal icon of Christ, the Priest and head, in the local Church. He is also the principal animator of the *ars celebrandi* in the local Church.

The priest, as with the bishop, with the power that comes with the Sacrament of Holy Orders, offers the Sacrifice of the Lord in the person of Christ. Again, the Second Vatican Council clearly articulates this point of faith in *Lumen gentium* and *Presbyterorum ordinis* (Decree on the Ministry and Life of Priests).[7] What is also presented at this point in the *General Instruction* are the duties of both the bishop and the priest throughout the course of the Eucharist as they celebrate and preside in the person of Christ. The bishop with his priests or the priest alone presides over those assembled for the Eucharist in their prayer, announces to them the word of salvation, joins them to himself in the Eucharistic Sacrifice, and gives them as well as himself the Body and Blood of the Lord. These chief duties, corresponding to the order of rites of the Mass, are all carried out as the actions of Christ through the bishop and the priest. This point gives particular force to the concluding sentence of this article, which bears repeating: "Therefore, when [the priest] celebrates the Eucharist, he must serve God and the people with dignity and humility, and by his bearing and by the way he pronounces the divine words he must convey to the faithful the living presence of Christ" (GIRM 93). This is the theological and liturgical foundation for the *ars celebrandi*. The actual manner of celebrating the Eucharist, on the part of the bishop and the priest, is a significant dimension of the manifestation of the Mystery celebrated in the Eucharist.

The Eucharist is a divine event. It is the complete expression of the Paschal Mystery of Christ — his saving death and resurrection. The Eucharist is the most excellent manifestation of this action of Jesus at the right hand of the Father in glory. This is the place of the perpetual Sacrifice of Christ which — through the action of the Holy Spirit, the cooperation of the priest and the faithful, and with the signs received from the Church — occurs in our time and in our midst with the Mass. Thus, when the bishop and the priest carry out their duties, they are in the service of God (who gives us the saving Mystery of his Son celebrated in the Liturgy), in the service of this same Mystery, and in the service of the people for whom the Mystery is given. This service, which is directed to the Lord and for the benefit of the faithful, requires an artfulness, a dignity that always indicates that the Mystery belongs to heaven and earth. This same service requires a humility, a bowing down before the Lord, because the Mystery is not of our own making but belongs completely to the power of God shared with us. Thus, the priest, like the bishop, in every celebration of Mass, mindful that his service to the Mystery of the Lord is to be dignified and humble, carries out his particular duties — what he does and what he says — with conviction that "he must convey to the faithful the living presence of Christ" (GIRM 93). This habitual disposition on the part of the bishop and the priest anchors their presidential role in the service of God and heaven's Mystery celebrated on earth.

The Deacon shares in the priesthood of Christ in his servant ministry and not in his sacerdotal ministry (see CCC 1570). As such, the Deacon is the first among all those who assist the bishop and the priest in the celebration of the Eucharist. And, imitating the duties of the Deacon from antiquity, he is an example and model for the participation of the baptized in the Mass with regard to gestures and postures. As will be noted in the following chapters, a Deacon has duties in the celebration of the Eucharist which are proper to his order. These include proclaiming the Gospel, declaring the intentions of the Universal Prayer, and assisting the bishop and the priest at the altar, especially with regard to the sacred vessels and the distribution of the Precious Blood.

The duties of those in Holy Orders — the bishop, the priest, and the Deacon — belong to them uniquely through the Sacrament of Holy Orders and fix their relationship to one another as sacred ministers and then to the baptized for the celebration of the Eucharist. Disregard for these proper duties and how they are ordered compromises the authentic presentation and celebration of the Mystery of Christ. When each of these sacred ministers carries out his respective duties, following the directions in the liturgical books, even when there is the possibility for one to carry out the duties of the other (such as a priest carrying out the duties of a Deacon), a stability is achieved in the communication of the Faith with the liturgical celebration. The stability of this relationship among those in Holy Orders is an important and expected dimension of the *ars celebrandi*.

Those among the baptized

"The People of God" ... "the faithful" ... "the baptized" — these are all ways to describe those associated with the bishop and the priest as the Sacrifice of Christ is offered with the Eucharist. The *General Instruction* identifies the baptized according to their primary duty in the celebration of the Eucharist as sharers in the priesthood of Christ. This is a true sharing but distinct from those in Holy Orders:

> In the celebration of Mass the faithful form a holy people, a people of God's own possession and a royal Priest-

> hood, so that they may give thanks to God and offer the unblemished sacrificial Victim not only by means of the hands of the Priest but also together with him and so that they may learn to offer their very selves. They should, moreover, take care to show this by their deep religious sense and their charity toward brothers and sisters who participate with them in the same celebration.
>
> They are consequently to avoid any appearance of singularity or division, keeping in mind that they have only one Father in heaven and that hence are all brothers or sisters one to the other. (95)

The *General Instruction* envisions a number of functions or ministries for the baptized to assume in the course of the celebration of the Eucharist. Before listing the possible ministries, however, it identifies the baptized as a people, forming one body as they listen to the word of God, engage in the prayers and singing, and most of all participate in the offering of the Sacrifice of Christ and the reception of Holy Communion (see GIRM 96). All of these actions of the baptized in the Eucharist become their right and duty as sharers in the common priesthood of Christ. The primary ministry of the baptized is to "give thanks to God and offer the unblemished sacrificial Victim" (95). They are united to the action of the priest as he offers the Sacrifice at his hands, which includes the offering of themselves. Every effort is to be made in the arrangement of the celebration of the Eucharist to ensure that the baptized are not unnecessarily divided from one another and that they have a sense of this communion in baptism with all the baptized assembled. This unity, as will be seen later, is especially assured when they observe gestures and postures in common (see 96).

With the reforms of the rites of the Mass subsequent to the Second Vatican Council, there has also been a reform of the functions and ministries now possible and normative among the baptized. Two of these call for special notice at this point: the ministry of the Instituted Acolyte and of the Instituted Reader (lector). The functions of these particular ministries respectively, as established in the 1972 decree *Ministeria quaedam*, are described in the *General Instruction*:

> The acolyte is instituted for service at the altar and to assist the Priest and Deacon. It is his place principally to prepare the altar and the sacred vessels and, if necessary, to distribute the Eucharist to the faithful as an extraordinary minister.
>
> In the ministry of the altar, the acolyte has his own proper functions, which he must carry out in person.
>
> The lector is instituted to proclaim the readings from Sacred Scripture, with the exception of the Gospel. He may also announce the intentions for the Universal Prayer and, in the absence of a psalmist, recite the Psalm between the readings.
>
> In the celebration of the Eucharist, the lector has his own proper function, which he himself must carry out. (98–99)

Prior to the establishment of these two instituted ministries in their current form in 1972, they belonged to the pattern of minor orders for those preparing for the Sacrament of Holy Orders. Their suppression as minor orders now allows for these particular ministries to have their own proper functions among the baptized in the celebration of the Mass. The insistence of the *General Instruction* on the point that both the instituted acolyte and the reader must carry out their proper functions is indicative that these particular ministries are normative. Unfortunately, the near universal practice that these instituted ministries continue to be for those preparing for Holy Orders has deprived the celebration of the Eucharist in most places of the service of these particular ministries. Nonetheless, the following chapters identify the proper functions of the instituted acolyte and reader in the course of the celebration of the Mass. The acolyte principally serves as needed by the bishop, priest, or Deacon and assists at the altar. The reader principally proclaims the word of God, except for the Gospel.

The instituted acolyte and reader allow for the baptized to carry out ministries that properly assist the bishop or the priest in his role of headship and at the same time assist all the baptized in their duty to participate in the same Eucharistic action. This need for assistance continues even when instituted acolytes and readers are not present, which is most often the situation. The *General Instruction* allows for other members of the faithful to be deputed to assist in the same way as the instituted acolyte and reader:

> In the absence of an instituted acolyte, there may be deputed lay ministers to serve at the altar and assist the Priest and the Deacon; these carry the cross, the candles, the thurible, the bread, the wine, and the water, or who are even deputed to distribute Holy Communion as extraordinary ministers.
>
> In the absence of an instituted lector, other lay people may be deputed to proclaim the readings from Sacred Scripture, people who are truly suited to carrying out this function and carefully prepared, so that by their hearing the readings from the sacred texts the faithful may conceive in their hearts a sweet and living affection for Sacred Scripture. (100–101)

When the baptized are deputed to carry out the functions of the acolyte and the reader, as with the instituted acolyte and reader, they do so to assist the bishop and the priest in their role of presiding over all the faithful assembled and aiding the participation of the body of the assembly in the Eucharist. In all cases, the instituted and deputed acolyte, as well as the instituted and deputed reader, must be truly suited to carry out their functions with a genuine understanding and thorough preparation for their respective ministries. This point, combined with the knowledge of how to carry out their liturgical roles, ensures and maintains an artful and careful observance of the rites of the Mass on the part of the liturgical ministers. The proper training and formation of liturgical ministers in the *ars celebrandi,* associated with their functions, contributes significantly to an overall reverent and beautiful celebration of the Mystery of Christ in the Eucharist.

In addition to the functions of an acolyte and a reader, the *General Instruction* lists two other types of functions that should be typical in the celebration of the Eucharist. The first pertains to what is needed to sing the Eucharist (more will be said about this in subsequent chapters), and the second to what may be needed for good order and hospitality.

The *General Instruction* identifies four liturgical music ministries. These are the psalmist, the *schola cantorum* or choir, the organist, and the cantor or choir director:

> It is the psalmist's place to sing the Psalm or other biblical canticle to be found between the readings. To carry out this function correctly, it is necessary for the psalmist to be accomplished in the art of singing Psalms and have a facility in public speaking and elocution.
>
> Among the faithful, the *schola cantorum* or choir exercises its own liturgical function, its place being to take care that the parts proper to it, in keeping with the different genres of chant, are properly carried out and to foster the active participation of the faithful by means of

> the singing. What is said about the *schola cantorum* also applies, with due regard for the relevant norms, to other musicians, and especially the organist.
>
> It is fitting that there be a cantor or a choir director to direct and support the people's singing. Indeed, when there is no choir, it is up to the cantor to direct the different chants, with the people taking the part proper to them. (102–104)

Each of these liturgical music ministries provides a talent that might not be shared by all the assembled baptized, yet they are among the baptized and in the service of the whole body. As with the liturgical ministries of acolyte and reader, understanding and preparation are essential, especially to assist the participation of all in the celebration of the Eucharist. The singing of the Psalm and the other parts of the Mass, especially when such singing is supported by the music minister, enhances the beauty of the celebration as well as the carrying out of the various rites and liturgical actions.

The *General Instruction* further identifies as liturgical ministries the functions of the sacristan, the commentator, those who take up the collection and greet and guide the assembly, as well as the master of ceremonies (see GIRM 105–106). These functions, although not always in place for the celebration of the Eucharist, provide for a good sense of order in distinct ways and as such add to the reverence and dignity of the celebration of the Mass. The sacristan provides for the arrangement of the liturgical books, sacred vestments, sacred vessels, and other needed elements for the celebration. The commentator, although a rare function today, provides brief and well-prepared remarks to help the baptized understand the liturgical action. This ministry was more common in the earlier stages of the liturgical reform and with the introduction of new rites. However, it can still be helpful when various rites are combined with the Eucharist and would require some explanation for a better understanding. For example, a commentator would benefit the assembly during the dedication of a church. Those who collect the offerings and those who greet and guide the assembly carry out an obvious and quite practical function. Finally, the master of ceremonies, usually in place for the bishop and larger celebrations, sees "to the appropriate arrangement of sacred actions and to their being carried out by the sacred ministers and lay faithful with decorum, order, and devotion" (106).

The celebration of the Eucharist as an action of the whole Christ, Head and members, anticipates the stable relationship among those in Holy Orders with the baptized. The Mass in every form also expects among the baptized those who willingly assist in a variety of liturgical ministries. In fact, the *General Instruction* instructs the faithful not to "refuse to serve the People of God in gladness" whenever they are invited to carry out some function or ministry in the course of the Mass (see GIRM 97). Often it happens that several bishops and/or priests are present for the same Eucharist, as well as Deacons and liturgical ministers. The *General Instruction* offers guidance on how the duties of those in sacred orders and the functions and ministries of the faithful are distributed in such cases.

There is always only one head to the body. This is an important principle to keep in mind when several bishops and/or priests are present for the celebration of the Eucharist, whether as concelebrants or in attendance in choir. So if the bishop or the priest is the celebrant of the Eucharist, he alone exercises all of the presidential functions in all their parts (see GIRM 108). An arbitrary separating out of these parts breaks down the sacramental integrity of the action, in which the celebrant is acting in the person of Christ, the Head. Unfortunately, this is often the case when another sacrament occurs in the course of the celebration of the Eucharist, such as baptism or marriage. As a general rule, the bishop or priest who prays the Eucharistic Prayer is also the one who carries out the other sacraments in the same celebration. At times this also occurs when a celebrant gives away a part of a rite — for example, the Final Commendation at the Funeral Mass. In the past, this rite was not part of the Funeral Mass but followed the Mass for the Dead. Today, it is a constitutive element of the Funeral Mass and a presidential function to be carried out by the celebrant of the Eucharist.

The body has many members. The norms for the celebration of the Eucharist recognize that on many occasions several people are present who can properly carry out the liturgical functions and ministries needed:

> If there are several present who are able to exercise the same ministry, nothing forbids their distributing among themselves and performing different parts of the same ministry or duty. For example, one Deacon may be assigned to execute the sung parts, another to serve at the altar; if there are several readings, it is well to distribute them among a number of readers, and the same applies for other matters. However, it is not at all appropriate that several persons divide a single element of the celebration among themselves, e.g., that the same reading be proclaimed by two readers, one after the other, with the exception of the Passion of the Lord. (109)

Often, the occasion for the celebration of the Eucharist requires a certain number of Deacons and liturgical ministers, such as the Stational Mass with a bishop, or a parish or community solemn celebration of Mass. And at times only one Deacon and/or liturgical minister may be available. Several points come together when making decisions about the distribution of liturgical functions and ministries. The celebration itself calls for the service of liturgical ministries (see GIRM 116), but Deacons and liturgical ministers should carry out only those functions proper to them. The number of Deacons and liturgical ministers should not exceed the liturgical and practical needs of the celebration that is taking place. For example, a Sunday Solemn Mass in a parish setting would be overburdened if every Deacon available vested to assist. As the *General Instruction* suggests, one Deacon might carry out the sung parts and the other proclaim the Gospel or assist at the altar. The practice of assigning a Deacon to the Liturgy of the Word and to the Liturgy of the Eucharist cannot be found in the liturgical books, yet it is a practical way with liturgical good sense to distribute the functions between two Deacons. Likewise with liturgical ministers — when several are available, their functions may be distributed, and the distribution should have some reasoning behind the arrangement. For example, if two acolytes are present, one could carry the cross, the other minister the *Roman Missal*, and both assist at the altar. If three are present, then one could carry the cross and the other two carry processional candles with one of them ministering the *Roman Missal*.

The formation and preparation of liturgical ministers, as already mentioned, is an indispensable aspect of the *ars celebrandi*. Simply because people are available to carry out liturgical ministries does not in itself indicate a suitability for the service expected. For that matter, the celebration of the Sacred Liturgy never simply falls into place. The *General Instruction* makes this excellent point for the contemporary celebration of the Eucharist:

> There should be harmony and diligence among all those involved in the effective preparation of each liturgical celebration in accordance with the Missal and other liturgical books, both as regards the rites and as regards the pastoral and musical aspects. This should take place

> under the direction of the rector of the church and after consultation with the faithful in things that directly pertain to them. (111)

The preparation of every aspect of the celebration of Mass, which presumes the formation of the ordained and the baptized, especially those engaged in liturgical ministries, should include a fitting regard for the distinct roles and the competent observance of duties. This fitting regard includes the following of the norms found in the liturgical books by all those celebrating and for all parts of the celebration. This is the harmonious and diligent preparation anticipated by the *General Instruction*, which likewise anticipates an artful and careful celebration.

Conclusion

A proper understanding of the concept of the *ars celebrandi* and the Sacred Liturgy must precede any presentation of its application. Fidelity to the rubrics for the celebration of the Sacred Liturgy is a respectable value in itself. However, the *ars celebrandi* moves beyond this to a focused engagement of the rites, which ultimately is a focused engagement of the Mystery of Christ celebrated in the Eucharist. Such an engagement allows for the celebration of the Sacred Liturgy to manifest more fully what God is doing and revealing in this divine event. The *ars celebrandi* becomes an aid, a resource, a way for liturgical theology. The authenticity and objectivity of this liturgical theology requires a stable and ordered carrying out of the Eucharist by the ordained and baptized as intended by their sacramental roles. The next chapter will address the important topic of liturgical participation on the part of the ordained and the baptized, as well as aspects of the celebration that foster this type of participation. Proper and authentic liturgical participation evolves from the *ars celebrandi.*

CHAPTER TWO
A Pathway to Authentic Liturgical Participation

Liturgical participation allows for an actual encounter with the Mystery of Christ celebrated in the Eucharist. A proper understanding of liturgical participation derives from the priesthood of both the ordained and the baptized at work in the celebration of the Eucharist. Singing, the use of gestures and postures, and observing silence throughout the course of the celebration of Mass have as their end the fostering and promoting of liturgical participation by all in the Mystery of Christ. In fact, the arrangements for the Mass, according to its many variable parts and the more or less solemn ways to celebrate it, are directed toward true liturgical participation. The *ars celebrandi*, as it focuses on the Mystery of Christ in the celebration, becomes a pathway to authentic liturgical participation in this same Mystery for the whole liturgical assembly.

Liturgical participation in general

Liturgical participation ranks by far as the most discussed and debated aspect of the reform of the rites following the Second Vatican Council. It is the overarching theme of the Council's *Sacrosanctum concilium.* In fact, the *General Instruction of the Roman Missal* references directly article 14 of the Council document on this point of liturgical participation of the ordained and baptized:

> It is, therefore, of the greatest importance that the celebration of the Mass or the Lord's Supper be so ordered that the sacred ministers and the faithful taking part in it, according to the state proper to each, may draw from it more abundantly those fruits, to obtain which, Christ the Lord instituted the Eucharistic Sacrifice of his Body and Blood and entrusted it as the memorial of his Passion and Resurrection to the Church, his beloved Bride.
>
> This will fittingly come about if, with due regard for the nature and other circumstances of each liturgical assembly, the entire celebration is arranged in such a way that it leads to a conscious, active, and full participation of the faithful, namely in body and in mind, a participation fervent with faith, hope, and charity, of the sort which is desired by the Church and which is required by the very nature of the celebration and to which the Christian people have a right and duty in virtue of their Baptism. (17–18)

Liturgical participation — encountering the Mystery of Christ in the actual celebration — as evolving from the artful and careful celebration of the Eucharist requires an authentic and unambiguous description. It is not something that simply occurs with the celebration of Mass. It properly belongs to every liturgical assembly yet varies with the circumstances of each one. The revised *Order of Mass* has been so reformed that its many elements — outlined for the bishop or the priest celebrant, for the baptized faithful, and for all of them together — center on the engagement of the liturgical action.

The *General Instruction* adds to the description of liturgical participation — "conscious, active, and full" as in *Sacrosanctum concilium* — that it is "namely in body and in mind, a participation fervent with faith, hope, and charity, of the sort which is desired by the Church" (18). Liturgical participation includes the whole person, in body and in mind — the whole Christian, every part of the particular member of the Body of Christ who enters into the celebration of the Mystery of Christ as ordained or baptized with all the virtues of the Christian life. This is the "sort" of liturgical participation desired by the Church. In fact, it is the only participation that makes theological sense, and it is expected of the Christian baptized in the same Mystery of Christ.

When a person is baptized, he or she rises from the saving waters of baptism as a sharer in the priestly action of Christ on the cross. As a sharer in the priestly action of Jesus with baptism, the Christian then gives expression to this sharing when he or she participates "in body and in mind" in every part of the Eucharist, in complete communion with Christ in his offering to his Father.

The bishop or the priest celebrant participates in every celebration of the Eucharist equally as both a baptized Christian and as someone configured to Christ the Priest as a ministerial priest. The priest unites himself to the offering of the Lord just as everyone else does in the liturgical assembly. By virtue of his sacramental ordination, he also perfects the offering of the baptized as he carries out the Eucharist and unites the offering of the baptized with the offering of the holy Body and Blood of the Lord in the Eucharistic Prayer. The *Pray, brethren,* during the preparation of the altar illustrates this point rather clearly. After the altar has been prepared and the gifts have been placed on it for the Sacrifice of Christ, the bishop or the priest celebrant, facing the people, sings or says: "Pray, brethren (brothers and sisters), that my sacrifice and yours may be acceptable to God, the almighty Father." This invitation to the faithful indicates that there are two distinct offerings or two manners of liturgical participation — *my sacrifice and yours* — that will be pleasing to God. The one is the offering of the bread and wine by the ministerial priest that will take place with the Eucharistic Prayer; the other is the offering by the baptismal priests, the assembled faithful, that accompanied this same bread and wine to the altar. This includes the offering of their very selves, "in body and in mind … with faith, hope, and charity."

The response that the faithful make to the bishop or priest celebrant's invitation reveals the purpose of liturgical participation: "May the Lord accept the sacrifice at your hands for the praise and glory of his name, for our good and the good of all his holy Church." What is the sacrifice at the hands of the bishop or the priest? It is the bread and wine placed on the altar. It is also all that is to be joined to this offering of the bread and wine, all that is in the body and mind of the faithful (including that of the bishop or priest celebrant), offered in faith, hope, and charity. This is the sacrifice at the hands of the celebrant. The faithful pray that this sacrifice, which is Christ and all who belong to Christ, be accepted as a priestly act: an action of Christ the Priest and those who share in his priesthood, for the glory of God and for the redemption and salvation of all.

Following the Second Vatican Council, as the reformed rites were introduced throughout the Church, a limited view of the meaning of "conscious, active, and full" participation frequently prevailed. The *Order of Mass*, as already mentioned, was so revised that the action of the people was significantly enhanced, both in terms of roles and the variety of ways to speak, to sing, and to do. As a result, liturgical participation frequently became a matter of exterior participation. While the exterior is valid and to be valued, participation only truly accords with "the very nature of the celebration" and for the faithful "a right and duty in virtue of their Baptism" when what is external is founded on the interior priestly offering with Christ in his offering, which occurs at the hands of the bishop or priest.[1]

The debates surrounding liturgical participation over the years since the Council often focused on a supposed clash in possibilities between an artful and careful celebration of the Eucharist and encouraging the engagement of the faithful. Pope Benedict XVI squarely addressed this point in *Sacramentum caritatis*, the Apostolic Exhortation that followed the Synod on the Eucharist. He wrote:

> In the course of the Synod, there was frequent insistence on the need to avoid any antithesis between the *ars celebrandi*, the art of proper celebration, and the full, active and fruitful participation of all the faithful. The primary way to foster the participation of the People of God in the sacred rite is the proper celebration of the rite itself. The *ars celebrandi* is the best way to ensure their *actuosa participatio*. The *ars celebrandi* is the fruit of faithful adherence to the liturgical norms in all their richness; indeed, for two thousand years this way of celebrating has sustained the faith life of all believers, called to take part in the celebration as the People of God, a royal priesthood, a holy nation.[2]

The *ars celebrandi* serves as a guarantor, "the primary way to foster the participation of the People of God." This participation is the "sort" intended by *Sacrosanctum Concilium* and directed by the *Order of Mass*: an interior participation expressed through exterior participation. This interior participation grounds and orients the *ars celebrandi* as it becomes a dimension of exterior participation.

Liturgical participation on the part of the bishop or priest celebrant

The celebration of the Eucharist with a bishop celebrant carries a significance that informs every other celebration of the Eucharist. In fact, canonically, every other celebration in the local Church is dependent on the local bishop. This is brought forward when the priest prays the Eucharistic Prayer and says, "N., our Bishop." This significance is two-fold. The whole of the local Church is liturgically structured around and under the bishop. And, the form of the celebration, especially the Stational Mass with the bishop, uniquely manifests the Church according to this structure. The *General Instruction* succinctly summarizes this dual significance:

> For the Diocesan Bishop, the prime steward of the mysteries of God in the particular Church entrusted to his care, is the moderator, promoter, and guardian of the whole of liturgical life. In celebrations that take place with the Bishop presiding, and especially in the celebration of the Eucharist by the Bishop himself with the Presbyterate, the Deacons, and the people taking part, the mystery of the Church is manifest. Hence, solemn celebrations of Mass of this sort must be exemplary for the entire diocese. (22)

The bishop participates in the celebration of the Eucharist in his sacramental role of representing Christ, the High Priest, in the local Church and in the liturgical action. He brings to the celebration one of his principal duties as the bishop of the local Church: to be "the prime steward of the mysteries of God in the particular Church entrusted to his care." As the prime steward, in his oversight of an artful and careful celebration of the Eucharist and his manner of celebrating in such a way, he helps build up faith in the mysteries celebrated and provides a formative model for all the members of the local Church, especially for priests. A bishop ought to be vigilant in his oversight of the liturgical life of the local Church; moreover, it is foolish to presume that the bishop can easily celebrate the Eucharist with care and attention simply because of his sacramental role. Rather, a prayerful, studied, and disciplined engagement of the rites is what assures the *ars celebrandi* for the bishop celebrant.

The *General Instruction* typically speaks only of the priest as the celebrant, and it is understood that the same would apply to the bishop when he celebrates. So, in what follows, what is said of the priest is also intended for the bishop. By virtue of the Sacrament of Holy Orders, the priest celebrant of the Eucharist, in addition to his interior personal participation, participates in the Eucharist in an external way that corresponds to his sacramental role to offer sacrifice in the person of Christ (see GIRM 93). Certain prayers and parts of the Eucharist that belong to the priest celebrant are outlined in the *General Instruction* in this way:

> Among those things assigned to the Priest, the prime place is occupied by the Eucharistic Prayer, which is the high point of the whole celebration. Next are the orations, that is to say, the Collect, the Prayer over the Offerings, and the Prayer after Communion. These prayers are addressed to God by the Priest who presides over the assembly in the person of Christ, in the name of the entire holy people and of all present. Hence they are rightly called the "presidential prayers."

> Likewise it is also for the Priest, in the exercise of his office of presiding over the gathered assembly, to offer certain explanations that are foreseen in the rite itself. Where this is laid down by the rubrics, the celebrant is permitted to adapt them somewhat so that they correspond to the capacity for understanding of those participating. However, the Priest should always take care to keep to the sense of the explanatory text given in the Missal and to express it in just a few words. It is also for the presiding Priest to regulate the Word of God and to impart the final blessing. He is permitted, furthermore, in a very few words, to give the faithful an introduction to the Mass of the day (after the initial Greeting and before the Penitential Act), to the Liturgy of the Word (before the readings), and to the Eucharistic Prayer (before the Preface), though never during the Eucharistic Prayer itself; he may also make concluding comments regarding the entire sacred action before the Dismissal. (30–31)

With the Eucharistic Prayer all the duties of the priest combine and become manifest in the singular expression of his configuration to Christ the Priest as he speaks in the first person, as Christ, with the words of institution and consecration: "This is my Body" and "This is the Chalice of my Blood." In a sacramental way the priest represents Christ and so acts in his name in this present celebration of his Sacrifice to the Father. At the same time, the priest brings forward the offering of Christ to his Father in the name of all those assembled and, in fact, in the name of all who continue to benefit here and now from the redemption and salvation that flow from this Sacrifice. In a related way, the principal orations of the *Order of the Mass* — the Collect, the Prayer over the Offerings, and the Prayer after Communion —

when prayed by the priest celebrant are carried out likewise in the person of Christ and on behalf of all. Acting in the person of Christ and on behalf of the baptized identifies a primary way of liturgical participation of the priest in the celebration of the Eucharist. The *General Instruction* reminds us that these prayers — the Eucharistic Prayer and the three orations — are properly named "presidential prayers." This name implies the particular association of these same prayers with the priest celebrant's liturgical participation.

The given parts and prayers that belong to the priest are clearly indicated throughout the current *Roman Missal.* The *General Instruction* additionally notes, "Likewise it is also for the Priest, in the exercise of his office of presiding over the gathered assembly, to offer certain explanations that are foreseen in the rite itself." In many instances the rites are introduced with a scripted introduction, which the priest celebrant may modify for the benefit of the assembled faithful when necessary for their more complete understanding of the liturgical action at hand. However, the caution of the *General Instruction* should be heeded thoughtfully: The priest celebrant should modify a text only as necessary, keeping the sense of what has been provided. Today, following the scripted texts in the *Roman Missal* appears to be the norm. Any modifications that might be introduced should be done with a previous study of the given texts.

As noted above, the priest celebrant may also provide helpful explanations throughout the course of the *Order of Mass*. These explanations require a liturgical and theological understanding of the rite to follow as well as a judicious exercise of this option. The intention of these explanations is for the priest celebrant to guide the authentic liturgical participation of the assembled faithful in the celebration of the Eucharist. Each of the opportunities listed for such an explanation leads directly into what follows.

So, for example, following the Greeting of the Introductory Rites, the Mass of the day may be introduced in a few words. This is not the occasion for another greeting (such as "good morning") but rather the occasion to invite the assembled faithful to participate in the whole of the Mystery of Christ as it now occurs with this celebration of the Eucharist. This introduction may reference the liturgical commemoration or occasion as well as lead the faithful into the event of the Eucharist. A similar introduction can take place prior to the beginning of the Liturgy of the Word. The *Roman Missal* provides two splendid samples of this type of introduction to the Liturgy of the Word for the Easter Vigil and the Extended Vigil of Pentecost. The assembled faithful are invited to listen to the Word as God reveals himself anew in the announcement of his saving Mysteries with the proclamation of the Sacred Scriptures. The whole of the Eucharistic Prayer may be introduced immediately prior to the dialogues of the Preface. This introduction takes the assembled faithful into the very heart of the Sacrifice of the Lord and calls them to offer themselves with the offering of Christ. Finally, before the Greeting and Blessing that are part of the Concluding Rites, there may be remarks that reference the Mysteries celebrated so as to send the faithful forth from the celebration mindful of its grace and power. All these opportunities arise from the primary role of the priest presiding over the baptized and orienting fittingly their liturgical participation in the Eucharist.

These opportunities for a few words of introduction take place most frequently with the introduction to the Mass and the remarks prior to the conclusion of Mass. Serious consideration should be given to the two other opportunities — before the Liturgy of the Word and the Preface of the Eucharistic Prayer. Also, these specified and limited opportunities for the priest celebrant to interject his own words in the course of the *Order of Mass* have in some cases been seen as license for comments all throughout the Mass, including even adding phrases to the given texts and prayers. The *General Instruction* is specific in stating that this should never happen during the Eucharistic Prayer (see 31); for that matter, it should not happen in the course of any of the other given texts and prayers. The priest celebrant, ever mindful of the *ars celebrandi*, should approach any modification of texts, when permitted, and these four introductions with seriousness of purpose and clarity of composition so that the faithful are indeed truly aided in their liturgical participation.

Above all, as the priest carries out his presidential role in the course of the Eucharist, those assembled should be able to hear him distinctly. This is an obvious initial step to promoting the liturgical participation of the faithful. "The nature of the 'presidential' parts requires that they be spoken in a loud and clear voice and that everyone listen to them attentively" (GIRM 32). Often, there is more of a concern about the declaration of the texts than there is about their reception — their being heard easily by those listening. Whatever is needed to amplify the voice of the priest should be in place (see 306), so that nothing impedes the faithful from hearing clearly the voice of the priest, especially as he prays the presidential prayers. There should be no sounds competing with the voice of the celebrant in the course of the celebration of the Eucharist, whether spoken or sung or played by a musical instrument (see 32).

In contrast to the presidential prayers and whatever fitting explanations that the priest may provide in the course of the celebration, there are other prayers proper to his role which are always prayed quietly. These prayers, which occur before the proclamation of the Gospel, during the Preparation of the Gifts, and during the Communion Rite, give expression to the priest's personal participation, as he prays in his own name so that "he may exercise his ministry with greater attention and devotion" (GIRM 33), to celebrate in an artful and careful manner. Often these prayers are recited in the same voice as the presidential prayers, which is contrary to their purpose. These quiet prayers belong to the priest personally to aid his liturgical participation and are not in any way directed to the assembled faithful.

Liturgical participation on the part of the baptized

The *Order of Mass* manifests the theological reality that the ministerial priesthood in every way is oriented to the baptismal priesthood. When the priest says, "The Lord be with you," he does so in his role as head of the liturgical assembly, representing Christ, the Head of his Body. When the people respond, "And with your spirit," they express the recognition of the spirit or character in the ministerial priest that links all the baptized to Christ, the Head, as members of his Body. In this dialogue the whole Christ is made present sacramentally for the work of Christ in his Church, in the offering of the Eucharist for the glory of the Father, and for the redemption and salvation of those participating and for the whole world. The liturgical participation of the faithful in the Mystery of Christ takes place through the presidency of the priest celebrant.

The *General Instruction* highlights several ways that this occurs in the *Order of Mass*, primarily with the dialogues between the priest celebrant and the baptized:

> Since the celebration of Mass by its nature has a "communitarian" character, both the dialogues between the Priest and the assembled faithful, and the Acclamations are of great significance; for they are not simply outward signs of communal celebration but foster and bring about communion between Priest and people.
>
> The Acclamations and the responses of the faithful to the Priest's greetings and prayers constitute that level of active participation that is to be made by the assem-

> bled faithful in every form of the Mass, so that the action of the whole community may be clearly expressed and fostered.
>
> Other parts, most useful for expressing and fostering the active participation of the faithful, and which are assigned to the whole gathering, include especially the Penitential Act, the Profession of Faith, the Universal Prayer, and the Lord's Prayer.
>
> Finally, among other formulas:
>
>> a) Some constitute an independent rite or act, such as the Gloria in excelsis (Glory to God in the highest), the Responsorial Psalm, the Alleluia and Verse before the Gospel, the Sanctus (Holy, Holy, Holy), the Memorial Acclamation, and the chant after Communion; b) Others, on the other hand, accompany some other rite, such as the chants at the Entrance, at the Offertory, at the fraction (Agnus Dei, Lamb of God) and at Communion. (37)

All the elements described above are a means of promoting the liturgical participation of the baptized in the celebration of the Eucharist. They highlight various aspects of the celebration and levels to this participation, particularly the importance and significance of all the dialogues throughout the course of the celebration. These dialogues both express and occasion the communion between the head and members in the liturgical assembly, in sacramental representation of the whole Christ worshiping his Father. These dialogues in all the forms of the Mass, even in the celebration of Mass at Which only One Minster Participates, emphasize that the Eucharist is an action of the community of the Church. However, not all the parts of the Mass in which the faithful participate are dialogical. Some are introduced by the priest celebrant with the priest and the faithful continuing together, such as the Penitential Act, the Universal Prayer, and the Lord's Prayer. For other elements, such as the *Gloria* and other chants (the so-called independent rites), the priest celebrant participates jointly with the baptized, without prejudice to specific roles in the celebration of the Eucharist. The Memorial Acclamation, the Mystery of Faith, listed among the independent rites, is more properly a dialogue between the priest celebrant and the faithful during the Eucharistic Prayer.[3]

Just as the priest celebrant in his role of presiding over the celebration of the Eucharist ought to speak in a loud and clear voice as he prays the prayers and parts assigned to him, in service of the text and for the benefit of the faithful, the responses of the faithful likewise should be made in a similarly loud and clear voice. This includes all members of the liturgical assembly when responding together or when carrying out a specific duty such as the proclamation of the Sacred Scriptures, the declamation of the intentions of the Universal Prayer, as well as any other introductions or explanations during the course of the Mass. The *General Instruction* makes the point that with the various texts for the celebration of Mass, there is also a variety of genre, which may be a prayer, a reading of a biblical text, an Acclamation, or an explanatory remark. Thus, there should be a correspondence between the voice employed and the type of text. Likewise, consideration should be given to the form of the Mass and to the occasion. Obviously, the character of the voice used at a Solemn Sunday celebration will be quite distinct from an early weekday morning celebration of the Eucharist (see GIRM 38).

The quality of the responses of the assembled faithful to the priest celebrant deserves some serious attention and refinement to ensure that they "foster and bring about communion." This is especially true when the faithful respond together with longer texts throughout the course of the Mass, such as during the response to the "Pray, brethren ..." and the "Behold the Lamb of God." Often, it is difficult to distinguish the individual words of these responses when so many people speak them at the same time, and with little attempt to be in unison with others. Occasionally rehearsing these longer responses for the purpose of promoting a communion within the assembly can definitely enhance the quality of the dialogue with the priest celebrant.

With regard to pronouncing different texts in the celebration of Mass the *General Instruction* states, "Therefore, in the rubrics and in the norms ... words such as 'say' and 'proclaim' are to be understood either of singing or of reciting" (38). Whether they are sung or recited is a question of the norm of singing certain elements of the Sacred Liturgy and the application of the principle of progressive solemnity, which is addressed later in this chapter. As far as the quality of responses on the part of the faithful, whether responses are sung or recited, in all cases there is to be a fitting attention to volume, clarity, and the genre of the text.

Singing

The *General Instruction* only briefly presents norms and patterns for singing the Eucharist. The 1967 Instruction *Musicam sacram* of the Sacred Congregation of Rites is the foundation for these norms and patterns. The *Order of Mass* is quite comprehensive in its presentation of the musical notations for those parts expected to be sung, with the additional information on singing the Mass as found in the appendices of the *Roman Missal*. The appendix to the *Roman Missal* gives direction for the choice of tones, solemn and simple, and for many of the sung parts of the Mass.

The chief norm is this: The celebration of the Eucharist is sung with regard for the particular liturgical assembly and its capacity to sing. A corollary norm is that while every part of the *Order of*

Mass may be sung, not every Mass is to be sung in this fashion. Rather, Sundays and similar observances, because of their rank in the liturgical calendar, call for greater use of singing as compared to a weekday celebration. In addition, there are preferences as to what should be sung when a choice for singing is to be made. These choices are guided by the theological value of the liturgical text. For example, as indicated in the *General Instruction*, the dialogues in the *Order of Mass*, expressive of the action of the whole of the liturgical assembly, head and members, and those elements sung by the whole liturgical assembly together are preferred to be sung above other texts (see 40). The *Order of Mass* in the current *Roman Missal* first provides the musical notations and texts for all the dialogues and then follows the text alone of the same dialogue. This emphasizes that the norm is to sing. In subsequent chapters, the specific norms for singing the chants at the Entrance, the Offertory, and the Communion will be presented, as well as those that occur during the Liturgy of the Word.

The discipline of the Roman Rite regarding musical forms to be employed, especially with the celebration of the Eucharist almost universally in the vernacular language, is rather broad and governed by two principles: The musical forms used must necessarily "correspond to the spirit of the liturgical action and ... foster the participation of all the faithful" (GIRM 41). The application of these two principles — a correspondence to the liturgical action and the liturgical participation of the faithful — does not happen by chance. Rather, always with the aim toward the *ars celebrandi*, this application requires a studied review of the type of music chosen for its fittingness in heightening the theological meaning of the action. This ensures the true liturgical participation of the liturgical assembly. The *General Instruction* prizes the use of Gregorian chant as a choice of a musical form for singing the Mass (see 41). Gregorian chant masterfully reveals the theological meaning of the liturgical action. That is, it points to its meaning with sound, and thus supports the texts with the music. The genius of Gregorian chant is how it models other musical forms for the Eucharist and enhances liturgical participation.

Gregorian chant belongs to the patrimony of the Roman Rite and continues to bring forward the sung faith of the centuries in the Mystery of the Eucharist. Gregorian chant also proposes a type of universality regarding a musical form for the celebration of the Eucharist. Likewise, the singing of parts of the *Order of Mass* in simpler Latin settings allows for a communal liturgical participation in the Eucharist not only in international assemblies but also in the first language of the Roman Rite (see GIRM 41). Practically speaking, these suggestions of the *General Instruction* on the use of Gregorian chant and even the use of sung Latin texts for the *Order of Mass* receive very little attention today and would seem quite foreign to most contemporary liturgical assemblies. However, as just illustrated, Gregorian chant and sung Latin texts have values in themselves. They also lend themselves to a liturgical participation that promotes an artful and careful celebration of the Eucharist.

Singing the Sacred Liturgy, especially singing the celebration of Mass, is a most important topic and one that seriously affects the *ars celebrandi* and the Eucharist. Other than stating the norms for singing found in the *General Instruction* and presenting what is directed in the *Order of Mass*, a more complete discussion of the topic is beyond the scope of this book. However, a consistent application of the above norms for singing the Eucharist, along with what is directed in the *Order of Mass*, will be found in the presentation of each part of the Mass in part two of this book.

Gestures and postures

The ordained and baptized significantly express their liturgical participation with gestures and postures for different elements of the celebration as well as when directed for individuals and then for all members at different parts of the same celebration. The *General Instruction* offers three interacting reasons for the significance of these gestures and postures: First, such gestures and postures contribute to the beauty and noble simplicity of the celebration; second, they assist with manifesting the "true and full meaning" of the different elements and parts of the celebration; and finally, above all, they allow for the external participation of all taking part in the celebration (see 42). The ordered and dignified manner in which the gestures and postures are assumed in the course of the Eucharist, founded on the above reasons, promotes an artful and careful liturgical celebration.

It should be noted that the gestures and postures employed during the Mass are neither arbitrary nor accidental. Rather, they arrive today from the tradition of the Roman Rite. The gestures and postures currently prescribed in the *General Instruction*, with some adaptation in the United States and in a local Church, belong to an understanding of participation that is for the benefit of all (see GIRM 42). It is rather careless and shortsighted when the priest celebrant or another member of the liturgical assembly suggests that some or all members assume a gesture or posture contrary to those prescribed. For example: inviting the faithful to sit for the Gospel because of its length ignores the fact that standing is a visible sign of being in the Risen One who is speaking his own Gospel to us. Inviting people to sit during the Eucharistic Prayer encourages a posture of passive receptivity, when kneeling (and, if necessary, standing) identifies a posture of engagement in the offering. Inviting some to stand or sit or kneel based on preference or choice shows a disregard for the connection between posture and the unity among the members of the assembly. "A common bodily posture, to be observed by all those taking part, is a sign of the unity of the members of the Christian community gathered together for the Sacred Liturgy, for it expresses the intentions and spiritual attitude of the participants and also fosters them" (42).

The *Order of Mass* indicates the gestures and postures of the priest celebrant throughout the celebration, as well as those to be observed by liturgical ministers as they carry out their duties. In most instances the *Order of Mass* provides the same for the faithful as they participate in the various parts of the Eucharist. Additionally, the *General Instruction*, in accord with an already standard use of certain gestures and postures, precisely outlines the pattern for the faithful:

> The faithful should stand from the beginning of the Entrance Chant, or while the Priest approaches the altar, until the end of the Collect; for the Alleluia Chant before the Gospel; while the Gospel itself is proclaimed; during the Profession of Faith and the Universal Prayer; and from the invitation, Orate, fratres (Pray, brethren), before the Prayer over the Offerings until the end of Mass, except at the places indicated here below.
>
> The faithful should sit, on the other hand, during the readings before the Gospel and the Responsorial Psalm and for the Homily and during the Preparation of the Gifts at the Offertory; and, if appropriate, … during the period of sacred silence after Communion.
>
> In the Dioceses of the United States of America, they should kneel beginning after the singing or recitation of the Sanctus (Holy, Holy, Holy) until after the Amen of the Eucharistic Prayer, except when prevented on occasion by ill health, or for reasons of lack of space, of the large number of people present, or for another reasonable cause. However, those who do not kneel ought to make a profound bow when the Priest genuflects after the Consecration. The faithful kneel after the Agnus Dei (Lamb of God) unless the Diocesan Bishop determines

> otherwise.
>
> For the sake of uniformity in gestures and bodily postures during one and the same celebration, the faithful should follow the instructions which the Deacon, a lay minister, or the Priest gives, according to what is laid down in the Missal. (43)

The above directions emphasize standing for the faithful throughout most of the celebration of the Eucharist. When the faithful stand, they are in the same posture as the priest celebrant. This same standing posture for the head and members of the liturgical assembly manifests their shared sacramental stature in the Risen One in the celebration of his Mystery. The observance of the proper gestures and postures, especially in their variety, belonging to the faithful throughout the Eucharist augments liturgical participation as related to the liturgical action. This is why caution for adaptation — even occasional adaptation — must be heeded with seriousness. With any adjustment to prescribed postures "these adaptations must correspond to the character and meaning of each part of the celebration."[4] This regard for correspondence to the meaning and character of the parts of the celebration with the respective gestures and postures simultaneously contributes to the *ars celebrandi* through the celebration of the Eucharist.

The "profound bow" called for when the faithful are not kneeling for the Eucharistic Prayer is often overlooked, or the faithful may not even be aware of this possible gesture that belongs to them in this circumstance. The bow here is not simply a concession when standing replaces kneeling. Rather, it is an example of a provided adaption that "corresponds to the meaning and character" of the Consecration during the Eucharistic Prayer, as it links the faithful to the priest celebrant in the adoration that follows the showing of the consecrated Host and the chalice to the people. This union in adoration is already present when the faithful are kneeling at the point of the Consecration.

The processions that occur throughout the celebration of the Eucharist are constitutive features of the rites. They have profound meaning and are not simply functional. The processions are always indicative of the liturgical assembly's movement toward God in the Paschal victory of his Son. The processions that occur during the celebration of the Mass vary with the occasion and the solemnity of the celebration but are always in place in some way. These processions include the entrance of the priest, possibly along with an assisting Deacon and ministers; the procession of the Deacon or priest to the ambo for the proclamation of the Gospel; the procession of those with the gifts for the Eucharist; and the procession of the faithful for the reception of Holy Communion. These processions will be considered in greater detail in subsequent chapters. It is important to note at this point that, as all the other gestures and postures of the liturgical assembly have particular meaning, these processions play a major role in grasping the progressive movement within the celebration of the Mystery of Christ and so should be carried out with an intentional dignity (see GIRM 44).

Under the heading of gestures and postures, two deserve special consideration because of the uniqueness and the distinct meaning applied to each: the genuflection and the bow. They are not the same gesture, nor do they have the same meaning in the Roman Rite. The *General Instruction* treats both according to their meaning and their use in the celebration of the Eucharist. The use of the genuflection and the bow described below extends beyond what is called for in the *Order of Mass*:

> A genuflection, made by bending the right knee to the ground, signifies adoration, and therefore it is reserved for the Most Blessed Sacrament, as well as for the Holy

Cross from the solemn adoration during the liturgical celebration on Good Friday until the beginning of the Easter Vigil.

During Mass, three genuflections are made by the Priest Celebrant: namely, after the elevation of the host, after the elevation of the chalice, and before Communion. Certain specific features to be observed in a concelebrated Mass are noted in their proper place (cf. nos. 210–251).

If, however, the tabernacle with the Most Blessed Sacrament is situated in the sanctuary, the Priest, the Deacon, and the other ministers genuflect when they approach the altar and when they depart from it, but not during the celebration of Mass itself.

Otherwise, all who pass before the Most Blessed Sacrament genuflect, unless they are moving in procession.

Ministers carrying the processional cross or candles bow their heads instead of genuflecting.

A bow signifies reverence and honor shown to the persons themselves or to the signs that represent them. There are two kinds of bow: a bow of the head and a bow of the body.

a) A bow of the head is made when the three Divine Persons are named together and at the names of Jesus, of the Blessed Virgin Mary, and of the Saint in whose honor Mass is being celebrated.

b) A bow of the body, that is to say, a profound bow, is made to the altar; during the prayers Munda cor meum (Cleanse my heart) and In

> spiritu humilitatis (With humble spirit); in the Creed at the words et incarnatus est (and by the Holy Spirit ... and became man); in the Roman Canon at the Supplices te rogamus (In humble prayer we ask you, almighty God). The same kind of bow is made by the Deacon when he asks for a blessing before the proclamation of the Gospel. In addition, the Priest bows slightly as he pronounces the words of the Lord at the Consecration. (GIRM 274–275)

The genuflection means adoration of Christ himself in his holy Body and Blood. The bow means reverence of persons or signs of persons. It is quite common today to see an arbitrary replacement of the genuflection with the bow, and at times vice versa. This practice compromises the meaning of these two gestures and impedes the clarity of "the true and full meaning" of the rite when it calls for a genuflection or a bow. Only when it is truly not possible to genuflect — for example, when a person has a physical limitation — is a profound bow to be used. Additionally, there is no need to accompany the genuflection with the Sign of the Cross. The *General Instruction* is clear that the genuflection takes place during Mass when the Most Blessed Sacrament is reserved in the sanctuary. On all other occasions, a profound bow is made to the altar. In cases where the tabernacle is in the sanctuary and someone is passing by the altar, the profound bow should be made to the front side of the free-standing altar and not between the altar and the tabernacle.

It may seem insignificant that the *General Instruction* makes a distinction between the bow of the head and a more profound bow. The bow of the head for the occasions listed above happens all throughout the course of the celebration of the Eucharist. The prescribed profound bows are integral to the rites during which they take place and as such give additional meaning to the rite as it unfolds. As with all the gestures and postures indicated so far in the celebration of the Mass, the genuflection and the bow are again another form of liturgical participation that brings the expression of the body to accord with a concurrent interior participation. This harmony between an interior and an external engagement of the Mystery with gestures and postures contributes to an overall artful and careful celebration of the Eucharist.

It should be noted that in the directions offered in the current edition of the *Roman Missal*, both in the *General Instruction* and the *Order of Mass*, the priest celebrant and the faithful face the same direction during certain parts of the Mass: the *ad orientem* posture (toward the East). This would be the posture for the Liturgy of the Eucharist only. Thus, there are moments during the Liturgy of the Eucharist when the priest celebrant is directed to turn and face the faithful, especially for some of the dialogues. The celebration of the Eucharist as a rule takes place today with the priest celebrant facing the faithful, *ad populum* (toward the people), and not *ad orientem*. However, for completeness, reference is made to the *ad orientem* posture in the chapters on the Liturgy of the Eucharist.

Silence

The use of silence during the celebration of the Eucharist requires a certain discipline and skill as well as a clear understanding of its role and purpose. The editions of the *Roman Missal* subsequent to the Second Vatican Council, especially the *Order of Mass*, have prescribed places for silence throughout the rites. These occasions of silence are much more than a pause; they are rather a true instance of liturgical participation. Liturgical silence does not mean simply that the members of the liturgical assembly become quiet following an introduction to a prayer or as part of a rite. This type of silence allows for a focused communion with others with the same intention without any common text. And depending on the part of the Mass when the silence occurs, its purpose varies. Silence is prescribed following the Penitential Act and the invitation to the Collect. This type of silence allows for recollection to enter more fully into the act of penance and the prayer that follows. Additionally, silence is to take place following the Readings and the Homily. This type of silence fosters meditation. Finally, silence follows the reception of Communion. This type of silence is meant to be a period of praise and thanksgiving (see GIRM 45).

The norms in the *General Instruction* additionally give value to silence in preparation for the celebration of the Sacred Liturgy: "Even before the celebration itself, it is a praiseworthy practice for silence to be observed in the church, in the sacristy, in the vesting room, and in adjacent areas, so that all may dispose themselves to carry out the sacred celebration in a devout and fitting manner" (45). Perhaps today this preparatory silence, more so than the silence to be observed during the Eucharist, requires considerable attention to become the norm. Silence observed before the celebration gives import and meaning to the silence during the celebration.

In many situations, periods of silence are not observed at all in the celebration of the Eucharist. In others, some periods of silence are observed and others ignored in the same celebration. As a liturgical action, silence is not a personal act. Rather, it is a corporate act of the whole liturgical assembly and provides for each member to engage in the action of the prayer or rite more fully. It is likewise an external expression of an interior participation in the Mystery of Christ. Silence, consistently observed at the proper times during the Mass, weaves itself seamlessly into a prayerful and reverent celebration, which is one of the aims of the *ars celebrandi.*

Arranging the celebration of Mass

The *ars celebrandi* applies not only to the ordered and reverent participation of everyone in the Mystery of Christ in the Eucharist but equally to the arrangement of all its elements and parts. Serious thought about this arrangement is the shared responsibility of the priest celebrant, the Deacon or Deacons, if in place, the liturgical ministers, and the faithful, depending on their duties and roles. Among these elements and parts, a primary element is the choice of Mass and its texts. Once this choice is in place, then the additional choices of the chants and the Sacred Scriptures are arranged to correspond to the choice of Mass. Most often the choice of Mass corresponds to the liturgical calendar which governs liturgical time and the observances of Sundays, solemnities, feasts, and obligatory and optional memorials. At times a choice of Mass, depending on the limits of the liturgical calendar, may be a Mass formula from the Ritual Masses, Masses for Various Needs and Occasions, and Votive Masses, or the Masses for the Dead. The norms for all of these choices and when they can and cannot be made are carefully described in the *General Instruction* (see 353–355, 368–385). The norms for the choice of Biblical Readings for each of these formulae for the Mass, although indicated in the *General Instruction* (see 357–362), are outlined as well in the *Introduction to the Lectionary for Mass.*[5] The choice of Mass also then indicates the options for the chants at the Entrance, Offertory, and Communion, as well as those that occur during the Liturgy of the Word.

The arrangement of the celebration of Mass, even when all is proper, is more pastorally effective if all the parts — the choice of Mass, the readings, and the chants — correspond to what will most benefit the faithful for their participation (see GIRM 352). All too frequently, these many choices are made in haste, or a choice for one part is made without consideration for others. Or, the choice of all things is determined by one person, perhaps the priest celebrant or the director of the liturgical music, without any regard for the common spiritual good and capacity of all or for those who carry out the many different parts (see GIRM 352).

At the same time, in arranging the celebration of Mass, with so many variable choices for a particular celebration, it is incumbent upon the sacred ministers and the liturgical ministers to know in advance the choices that have been made, especially the choice of parts which belong to their duties and roles (see GIRM 352). This intentional planning and preparation underscores the measure of disciplined seriousness required for an artful and careful celebration of the Eucharist. Likewise, this type of planning and preparation brings an ordered harmony to each of the rites and to the whole of the Mass, which fosters the liturgical participation of all, interiorly and exteriorly, and with a proper regard for the spiritual needs of all (see 20 and 352).

Progressive solemnity

The celebration of the Eucharist is the celebration of the Eucharist. However, a Sunday is not a weekday, and a cathedral is not a hospital chapel. The *Order of Mass*, as directed by the *General Instruction*, recognizes and allows for levels of solemnity with due regard for the occasion and place of the celebration. The celebration of Mass with a bishop celebrant, especially the Stational Mass, as already mentioned, represents one of the most solemn forms of the Mass and is to be celebrated as such. In addition to the *General Instruction*, Masses at which a bishop presides are directed by the *Ceremonial of Bishops*. The Stational Mass of the diocesan bishop receives detailed attention in the *Ceremonial of Bishops* with due regard for the liturgical and theological character of this form of the Mass.[6]

Progressive solemnity, a term first introduced in the arrangement of celebrations in *Musicam sacram*[7] and again with the reformed *Liturgy of the Hours*,[8] provides a guiding principle for arranging the celebration of Mass with the many options possible for liturgical music and ceremony, for vesture and vessels, and the complement of liturgical ministers in favor of greater or lesser solemnity. This principled arrangement corresponds to the occasion and place and the capacity and needs of all participating in the Eucharist. At one end of the range of progressive solemnity, an occasion of greater solemnity would have all the possible parts of the Mass sung with the use of incense, vestments, and vessels perhaps of a greater quality, and the needed ministers to provide for the full observance of the rites. At the other end of this range, an occasion of lesser solemnity would only have the dialogues sung as well as those parts belonging to the priest celebrant together with the faithful, dignified vestments and vessels, and perhaps only one server, one reader, and the cantor.

Prior to the introduction of the *Roman Missal* with its *General Instruction* following the Second Vatican Council, the levels of solemnity were much more rigidly defined, especially in the United States, with the Solemn Mass, the High (Sung) Mass, and the Low Mass. There were few options and variables to these levels. The current *General Instruction* and *Order of Mass* foresee a similar variety of levels, although less rigidly defined. This lack of definition of levels in many cases today has given way to no variation, with few options used toward greater solemnity when fitting. If the *ars celebrandi* is to become normative in the celebration of the Eucharist in the parish community or any other community, there must be a developed plan for progressive solemnity, which takes into account the varied observances in the liturgical calendar, the place of the celebration, and the needs and capacity for the liturgical participation of all. An imposed plan for progressive solemnity, as was the case prior to the current reform, mitigates the value of the great many options presently available with the celebration of Mass and the arrangement of these options to focus on the Mystery of Christ in greater and lesser solemn ways.

Conclusion

A solid connection links liturgical participation and the *ars celebrandi*. A true engagement of the Mystery of Christ in the Eucharist seeks and sustains a focus on this same Mystery for both the ordained and the baptized for an artful and careful celebration. All the liturgical expressions of participation — especially singing, gestures and postures, and silence — receive greater attention and become even more effective when there is authentic liturgical participation in the Mystery celebrated. The fitting arrangement of the many elements and parts of the Eucharist, with regard for liturgical participation and the liturgical observance, is more diligently realized when governed by the *ars celebrandi*. The *ars celebrandi*, as a pathway to liturgical participation, must more and more become a normative aspect of liturgical celebration.

The place of the celebration of the Eucharist and its proper arrangement likewise fills an important role in fostering liturgical participation. The next chapter looks at the place of the celebration and the proper arrangement of the physical elements that are a part of it. Both the place for the Eucharist and these physical elements properly understood and employed explicitly for the Sacred Liturgy belong to an environment that shapes the *ars celebrandi*.

CHAPTER THREE
Some General Considerations

The celebration of the Eucharist makes use of many physical elements which in themselves are signs of something greater. As signs they reveal theological meaning to those assembled to celebrate the sacred Mysteries. In fact, they manifest many layers of meaning — liturgical and theological — in the Mystery of Christ. They point to the profound reality that the here and now celebration is a temporal experience of the eternal celebration of this same Mystery with the angels and saints in glory.

The celebration of the Eucharist requires that even before the singing of the Entrance Chant, these many elements, these signs, be properly understood and engaged so that their full import may be realized, especially as a contribution to the *ars celebrandi*. Some of these more important elements or signs include the place of the celebration and its arrangement for the roles and duties of the ordained and the baptized; the sacred vestments and sacred vessels; the bread and wine; the liturgical books; and the use of incense in the course of the liturgical action. When these elements are considered for the sign value they hold during the celebration, this dimension further promotes an authentic *ars celebrandi*, an artful and careful celebration, on the part of everyone assembled for the saving Mystery of Christ. Reverence as well for these same elements prepares everyone assembled to receive the many meanings they reveal.

The place of celebration of the Eucharist

It is too simple to say that the Eucharist takes place in a church. The church room is not the starting point for an understanding of the celebration of Mass. Rather, the Mystery of Christ, that is the Eucharist, defines the place for its celebration. This includes not only a place deemed suitable for the Eucharist but also a place that allows for the full observance of the rites and the participation of all in these rites. In summary, the *General Instruction of the Roman Missal* states that the place for the celebration of the Eucharist should be truly worthy and beautiful and be a sign of the heavenly realities (see 288, 318). At one and the same time, the church room needs to be functional for the needs of the liturgical celebration and remarkable in dignity and beauty to highlight that what occurs is a foretaste of the heavenly realities.

The church building itself carries its own *ars celebrandi*, a focus on the Mystery, which is to serve the fitting celebration of the Sacred Liturgy. Church buildings throughout the ages and in every part of the world, with the benefit of the arts, in most instances point to the Mystery of Christ celebrated within them. When a church is dedicated or blessed, the rites and prayers teach us to engage the church as the dwelling place of Christ, in the divine event of his offering and in those who will celebrate it.

The disciples received the instruction from the Master to find the room for his final Passover meal that was "furnished and ready" for so great an event (see Mk 14:15). And so the Church, especially on the part of her ministers, must do the same for the Mass. The fitting celebration of the Eucharist needs more than an available church. Everything within and without the church, without prejudice to any particular form or style, must be intended for the celebration of the Mystery of Christ. In other words, what is used for the celebration of Mass, especially furnishings and appointments, should not suggest a household item or something that could easily be exchanged for household use. Just like the place for the celebration of the Eucharist, so those elements needed for the celebration likewise should be truly worthy and beautiful and be a sign of the heavenly realities. The *General Instruction* further notes that "the ornamentation of a church should contribute toward its noble simplicity rather than to ostentation. Moreover, in the choice of elements attention should be paid to authenticity and there should be the intention of fostering the instruction of the faithful and the dignity of the entire sacred place" (292).

While on the one hand the liturgical and theological value of the place for the celebration of the Eucharist invites a reverence for the very place, on the other hand there are practical aspects that deserve equal attention to promote a focus on the Mystery of Christ. The *Order of Christian Initiation of Adults* has a preface document, *Christian Initiation, General Introduction*, which in its description of the Sacraments of Christian Initiation presents primarily the dignity of baptism, the offices and ministries, and the requirements for celebration. In the section describing the requirements, there are two articles that provide an overarching understanding of the practical aspects that call for special attention so that the theological and liturgical value of the signs and place are more clearly accessible. The first is that "the water used in baptism should be true water and, both for the sake of authentic sacramental symbolism and for hygienic reasons, should be pure and clean."[1] The second is that "the baptismal font, or the vessel in which on occasion the water is prepared for celebration of the sacrament in the sanctuary, should be spotlessly clean and of pleasing design."[2] The water is to be true, pure, and clean! The place for the celebration of the sacrament should be spotlessly clean!

The church building for the Mystery of Christ should be so ordered as to raise the minds and hearts of those assembled to the heavenly realities present in the liturgical celebration. As far as a practical expression, great care for the place for the celebration of the Eucharist — with its furnishings and appointments — should be exercised so that the church is also clean and not cluttered. This allows for an unencumbered engagement of the liturgical signs and their many meanings. Special regard is to be shown to the altar and everything associated with the divine action at the altar so that it is in relief as a true sign of Christ and his offering (see GIRM 350). The *General Instruction* gives little direction about decorating the place for the celebration of the Eucharist. Moderation is the norm when it comes to decoration (see 305). The signs themselves have their own value and attractiveness. To emphasize this point, the *General Instruction* notes:

> During Advent the floral decoration of the altar should be marked by a moderation suited to the character of this time of year, without expressing in anticipation the full joy of the Nativity of the Lord. During Lent it is forbidden for the altar to be decorated with flowers. Exceptions, however, are Laetare Sunday (Fourth Sunday of Lent), Solemnities, and Feasts. Floral decoration should always show moderation and be arranged around the altar rather than on the altar table. (305)

There are two further considerations about the decoration of the church. Often the focus is only on the action at the altar. This comes through even in what is directed in the *General Instruction* as seen above. First, the whole church is the place for the celebration of the Eucharist, and decoration needs to expand in a regular way beyond the area of the altar and its action. Second, while the indications for the placement of flowers for the altar are clear (around it rather than on it), they are insufficient. Floral arrangements around the altar typically move the eye to the flowers and away from the centrality and action of the altar. Additionally, these same arrangements often impede the actions at the altar, such as walking around it for its incensation. Likewise, with a sense that the whole of the church ought to be decorated, so ought the area of the sanctuary, and not just one piece of furnishing in the sanctuary.

The arrangement of the place for the celebration of the Eucharist

The place for the celebration of the Eucharist is a sacramental environment in all its dimensions, disposing everyone to encounter the sacred Mysteries to be celebrated. This sacramental environment includes the specific places within the church as they are arranged, or ordered, to each other with meaning and purpose. When the church building was discussed above, the place for the celebration was the primary consideration. Now, when looking at specific places within the church, the focus becomes twofold: First, those who fill the specific places are considered; second, the specific places for them (for the ordained and baptized) within the church itself are then considered. The *General Instruction* gives a succinct overview of these two considerations:

> The People of God which is gathered for Mass is co-

> herently and hierarchically ordered, and this finds its expression in the variety of ministries and the variety of actions according to the different parts of the celebration. Hence the general arrangement of the sacred building must be such that in some way it conveys the image of the assembled congregation and allows the appropriate ordering of all the participants, as well as facilitating each in the proper carrying out of his function.
>
> The faithful and the schola cantorum (choir) shall have a place that facilitates their active participation.
>
> The Priest Celebrant, the Deacon, and the other ministers have places in the sanctuary. There, also, should be prepared seats for concelebrants, but if their number is great, seats should be arranged in another part of the church, though near the altar.
>
> All these elements, even though they must express the hierarchical structure and the diversity of functions, should nevertheless bring about a close and coherent unity that is clearly expressive of the unity of the entire holy people. Indeed, the nature and beauty of the place and all its furnishings should foster devotion and express visually the holiness of the mysteries celebrated there. (294)

An artful, careful celebration of the Eucharist expands beyond carrying out the rites with attentiveness to the texts and actions at hand. The *ars celebrandi* further requires a clear understanding of the relationship among those celebrating, as already presented in chapter one, and how this relationship is articulated in the arrangement of specific places for them within the church. The *General Instruction* on the one hand clearly expresses that those assembled for Mass be "coherently and hierarchically ordered." On the other hand, it insists that this ordering serve to "bring about a close and coherent unity." In more theological language, the celebration of the Eucharist signifies an action of the whole Christ, head and members, each with respective roles and duties and properly oriented to each other with a specific place within the church room. Attention to this theological point underscores the sensibility of a specific place for the ordained (the sanctuary), and a specific place for the baptized (the body of the church or the nave). These two distinct places within the church should be arranged in such a way so as to ensure that the ordained and the baptized participate accordingly with one another as directed by the rites. This prescribed arrangement should be unambiguous and easily perceived by all. Likewise, this same arrangement from a visual perspective needs to be beautiful and attractive so as to clearly manifest the one Body of Christ at work, in the head and members, ordained and baptized, in the divine event of Christ's Sacrifice.

The arrangement of the sanctuary and its furnishings

The ordering of the church building itself sacramentally announces that the Eucharist is an action of Christ, in his head and members, with the sanctuary as the place for the priest, Deacon, and other ministers, oriented to the body of the church as the place for the faithful. The *General Instruction*, in accord with a long-standing Roman tradition, states that the sanctuary "should be appropriately marked off from the body of the church either by its being somewhat elevated or by a particular structure and ornamentation" (295). The altar, the ambo, and the chair for the priest celebrant are located in the sanctuary as the needed furnishings for singular actions of the Mystery of Christ in the Eucharist. The ordained and the baptized, equally, should possess a multivalent grasp of the significance of the altar, ambo, and chair as signs of the presence of Christ and as occasions of this presence in the course of the liturgical action. Reverence and understanding of these furnishings both outside and during the celebration of the Eucharist foster the *ars celebrandi* on the part of the ordained and the baptized.

The Altar

The altar, more than the ambo and the chair for the priest celebrant, is to have a central location in the sanctuary. Its placement in the sanctuary becomes the focal point for the entire celebration of the Eucharist as the place of the Sacrifice, the actual event of the death and rising of the Lord, and everyone's participation in this divine event, both the ordained and the baptized. The death and rising of the Lord celebrated at the altar gives meaning to the whole church, to each part of the church, to the ambo and to the chair, to the role of the priest and other sacred ministers, and to the role of the faithful. The Sacrifice at the altar defines our posture, our gestures, and even our attitude toward the altar, and invites us to a deeper faith in the Mystery that occurs on this holy table. The *General Instruction* speaks of the altar as actually convoking the ordained and the baptized to participate in the Eucharist because upon it "the Sacrifice of the Cross [is] made present under sacramental signs" (296).

The *General Instruction* guides the construction of the altar only to highlight its placement as "the center of the thanksgiving that is accomplished through the Eucharist" (296):

> The altar should be built separate from the wall, in such a way that it is possible to walk around it easily and that Mass can be celebrated at it facing the people, which is desirable wherever possible. Moreover, the altar should occupy a place where it is truly the center toward which the attention of the whole congregation of the faithful naturally turns. The altar should usually be fixed and dedicated. (299)

Ideally, the altar is fixed, that is, attached to the floor, and preferably constructed of natural stone which expresses the permanence of the Christ event, his eternal offering on the cross. The offering of Christ engages our participation, shapes our reverent attitude, and informs the artful and careful way the ordained and the baptized conduct themselves around it.

The vesting and appointing of the altar for the celebration of the Eucharist is specified in detail in the *General Instruction*:

> Out of reverence for the celebration of the memorial of the Lord and for the banquet in which the Body and Blood of the Lord are offered, there should be, on an altar where this is celebrated, at least one cloth, white in color, whose shape, size, and decoration are in keeping with the altar's structure. …
>
> For only what is required for the celebration of the Mass may be placed on the altar table: namely, from the beginning of the celebration until the proclamation of the Gospel, the Book of the Gospels; then from the Presentation of the Gifts until the purification of the vessels, the chalice with the paten, a ciborium, if necessary, and, finally, the corporal, the purificator, the pall, and the Missal. …
>
> The candlesticks required for the different liturgical services for reasons of reverence or the festive character of the celebration should be appropriately placed either on the altar or around it, according to the design of the altar and the sanctuary, so that the whole may be harmonious and the faithful may not be impeded from a clear view of what takes place at the altar or what is placed upon it.
>
> Likewise, either on the altar or near it, there is to be a cross, with the figure of Christ crucified upon it, a

> cross clearly visible to the assembled people. It is desirable that such a cross should remain near the altar even outside of liturgical celebrations, so as to call to mind for the faithful the saving Passion of the Lord. (304, 306–308)

The use of only a white cloth on the altar table itself, that only what is essential to the celebration ever be placed upon the altar, the reason for and placement of candles, and the required clearly visible cross with the crucified Lord point to the central role of the altar as the sign and place of the Redeemer's Sacrifice. These same details aid the ordained and the baptized in their encounter with the Mystery of Christ that occurs at the altar and orients the whole of the liturgical action. When the details listed above are put aside and instead the altar is set and appointed similarly to a dining room table, especially with the candles and flowers, its value as a sign of the salvific offering of Christ is seriously weakened.

The ambo

The ambo, with its own established location, follows the altar in the hierarchy of furnishings in the sanctuary. The same Mystery of Christ, realized sacramentally at the altar, is likewise announced at the ambo.[3] As the altar with its central location ought naturally to draw the attention of all to the sacred action that occurs upon it, so the ambo, for its role in the proclamation of the word of God, by its placement in the sanctuary and its design, likewise ought to draw the attention of all and allow for the participation of all during the Liturgy of the Word (see GIRM 309). A certain discipline is necessary to promote reverence for the ambo as a sign of the presence of Christ in his word. This discipline, to be observed by the ordained and the baptized, has its origin in the rites that surround the use of the ambo. It is meant to be used only by the proper ministers for the announcement of the word of God in the Biblical Readings, which includes the Responsorial Psalm; the Easter Proclamation (Exultet); and, at times, the Homily and the intentions of the Universal Prayer (see 309). Often for the sake of convenience, especially because of amplification, the ambo is used sometimes for announcements apart from the word of God, often given by someone who is not a minister of the word. This practice detracts from the dignity and significance of the ambo as a sign itself of the living word of God and, therefore, should be avoided.

The chair for the priest celebrant

The chair for the priest celebrant follows the altar and ambo in the order of furnishings in the sanctuary. This chair, like the altar and ambo, derives its significance from its use in the course of the celebration of the Sacred Liturgy. The *General Instruction* describes the chair for the priest celebrant with several points to keep in mind:

> The chair of the Priest Celebrant must signify his function of presiding over the gathering and of directing the prayer. Thus the more suitable place for the chair is facing the people at the head of the sanctuary, unless the design of the building or other features prevent this: as, for example, if on account of too great a distance, communication between the Priest and the congregation would be difficult, or if the tabernacle were to be positioned in the center behind the altar. In any case, any appearance of a throne is to be avoided. (310)

The chair's location in the sanctuary communicates a liturgical, theological purpose. It is a sign of the priest acting in the person of Christ, the Head of his Body, which he does all throughout the celebration of the Eucharist. Thus, its placement is not arbitrary, and even though the chair is frequently movable, it should have a permanent location that manifests its constant significance. The *General Instruction* indicates that the most fitting location is at the head of the sanctuary facing the faithful in the body of the church. The cautions given in this same instruction should be carefully heeded for good reasons. The chair fosters the relationship in the assembled Body of Christ and so practically it should not be out of reach or sight of the baptized, whose prayer is directed from the chair. Likewise, and perhaps even more obvious, if the Blessed Sacrament is reserved on the central axis in the church and directly behind the altar, then the chair for the priest celebrant should not compete liturgically, architecturally, or practically with the tabernacle. In this instance, it seems suitable that the chair be placed in the sanctuary to the left or right of the altar, opposite the ambo, and again facing the assembled faithful in the nave of the church.

There is always only one representative of Christ the Head in the celebration of the Sacred Liturgy and, as indicated above, this headship is communicated by the chair of the priest celebrant. So, in practice, every effort should be made to avoid joining other chairs for concelebrating priests and altar servers to the chair of the priest celebrant. As far as concelebrating priests, they should have chairs in the sanctuary in a location that distinguishes them in this role and does not have them mixed in with other liturgical ministers or the faithful. This would be true as well if these priests were in choir dress (cassock and surplice) and participating in Mass without concelebrating. The chair for the Deacon, however, can and should be placed near the priest celebrant whom he is assisting. If additional Deacons are assisting, they do not necessarily need to be placed near the priest celebrant but in a location in the sanctuary that allows them to carry out their roles with ease. The chairs for the servers should also be in a place in the sanctuary, but distinct from the clergy, that allows them to carry out their roles with reverence and ease (see GIRM 310).

The tabernacle

The location for the reservation of the Sacred Body of the Lord should be considered at this point not so much because it is linked to the altar, the ambo, and the chair, but because it is typically located in the sanctuary as well. The directions regarding the location of the tabernacle in the *General Instruction* represent a revised discipline with a preference for its placement in the sanctuary itself, while allowing for another location related to the church to foster prayer and adoration. These same directions highlight the significance of the tabernacle, its decoration, and traditional practices to indicate and protect the reserved Sacrament (see GIRM 315). In the course of the celebration of the Eucharist, although there are no directives for the use of it, the tabernacle is the focus of adoration, such as at the beginning and end of Mass and, at times, during the Communion Rite when recourse is made to it for additional Hosts and the reservation of Hosts.

The arrangement of the nave, the place for the baptized

The placement of the faithful in the nave, the body of the church, is to be oriented to the placement of the ordained in the sanctuary. The architectural ordering of those celebrating — the baptized to the ordained, the ordained to the baptized — signifies again the work of the whole Body of Christ, in its head and members, carrying out the Mystery of the Lord. The arrangement of the chairs or pews for the faithful should correspond to the liturgical aim of their actual participation in the Eucharist. The faithful need to see and be drawn into the rites as they unfold. The arrangement of chairs or pews should also lend itself to the various bodily postures carried out by the faithful throughout the celebration: standing, sitting, bowing, and kneeling. This same arrangement should also aid the several processions through the assembled faithful that take place during the course of the Mass: the Entrance, the Offertory, and the Communion. Every effort is to be made in every celebration of the Eucharist that the faithful, uniquely associated with the priest celebrant in the offering of Christ, can fittingly and adequately do so. This means that printed aids, amplification, and reasonable proximity to those in the sanctuary should be priorities (see GIRM 311).

In the nave, seats should be arranged for choirs and *scholae* who are one with all the faithful as they guide the musical participation of the whole liturgical assembly in the celebration of the Eucharist. In many situations, the placement of liturgical music ministers as part of the faithful within the body of the church has been unevenly observed. When they are set apart from the faithful, choirs and *scholae* can easily become performers on behalf of the faithful. The area within the nave for the placement of liturgical music ministers should allow for their participation throughout the celebration, especially with the full range of body postures and, even at times, joining the Communion procession (see 312).

The organ and other musical instruments are in the service of the whole liturgical assembly and so their placement, while typically near the location of liturgical music ministers, should take into consideration their use on behalf of everyone (see 313). The directives for the use of the organ and other musical instruments during certain times and on certain days of the liturgical year, especially when moderation and non-use are expected, promote the unique and overall character of these times which is likewise illustrated by other physical elements of the Eucharist such as sacred vestments.

Sacred vestments

One of the more variable signs in the celebration of the Eucharist is the vestments worn by the sacred ministers. In consideration of the sacred vestments for Mass, the starting point is not those garments worn by the priest and Deacon, but the garment worn by the members of the Body of Christ: the sacramental garment of the priesthood of Christ. It is this garment, the primary garment, which then allows for additional meaning in the vestments worn by the ordained and the baptized, each of whom share uniquely but distinctly in the priesthood of Christ. The different vesture worn by each give expression to the different and proper roles of both the ordained and the baptized and, at the same time, add to the beauty of an artful celebration (see GIRM 335). It must be remembered that sacred vestments, whether worn by the ordained or the baptized, are clothing and not mere appointments or decorations. As such, they require care in wearing them — that is, they should fit the body, and be clean and presentable for use in the celebration of the Sacred Liturgy.

The alb, which is always white in color as the origin of its name indicates, is the liturgical garment that belongs equally to the ordained and the baptized. The design of the alb, as such, covers all clothing under it from the neck to the top of the shoes and is gathered at the waist by a cincture. If the alb is not designed to cover the clothing at the neck or does so inadequately, then an amice is to be worn to do this. An alb is always worn under the chasuble or dalmatic and always worn when a stole may be worn without a chasuble or dalmatic (see GIRM 336). The practice continues with decorations and applications on the alb and material openings in the alb, which custom tolerates. However, it is more in keeping with the nature of the garment that it be solid white for the most part. A religious habit does not replace the alb.[4]

The chasuble, always worn over the stole, is the proper vestment of the priest celebrant for the Eucharist (see GIRM 337). The priest wears his stole around his neck with it hanging down his front side (340). The dalmatic, always worn over the stole, is the proper vestment of the Deacon for the Eucharist (338). The Deacon wears his stole over his left shoulder and diagonally across his chest and fastened on his right side (340). The chasuble is always worn without exception by the priest celebrant, and the dalmatic typically by the Deacon. However, the dalmatic may be omitted in rare instances; for example, when the vestment is not available or on a less solemn occasion (338). The alb, as described above, is the fitting vesture for liturgical ministers, especially formally instituted readers and acolytes (339). The traditional form and shape of the sacred vestments, especially the chasuble and dalmatic, should be maintained because they contribute to the sign value of the garment for the respective sacred minister and a common recognition of the meaning of the sign. Equally, the materials used in making sacred vestments contribute greatly to their beauty and highlight the liturgical action and the proper role of the minister (342, 343). Any ornamentation applied to the materials of the sacred vestments should point to the Mystery of Christ and not detract from it 344). The sign is the sacred vestment itself, not what is placed on it.

In addition to the various shapes and materials of the sacred vestments, especially of the chasuble and dalmatic, they are even further distinguished by a variety of colors associated with the liturgical year and the Mysteries of Christ, Our Lady, and the saints, as well as the liturgical rites (see GIRM 345). The traditional use of the colors — white, red, green, violet, black, and rose — is maintained in the current edition of the *Roman Missal.* It is also possible on more solemn and festive occasions to wear more precious vestments, such as gold or silver colored, even if not the appointed color of the day (346). The norms for the color of vestments for Ritual Masses, Masses for Various Needs, and Votive Masses should be carefully observed, again, because the color of the sacred vestments gives additional and specific meaning to the liturgical celebration (347).

The sacred vessels

The Liturgy of the Eucharist revolves around the sacred vessels that are required for the unfolding of the Mystery of Christ at the altar. The paten and chalice, above all, stand out in a singular way because with them the bread and wine that become the Body and Blood of the Lord are presented as the offering of the Savior, consecrated, and then consumed (see GIRM 327).

In recent times the paten and chalice as well as additional sacred vessels such as ciboria and other chalices have been constructed of a variety of materials and have even taken on different shapes. As far as the material for sacred vessels, the *General Instruction* provides precise guidance:

> Sacred vessels should be made from precious metal. If they are made from metal that rusts or from a metal less precious than gold, they should generally be gilded on the inside.
>
> In the Dioceses of the United States of America, sacred vessels may also be made from other solid materials which in the common estimation in each region are considered precious or noble, for example, ebony or other harder woods, provided that such materials are suitable for sacred use. In this case, preference is always to be given to materials that do not easily break or deteriorate. This applies to all vessels that are intended to hold the hosts, such as the paten, the ciborium, the pyx, the monstrance, and others of this kind.
>
> As regards chalices and other vessels that are in-

> tended to serve as receptacles for the Blood of the Lord, they are to have a bowl of material that does not absorb liquids. The base, on the other hand, may be made of other solid and worthy materials. (328–330)

The paten and chalice for the Eucharist — in fact, all the sacred vessels — are not simply functional; rather, in themselves they communicate a more profound reality — a divine reality. They do this not only in their use during the celebration of the Eucharist but also by their design, according to the prescribed directives for their fabrication. Worthy and beautiful vessels for the Eucharist are in the service of the immeasurable worth and beauty of the Mystery they contain. It is obvious, then, that any vessels that are intended for household use would not have a place in the celebration of the Sacred Liturgy.[5] The use of household dishes and cups seriously compromises the role of the vessels for the *ars celebrandi*.

In addition to the importance of the quality of the material for the sacred vessels, their form is equally important. These vessels are for the food and drink of the bread and wine, and so they resemble a plate and cup in their essential form. The paten and the chalice can be considered for the communion of many. The use of a single paten and chalice, when possible, manifests the theological reality that in the communion of many from the one paten with consecrated bread and the one cup of consecrated wine there is a new unity in the one Christ. So, when at all possible, a larger paten is fitting for the bread of the priest celebrant, other concelebrants, if any, the Deacon, if present, the liturgical ministers, and the faithful (see GIRM 331).

The liturgical books

Several different books are used in the course of the celebration of the Eucharist, especially the *Roman Missal* and the *Lection-*

ary for Mass. Each one, regardless of its service to the Mystery of Christ, deserves special care and to be handled intentionally. Above all, the *Book of the Gospels* and the *Lectionary for Mass*, textual vessels for the saving word of God that are venerated with a kiss like the altar, require reverent attention on the part of those who read from them. The *Book of the Gospels* is a sign of Christ present in the Sacred Liturgy and should be used in cathedrals and larger churches.[6] In fact, all liturgical books are "truly signs and symbols of higher realities and hence should be truly worthy, dignified, and beautiful" (GIRM 349). The size of the liturgical books should be appropriate to the size of the place where they are used. Worn and torn liturgical books should be replaced when necessary and no longer be used in the celebration of the Sacred Liturgy.

The bread and wine

The central sign of the Eucharist is the bread and wine. These are the very elements that the Lord Jesus took into his hands at the supper on the night before he died. These elements become the Sacrifice of the Lord on the cross and our communion with this same Sacrifice: "Following the example of Christ, the Church has always used bread and wine with water to celebrate the Lord's Supper."[7] Likewise, corresponding to tradition this bread must be unleavened and recently made from wheat and water only.[8] The wine as well must be natural, from the fruit of the grape, pure and incorrupt, and not mixed with any other substance.[9]

As central and multivalent as the bread and wine are for the Mystery of Christ, these essential elements often receive so little attention and care in the course of the Eucharist. The fact that we are so removed from the actual making of the bread and the production of the wine accounts for a perceptible indifference to their signification. The *General Instruction* speaks to our engagement of the sign of the bread especially:

> By reason of the sign, it is required that the material for the Eucharistic Celebration truly have the appearance of food. Therefore, it is desirable that the Eucharistic Bread, even though unleavened and made in the traditional form, be fashioned in such a way that the Priest at Mass with the people is truly able to break it into parts and distribute these to at least some of the faithful. However, small hosts are not at all excluded when the large number of those receiving Holy Communion or other pastoral reasons call for them. Moreover, the gesture of the fraction or breaking of bread, which was quite simply the term by which the Eucharist was known in apostolic times, will bring out more clearly the force and importance of the sign of the unity of all in the one bread, and of the sign of charity by the fact that the one bread is distributed among the brothers and sisters. (321)

The reality of the sign of bread and wine as true food and drink allows us to engage them in a human way for our sacramental use to communicate how the saving Mystery of Christ unfolds in the breaking and pouring, the eating and drinking. Precisely because bread and wine are indeed food and drink in the course of the Eucharist, every effort is to be made that these elements are fresh and not spoiled for their consecration as the Body and Blood of the Lord (see 323). Also, as the Body and Blood of Christ, reverent attention to every particle of bread and drop of wine is demanded.

The use of incense

The use of incense is optional in any form of the celebration of Mass, and there are also several optional ways to make use of it (see GIRM 276). The *General Instruction* references Sacred Scripture (Ps 141 [140]:2 and Rv 8:3) to make the point that the use of incense during the Eucharist evokes reverence and prayer. As with every option allowed both in the *General Instruction* and the *Order of Mass*, a liturgical and theological intelligence should inform the use of the option. The use of incense immediately lifts the celebration to a point of greater solemnity and festivity. The solemnity and festivity celebrated on a Sunday, a proper solemnity or feast, as well as certain liturgical occasions such as a Ritual Mass or a Mass celebrated by a bishop, are perceptibly enhanced with the use of incense.

When incense is used, further considerations are necessary. It may be used five times: 1) during the Entrance Procession; 2) to incense the cross and altar at the beginning of Mass; 3) during the procession before the Gospel and prior to the proclamation of the Gospel; 4) to incense the gifts once they have been placed upon the altar, the cross and the altar, as well as the priest and the baptized; and 5) at the showing of the Host and chalice following the Consecration (see 276). It is clear from the *General Instruction* that, while all five times of incensation are possible in the course of the Mass, choices can be made from among these five times. A reasonable choice on lesser solemn occasions may be to incense at the Gospel and during the Preparation of the Gifts, and on more solemn occasions, to use incense at all five possible times. Then again, for good reason, the choice on certain occasions may be to incense only during the showing that follows the Consecration of the bread and wine. In the fourth option above, the gifts, the cross, the altar, the priest, and the baptized are listed together, and this is intentional. All five of these recipients of the incensation at this point of the Mass combine to express in uniquely distinct but related ways the offering of Christ that occurs with the Liturgy of the Eucharist. The bread and wine will become the Sacrifice of Christ, represented by the cross on the Table of Sacrifice, offered together, albeit differently, by the priest and the baptized. It compromises the integrity of the liturgical action at this point when what is incensed is arbitrarily reconfigured not to include all five elements.

Incense as a sign of prayer and reverence needs to be clearly seen and have a pleasant fragrance. The lively movement of the smoke as it surrounds the cross, the altar, the Gospel, the gifts, the priest, the baptized, and the Body and Blood of the Lord evokes the reverence and prayer signified. Incensing during the celebration of the Sacred Liturgy, in addition to the choice to use it, requires some skill that should not be quickly dismissed. Likewise, the pattern of incensation provided for the current form of the Roman Mass underscores a theological point about the many presences of the same Christ.

The thurible and boat, the liturgical instruments for the use of incense, as with all the appointments and instruments for the celebration of the Sacred Liturgy, should be fitting for worship, clean, and serviceable. Of all the instruments used in worship, perhaps the thurible and boat may be the most neglected. The thurible with sufficient burning coals, once it is filled by the priest from the boat with a generous supply of incense, always receives a blessing with the Sign of the Cross without any words (see GIRM 277). The priest, the Deacon, and the acolyte (or server) who make use of the prepared thurible throughout the course of the liturgical celebration should grip the chain of the thurible in such a manner that the bowl of the thurible only moves toward what is to receive the incensation.

The pattern for incensing during the Sacred Liturgy is typically the same in each instance. There is only one Christ, and this one and the same Christ is present in multiple ways during the celebration of the Mass. Christ is present in those gathered for the Eucharist, in the Word, in the priest, and most excellently in his Holy Body and Blood. This same Christ is represented in other ways, such as the altar cross, relics of the Holy Cross and images of the Lord exposed for veneration, and the Paschal Candle. All these presences of Christ and representations of the same Christ receive a bow before and after the incensation and three single swings of the thurible (see 277). This explicit pattern of incensation described in the *General Instruction*, especially because of the sign value connoted regarding the presences of the single Christ, should be carefully observed so as not to distort this principal theological reality.

The altar, which is more a sign of the action of the Eucharist than of Christ (see 296), is incensed according to its own pattern. There is no bow before the altar when it is incensed (277). A single swing of the thurible is used whether the altar is freestanding or not. Typically, this single swing of the thurible is directed to the base of the altar and not the mensa as the celebrant walks completely around it (123). If the altar is not freestanding, then the celebrant incenses it first moving to the right and then to the left (277). The incensation of the altar cross is part of the action of the incensation of the altar. This cross can be on the altar, next to the altar, or hanging in the sanctuary area. This representation of Christ, as with the other representations identified above, receives a bow before or after it is incensed. If the altar cross is on the altar or next to it, then it is incensed first before the altar itself. If neither is the case for the altar cross, then it is incensed, with the accompanying bows, when the celebrant passes it as he is incensing the altar (277).

The offerings of the bread and wine for the Mass, as with the altar, have their own pattern for incensation. There is no bow to the offerings; rather, the celebrant incenses the bread and wine with three single swings of the thurible or with a Sign of the Cross over the gifts. Once the offerings have been incensed, the celebrant incenses the altar cross and altar as described above (see 277).

Occasionally, for certain festive celebrations, relics, images of the Blessed Virgin Mary, and images of the saints are placed near the altar for public veneration. These may also be reverenced with an incensation, especially when incense is employed during the celebration of the Mass. Two swings of the thurible, without any bows, are directed to the relics and images only at the beginning of Mass after the altar is incensed (277).

Conclusion

The *ars celebrandi* indeed focuses on the Mystery of Christ celebrated in the Eucharist, and a sense of it is expected on the part of all celebrating. Equally, the *ars celebrandi*, for its more effective impact on those celebrating, also requires that the place and arrangement of this place for the celebration of the Eucharist be ordered according to the plan given by the Church and Tradition — the liturgical and theological plan presented in this chapter. Likewise, all the furniture, especially in the sanctuary, as well as the other physical elements used in the celebration, lend themselves to the same focus on the Mystery of Christ when they actually point to this same divine Mystery in their beauty and reverent use. Everything about the church room and all that fills it and all that is used for the celebration of the Eucharist should declare without words the worship of God.

A firm grasp of the concept of the *ars celebrandi* — its role as a pathway to authentic liturgical participation and how it extends even to those elements used in the Eucharist — forms a necessary foundation for a more complete application to the celebration of the Mystery of Christ itself. An appreciation for all that has already been presented provides the fitting context for an artful and careful celebration of the Eucharist, a celebration that is serious, noble, simple, and beautiful.

PART TWO

Ars Celebrandi: An Artful and Careful Celebration of the Eucharist

Part two consists of seven chapters. The first reviews the various forms for the celebration of Mass and the preparation necessary for each form of celebration. The other six chapters look at the parts of the Mass: the Introductory Rites, the Liturgy of the Word, the Liturgy of the Eucharist, and the Concluding Rites. The Liturgy of the Eucharist is presented in three distinct chapters: the Preparation of the Gifts, the Eucharistic Prayer, and the Communion Rite.

The Mass with its four parts — the Introductory Rites, the Liturgy of the Word, the Liturgy of the Eucharist, and the Concluding Rites — forms a single act of worship of Almighty God (see GIRM 28). The discipline and the skill of the *ars celebrandi,* which is the task of the ordained and the baptized, a task that is born of faith in the Paschal work of Christ in the Liturgy, ensures that every aspect of each part of the Mass folds into this singular worship of Almighty God.

The *General Instruction of the Roman Missal* provides the content for the description of the elements within each part of the Mass. The directions for the celebration of each part of the Mass are then extracted from both the *General Instruction* and the *Order of Mass.* At times, because the description and directions come from these complementary sources, there may be a repetition of information. Throughout each chapter, with the description of the elements and the directions for celebration, the *ars celebrandi* is highlighted as derived from what is intended by the *Roman Missal* for the celebration of the Eucharist. An authentic *ars celebrandi,* while it cannot be divorced from the personalities of those celebrating, of the ordained and the baptized, remains objective and universal when its application derives from the rites themselves.

In general, the governing principle of the *ars celebrandi* underscores the material presented in part two; namely, that in the celebration of the Sacred Liturgy, Christ is the artist. The Sacred

Liturgy is his work, his saving death and resurrection, and we participate in it. The primary *ars* belongs to Christ and his offering and so our *ars* is a communion with him in this offering and in the service of his Mystery for the glory of the Father and for our share in the holiness of God. In this way, the *ars celebrandi*, consciously observed, by the ordained and the baptized, also contributes to the worship of Almighty God that takes place with the celebration of the Eucharist.

CHAPTER FOUR
The Forms of Celebrating Mass and Preparing for Mass

The celebration of the Eucharist takes place in a great variety of settings and circumstances in the life of the Church. The Church responds to this legitimate variety with the arrangement of differing forms for the celebration of the same Mystery of Christ. Each of these forms then requires a corresponding preparation for the celebration and also of those who will celebrate. This chapter presents a description of these forms of celebrating Mass, the preparation needed for each form, and the important role of liturgical ministers. The *ars celebrandi* that surrounds the celebration of the Eucharist begins with the use of the appropriate form of Mass and its required preparation.

The different forms of celebrating Mass

While there is a structure to the *Order of Mass*, the two principal parts — the Liturgy of the Word and the Liturgy of the Eucharist, with the rites that introduce and conclude them — there are several different forms of celebrating Mass. The form of the Mass is determined by certain circumstances. Each form allows for adjustments to parts of the Mass which accord with the varying circumstances. The primary form is the Stational Mass, the celebration of the bishop with the local Church. The other forms of the Mass include, as titled in the *General Instruction of the Roman Missal*, Mass with the People without and with a Deacon, the Concelebrated Mass, and Mass at Which only One Minister Participates. The Stational Mass is not the subject of this book. However, it does have a role in fostering the *ars celebrandi*, as will be presented below. The forms of the Mass — the Mass with the People without a Deacon, the Mass with the People with a Deacon, the Concelebrated Mass, and the Mass at Which only One Minister Participates — are the subject of this book and will be discussed in detail in the subsequent chapters.

The Stational Mass

The Stational Mass, the celebration of Mass with the bishop and the local Church, is directed by its own ritual guide, the Ceremonial of Bishops.[1] However, the General Instruction highlights this form of the Mass and its meaning for the local Church: "In the local Church, first place should certainly be given, because of its significance, to the Mass at which the Bishop presides, surrounded by his Presbyterate, Deacons, and lay ministers, and in which the holy People of God participate fully and actively, for it is there that the principal manifestation of the Church is found" (112).

Every celebration of the Eucharist is a manifestation of the Church, the Church as the whole Christ in his sacramental Body, head and members, with the ordained and the baptized. When the bishop celebrates, however, he signifies the unity of the local Church in Christ as he points to the presence of the same Christ as the High Priest who assembles his priests and people for the worship of Almighty God.[2] In this way, then, the Stational Mass becomes the principal manifestation of the Church.

This unique manifestation unfolds expressly with the concelebration of the bishop with the priests of the local Church. The *General Instruction* gives special recognition of the concelebrated Stational Mass:

> To be held in particularly high regard is that concelebration in which the Priests of any given diocese concelebrate with their own Bishop at a stational Mass, especially on the more solemn days of the liturgical year, at the Ordination Mass of a new Bishop of the diocese or of his Coadjutor or Auxiliary, at the Chrism Mass, at the Evening Mass of the Lord's Supper, at celebrations of the Founder Saint of a local Church or the Patron of the diocese, on anniversaries of the Bishop, and, lastly, on the occasion of a Synod or a pastoral visitation.
>
> In the same way, concelebration is recommended whenever Priests gather together with their own Bishop whether on the occasion of a retreat or at any other gathering. In these cases the sign of the unity of the Priesthood and also of the Church inherent in every concelebration is made more clearly manifest. (203)

The concelebration of the bishop with the priests of the local Church further expresses the unity of the ministerial priesthood in and with the bishop and among all the priests. This is especially evident when the concelebrated Stational Mass takes place in the local Church on the principal days and more solemn occasions in the course of the liturgical year. Concelebration of priests with the bishop should be the norm and every effort made for this type of celebration, even when it is not an occasion for the Stational Mass. Additionally, concelebration, in itself, with and without the bishop, on other days and occasions, always points to this same unity of the ministerial priesthood and of the Church and is an indispensable reality which governs this form of the Mass.

The Stational Mass becomes the form of the Mass that guides and inspires the celebration of every other form of the Mass in the local Church. It is, in essence, the model for the celebration of the Eucharist throughout the diocese:

> The celebration of the Eucharist in a particular Church is of the utmost importance.
>
> For the Diocesan Bishop, the prime steward of the mysteries of God in the particular Church entrusted to his care, is the moderator, promoter, and guardian of the whole of liturgical life. In celebrations that take place with the Bishop presiding, and especially in the celebration of the Eucharist by the Bishop himself with the Presbyterate, the Deacons, and the people taking part, the mystery of the Church is manifest. Hence, solemn celebrations of Mass of this sort must be exemplary for the entire diocese.
>
> The Bishop should therefore be determined that the Priests, the Deacons, and the lay Christian faithful grasp ever more deeply the genuine significance of the rites and liturgical texts, and thereby be led to the active and fruitful celebration of the Eucharist. To that end, he should also be vigilant in ensuring that the dignity of these celebrations be enhanced and, in promoting such dignity, the beauty of the sacred place, of the music, and of art should contribute as greatly as possible. (GIRM 22)

The theological importance of the Stational Mass is complemented by its liturgical significance for the local Church. At the same time as the Stational Mass reveals the spiritual reality of the assembled Church, it becomes a primary example of the artful and careful celebration of the Sacred Liturgy. The bishop has among his chief responsibilities as "the prime steward of the mysteries of God" to be "the moderator, promoter, and guardian" of the celebration of the Sacred Liturgy so that it is indeed a worthy example of imitation and formation for the local Church. This example, this motive for the *ars celebrandi*, is to be rooted in the bishop's dedication to a profound and authentic understanding of the rites and texts of the Sacred Liturgy for both the ordained and the baptized. This understanding then allows for a true engagement and participation in these same rites on his part and the part of all. Side by side with such an understanding and participation in the rites is the recognition that the redemptive and salvific reality of the Sacred Liturgy becomes even more visible and compelling with a dignified celebration. A celebration marked by beauty in every dimension, especially the physical features of the place of celebration, the liturgical appointments, the carrying out of the rites on the part of all, and the liturgical music is the task of the *ars celebrandi*.

Each form of the Mass — Mass with the People without a Deacon, Mass with the People with a Deacon, the Concelebrated Mass, and Mass at Which only One Minister Participates — as with the Stational Mass, necessarily requires also on the part of the ordained and the baptized an understanding of the rites and texts, authentic participation, and genuine beauty as motives for the promotion of the *ars celebrandi*.

Mass with the People without a Deacon and with a Deacon

Mass with the People is the normative or typical form of the celebration of the Eucharist and is the first form of the Mass presented in the *General Instruction*:

> By Mass with the people is meant a Mass celebrated with the participation of the faithful. Moreover, it is appropriate, in so far as possible, and especially on Sundays and Holydays of Obligation, that the celebration take place with singing and with a suitable number of ministers. It may, however, take place even without singing and with only one minister. (115)

Mass with the People — Mass with the priest and the faithful — is ordinarily a sung celebration with servers and readers. The Mass with the People with the parish community — in fact, with any community — is of the greatest importance, as it signifies and represents the universal Church in a specified time and place. The principal expression of the Mass with the People is the Sunday celebration of the Eucharist (see GIRM 113). Additionally, Mass with the People may take place without or with a Deacon assisting. It is curious that the *General Instruction* first presents the form of the Mass without a Deacon assisting and then presents the Mass with a Deacon assisting. The *Order of Mass* gives directions for Mass without and with a Deacon. If a Deacon is present for any celebration of the Eucharist, he should carry out his particular duties (see 116). In the subsequent chapters, Mass with the People without a Deacon is presented distinctly from Mass with the People with a Deacon.

Concelebrated Mass

The next form of the Mass presented in the *General Instruction* is the Concelebrated Mass. This form of the Mass, likewise, can be celebrated without a Deacon, or with a Deacon present carrying out his particular duties. The Concelebrated Mass expresses the "unity of the Priesthood, of the Sacrifice, and also of the whole People of God" (GIRM 199) and as such is prescribed for certain rites, such as the Ordination of a Bishop and Priests and the annual Chrism Mass. At the same time, due to its liturgical and theological value and without neglect of the needs of the faithful, the *General Instruction* recommends concelebration at the Evening Mass of the Lord's Supper, the gatherings of bishops, the principal Mass in churches and chapels, and the gatherings of priests (see 199).

Concelebration has now become the norm when more than one priest celebrates the Eucharist at the same time and in the same place (see GIRM 114). Even with this norm, every priest has the right to celebrate Mass individually but not at the same time and in the same place as a Concelebrated Mass. The exception to this would be the Mass of the Lord's Supper and the Mass of the Easter Vigil when an individual celebration of Mass is not permitted (199). Any priest in good standing should be admitted to a Concelebrated Mass (200). Obviously, this good standing should be ascertained in advance of the concelebration. The *General Instruction* further specifies those occasions and days when a priest may celebrate or concelebrate more than once in the same day; for example, Mass with the bishop or on a liturgical day such as the Nativity of the Lord (204).

The Concelebrated Mass is probably the form of celebrating Mass that requires renewed attention for an artful and careful celebration. The liturgical value and theological meaning of the Concelebrated Mass cannot simply depend on principles; rather, they are also served by a proper carrying out of the Concelebrated Mass. Thus, the *General Instruction* states that the bishop regulates the discipline of concelebration in all churches and chapels in his diocese (see 202). Although there is a preference for concelebration, according to the nature of the Eucharist and for the unity of the ministerial priesthood, it is by no means a requirement for participation in the Mass for a priest. If a priest does not concelebrate the Eucharist, he takes a place apart from concelebrating priests, wearing "proper choir dress or a surplice over a cassock" (GIRM 114).

The manner of celebrating the Concelebrated Mass, whether it is with the bishop or with priests only, generally follows the directions given for Mass with the People without a Deacon or with a Deacon (see 205). The addition of one or several priests for the concelebration brings ritual adjustments which serve the liturgical value and theological meaning of the rite as already identified above. When a priest concelebrates the Mass, he concelebrates the whole of the Mass, which begins with the Entrance and concludes with the Dismissal. The concelebrating priest is uniquely linked and identified with the principal celebrating priest in his role as the head of the Body, of the whole Christ, celebrating the Mystery of Christ in the Eucharist. It would be absurd for the principal celebrating priest to be absent from any part of the Mass. Likewise, the same is the case for a concelebrating priest. Thus, the emphatic language of the *General Instruction* when it states that "no one is ever to join a concelebration or to be admitted as a concelebrant once the Mass has already begun" (206). The same would be true for a concelebrating priest leaving a concelebration before the Dismissal. When this norm is put aside, so are the theological and liturgical values inherent in the Concelebrated Mass, and the *ars celebrandi* is compromised.

Mass at Which only One Minister Participates

The *General Instruction* next presents the Mass at Which only One Minister Participates. The *Roman Missal* provides a distinct *Order of Mass* for this form of the Mass with the title, *The Order of Mass with the Participation of a Single Minister.* This title is not without theological significance. The celebration of the Eucharist is always an action of the whole Christ, head and members, and this action is manifested by those who participate in the Eucharist, namely, the ordained and the baptized. So, even in such instances when the Mass is celebrated without an assembly, it does not forfeit its fundamental nature as a communal event. Therefore, every effort is to be made for at least a server or someone else to be present to make the responses and be representative of the members of the Body of Christ.[3] The form of celebrating Mass at Which only One Minister Participates also generally follows the directions given for Mass with the People without a Deacon or with a Deacon (see GIRM 252). If the one person participating happens to be a Deacon, then he carries out his particular duties as described in a Mass with a Deacon as well as those parts carried out by the people (see 253). There are occasions when it is not possible for a priest to celebrate Mass with at least one member of the faithful.[4] On such occasions this form of the Mass is modified to account for the absence of another person with the omission of the greetings, the instructions, and the blessing at the end of Mass (254).

Preparation for Mass

Preparation for Mass happens on many levels and in different ways, including the observance of the Communion Fast, which, like the Paschal Fast, anticipates the divine taste of the Paschal Mystery.[5] The indispensable and primary preparation for everyone participating in the Mystery of Christ takes place on an interior level when both the ordained and the baptized unite themselves in their unique and respective ways to the offering of the Lord in the Eucharist. This interior preparation is enhanced for everyone celebrating when things are in order for the actual carrying out of the rites of the Mass.

In fact, the *Roman Missal*, in a section titled "Preparation for Mass," includes among prayers for the priest celebrant this

Formula of Intent:

> My intention is to celebrate Mass
> and to consecrate the Body and Blood of our Lord Jesus Christ
> according to the Rite of Holy Roman Church,
> to the praise of Almighty God
> and all the Church triumphant,
> for my good
> and that of all the Church militant,
> for all who have commended themselves to my prayers in general and in particular,
> and for the welfare of Holy Roman Church.
> Amen.
>
> May the almighty and merciful Lord
> grant us joy with peace,
> amendment of life,
> room for true repentance,
> the grace and consolation of the Holy Spirit
> and perseverance in good works.
> Amen.[6]

This prayer underscores a combination of ideas for the celebration of the Mystery of Christ in the Eucharist, the intention of the priest celebrant, and the fruits of the Mass. However, the significance of the phrase "according to the Rite of Holy Roman Church" highlights the liturgical and theological import of observing the structure and the deliberate manner of the celebration. The celebration of Mass according to the rite of the Church distinguishes the purpose and function of the rite as it manifests the Mystery of Christ, as the ordained and the baptized enter into the rite, and as they are formed by the rite for the praise of

God and for their own good. Whatever other preparations are required for the Eucharist, a readiness to enter into the rite of the Church and encounter the Mystery of Christ, again on the part of all, is the first stage of the necessary preparation for Mass and allows for an equal readiness to receive the abundant gifts that flow from the celebration of the Sacred Liturgy. The priest celebrant is charged in a particular way to prepare himself with prayer for Mass and, for that matter, to give thanks following the celebration.[7]

In general, what is described by the *General Instruction* for the preparation for Mass with the People without a Deacon and with a Deacon is also what is necessary for a Concelebrated Mass and Mass at Which only One Minister Participates. In addition to what is described below for the preparations for the celebration of each form of the Mass for the priest celebrant and Deacon, what is needed for the faithful must also be considered. Whatever worship aids are needed should be easily and readily available. Any instructions that will assist their participation should be made beforehand or printed in the worship aid. Lastly, there should be sufficient amplification for all to hear (see GIRM 306).

Mass with the People without a Deacon and with a Deacon

As far as what is to be prepared for the celebration of Mass, the *General Instruction* first draws our attention to what is needed for the altar, then the actual celebration, and finally the proper vesture for the priest, the Deacon, and the liturgical ministers. The altar is the centerpiece of the celebration of the Eucharist and so its appointments deserve serious attention:

> The altar is to be covered with at least one white cloth. In addition, on or next to the altar are to be placed can-

> dlesticks with lighted candles: at least two in any celebration, or even four or six, especially for a Sunday Mass or a Holyday of Obligation, or if the Diocesan Bishop celebrates, then seven candlesticks with lighted candles. Likewise, on the altar or close to it, there is to be a cross adorned with a figure of Christ crucified. The candles and the cross with the figure of Christ crucified may also be carried in the procession at the Entrance. On the altar itself may be placed a Book of the Gospels distinct from the book of other readings, unless it is carried in the Entrance Procession. (117)

In every instance (recalling what is described in chapter three about the altar and its appointments), the altar is covered with a white cloth from the beginning of the celebration, and candlesticks with lighted candles are placed on it or near it. If these candlesticks are not placed on the altar, then their position near the altar should be such that it is obvious that they appoint the altar itself. Sunday, the Lord's Day, is the original holy day[8] and so in any plan of progressive solemnity, as with a similar ranking solemnity, this fact is indicated by the number of candles beyond the minimum of two. In fact, a common practice today is to place six candles on or near the altar for a Sunday and solemnity, four for a feast, and two for weekdays and memorials. The traditional custom of seven candlesticks on or near the altar when the diocesan bishop celebrates has its origin in the ancient practice of seven candlesticks employed for Masses with the Bishop of Rome. There is no precise placement given for the arrangement of the seven candlesticks or, for that matter, for any number of candlesticks. The altar cross, with an obvious image of the crucified Christ, is to be placed on or near the altar. The explicit identification of the figure of Christ crucified makes the visible connection between this appointment and the action of the altar, the Sacrifice of the Lord. Again, if the altar cross is not placed on the altar, its placement near the altar should obviously relate it to the altar. These very same appointments, the candlesticks and altar cross, may also serve as the processional candles and cross during the Entrance. Although this is not a common practice, making use of these appointments in this way links the purpose of the Entrance, an entrance into the Mystery of Christ, which fully unfolds with the divine event at the altar. The *Book of the Gospels* may be placed on the altar on certain occasions in preparation for Mass when it cannot be carried, for some good reason, by the Deacon or a concelebrant or even the reader.

With the altar ready for the celebration of Mass, then what is needed for the actual celebration is prepared at the chair for the priest celebrant, at the ambo, and on the credence table:

> Likewise these should be prepared:
>
> a) next to the Priest's chair: the Missal and, if appropriate, a hymnal;
>
> b) at the ambo: the Lectionary;
>
> c) on the credence table: the chalice, corporal, purificator, and, if appropriate, the pall; the paten and, if needed, ciboria; bread for the Communion of the Priest who presides, the Deacon, the ministers, and the people; cruets containing the wine and the water, unless all of these are presented by the faithful in the procession at the Offertory; the vessel of water to be blessed, if the sprinkling of holy water takes place; the Communion-plate for the Communion of the faithful; and whatever is needed for the washing of hands.

> It is a praiseworthy practice for the chalice to be covered with a veil, which may be either of the color of the day or white. (GIRM 118)

The Introductory Rites always begin at the chair in the Mass with the People, and so it is necessary to have the *Roman Missal* available, even if the priest celebrant has committed to memory most of the texts for these rites. It is always permissible and fitting for these rites to have a stand for the *Roman Missal* at the chair when a server is unavailable. The priest celebrant, as a member of the liturgical assembly, not only leads prayer but also joins in prayer, so it is helpful that whatever is needed, such as a hymnal, is available as well for singing these rites. The *Lectionary for Mass*, closed, is set to the readings of the day and ready for use at the ambo.

In the sanctuary, there should be an additional table, a credence table, for items needed for the Liturgy of the Eucharist and other parts of the Mass. The use of a credence table or side table near the altar for these items preserves the altar's significance as the sign and place of the Sacrifice of Christ. The altar itself should not double as a credence table. The *General Instruction* at this point does not simply identify what might be on this table but also instructs about the items. The chalice and paten and all that is a part of their use during the Liturgy of the Eucharist are listed: the corporal, the purificator, and a pall, if it is to be used. When the paten and ciborium are mentioned, the instruction presumes that bread will be prepared for all those receiving Holy Communion at the Mass. Some of these items, including the cruets of wine and water, may be either on this table or be part of the procession at the Offertory. Finally, the Communion plate and those things needed to wash the hands of the priest are also at this table. On certain occasions, other items may be placed on the credence table, such as additional chalices with purificators for the Precious Blood. The vessel of water would be an element not needed for the Liturgy of the Eucharist but, if needed for the Introductory Rites, may also be on the credence table.

The note about veiling or vesting the chalice should not be easily put aside. In fact, the practice of veiling the chalice in either the vestment color of the day or white is considered praiseworthy because of the meaning it communicates. In the same way that the word of God is vested with fine book covers as an indication that the texts of Scripture give voice to God himself, the vesting of the chalice with the veil indicates that this sacred vessel is for the very Body and Blood of the Lord. If additional chalices for Communion will be used for the distribution of the Blood of Christ, then there is no reason that prevents a veil being placed over all the chalices.

Finally, the proper vesture needed for the priest, Deacon, and liturgical ministers must be prepared:

> In the sacristy, according to the various forms of celebration, there should be prepared the sacred vestments (cf. nos. 337–341) for the Priest, the Deacon, and other ministers:
>
> > a) for the Priest: the alb, the stole, and the chasuble;
> >
> > b) for the Deacon: the alb, the stole, and the dalmatic; the latter may be omitted, however, either out of necessity or on account of a lesser degree of solemnity;
> >
> > c) for the other ministers: albs or other lawfully approved attire.

> All who wear an alb should use a cincture and an amice unless, due to the form of the alb, they are not needed.
>
> When the Entrance takes place with a procession, the following are also to be prepared: a Book of the Gospels; on Sundays and festive days, a thurible and incense boat, if incense is being used; the cross to be carried in procession; and candlesticks with lighted candles. (GIRM 119)

The vesture proper to the priest, the Deacon, if he is assisting, and the liturgical ministers specified above received a fuller treatment in chapter three. Vesting takes place apart from the place of the liturgical celebration, in a place that allows for preparation for the Entrance to the Mass. The chasuble is always required for the priest celebrant, along with the alb and stole. The dalmatic for the Deacon may be omitted for serious reasons; for example, if one is not available, but the Deacon always wears an alb and stole. Liturgical ministers should be vested. The alb is preferred unless something else is locally determined. The use of the amice and cincture, typically white, are expected with the alb unless the garment allows for their purpose in some other form. The vesting of the sacred ministers and the liturgical ministers should take place in the vesting room in silence to foster the needed interior preparation for the celebration of the Sacred Mysteries (see GIRM 45). Making use of the traditional vesting prayers assists with this focused preparation.

If the Entrance includes a procession (which is determined according to the liturgical day, occasion, and/or place for the celebration), then incense is prepared, if it is to be used. The cross and lighted candlesticks are readied as well. The *Book of the Gospels* is also to be prepared if it will be carried in the Entrance. All of these items or the cross alone may be part of the Entrance depending on the local plan for progressive solemnity.

Preparation for Concelebrated Mass

In addition to what is listed above as to what things are to be prepared for the celebration of Mass with the People, for a Concelebrated Mass additional seats for the concelebrants and any texts that they might need — for example, copies of the Eucharistic Prayer and hymnals — should also be prepared. On the credence table, a chalice with a larger cup or additional chalices should be prepared for the concelebrants' reception of the Blood of the Lord (see GIRM 207). Part of the preparation of a Concelebrated Mass is the distribution of roles beforehand among concelebrants. As already mentioned, in any form of the Mass, if a Deacon is present, then he vests and carries out his proper duties. However, if a Deacon is not present for a Concelebrated Mass, then one or several concelebrants carry out the duties of the Deacon but always vested as a concelebrating priest. One or several concelebrants are to assist the priest celebrant in proclaiming the Gospel, preparing the altar and the gifts, raising the chalice at the doxology of the Eucharistic Prayer, giving the invitation to the sign of peace, and announcing the Dismissal. If liturgical ministers are absent from the celebration and members of the faithful are unable to carry out their duties, then one or several concelebrants serve the Mass, proclaim the readings, and lead the singing of the Mass (see 208). Concelebrants likewise vest in a location apart from the place of the celebration of the Eucharist and with the same vesture worn by the priest celebrant when celebrating Mass individually. Only out of necessity is the chasuble omitted by a concelebrant; for example, if one is not available, but in every case the concelebrants wear the alb and stole (see 209).

Preparation for Mass at Which only One Minister Participates

The things to be prepared for Mass at Which only One Minister Participates are the same as for Mass with the People. The only difference is that the sacred vessels may be "at the credence table or on the right hand side of the altar" (GIRM 255). The preference even in this form of the Mass, presuming the presence of a Deacon or a server, is that these vessels be at the credence table.

Instituted and Deputed Ministers

In the subsequent chapters, the duties of the instituted and deputed ministers in serving Mass will be described for each part of the Mass. The presence and assistance of these liturgical ministers, whether as instituted acolytes or deputed servers, allows for a more careful and reverent celebration of the Eucharist. In fact, the arrangement of the rites anticipates that these liturgical ministers assist the priest celebrant and the faithful. Thus, an important dimension of each form of the Mass and the required preparation is the suitable training and formation of ministers to serve the Mass. Due consideration should be given to the form of the Mass and the solemnity of the occasion in determining the number of ministers needed and their respective duties.

Conclusion

The *ars celebrandi* not only guides the celebration of the Eucharist but also applies to the form of the Mass celebrated and the preparation for it. Regardless of the form of the Mass, the ordained and the baptized ought to dispose themselves for the celebration with an awareness of what is distinct about each form and what to expect liturgically and theologically with a particular form. The choice of form is not accidental but specific with regard to solemnity, circumstance, and occasion. Mass with the People without or with a Deacon, the typical parish celebration, brings with it notions of the Church celebrating the Mystery of Christ and with everyone anticipating his or her proper role. The Concelebrated Mass, which happens rather frequently, in addition to a focus on the whole People of God offering the Sacrifice of the Lord, highlights the notion of the unity of the priesthood. Mass at Which only One Minister Participates gives expression to the unique role of the priest to act on behalf of the salvation of all with the Eucharist.

An awareness beforehand of the form of the Mass to be celebrated allows for the fitting and necessary preparation associated with that form. The careful and complete preparation of all things needed for the Eucharist corresponding to the form of the Mass is another dimension of the *ars celebrandi*. When all is ready for the celebration of the Eucharist with respect to its form, then there is confident assurance that the actual celebration will be carried out in an artful and careful manner on the part of the ordained and the baptized. Preparation of all things needed for the Eucharist underscores the expected *ars celebrandi* throughout the celebration.

Preparation for the celebration of Mass on the part of the ordained and the baptized connects directly with the indispensable place of the Eucharist in the Christian life. Focused engagement and authentic participation in the Mystery of Christ are promoted when there is interior preparation, especially with prayer and the union of self with the offering of Christ that will take place, combined with the physical and external preparation required. The grace of this engagement, this participation, in the divine event of the Liturgy carries over into the living out of this same Mystery with the routines and demands of the Christian life.

The next chapter looks at the Introductory Rites of the Mass, and provides a description of the several elements and directions for their celebration for each form of the Mass.

CHAPTER FIVE
The Introductory Rites

This chapter looks at the Introductory Rites of the Mass. Each element of the Introductory Rites is presented as described in the *General Instruction of the Roman Missal*. Then follow the directions for carrying out the Introductory Rites as given in both the *General Instruction* and the *Order of Mass* for each form for the celebration of the Eucharist — the Mass with the People without and with a Deacon, the Concelebrated Mass, and the Mass at Which only One Minister Participates. Looking at the directions for each form for the celebration of the Eucharist will be the pattern for the subsequent parts of the Mass as well. The directions given are supplemented with ideas and suggestions that should be considered for an authentic and careful observance of the rites. The choice of Collect, the highpoint of the Introductory Rites, is specifically addressed. Finally, the important duties of the liturgical ministers for the Introductory Rites are outlined. The *ars celebrandi* of the whole celebration of the

Eucharist begins with a primary consideration of this discipline with the Introductory Rites of the Mass.

The Introductory Rites

The manner in which the Introductory Rites are carried out deserves special attention so that the whole of the celebration of the Eucharist is focused on the saving Mystery of Christ. The several elements of the Introductory Rites are not meant to pile up as one on top of the other or project a cumbersome arrangement of these same elements. Rather, these rites — the Entrance, Reverence to the Altar and Greeting of the Assembled People, the Penitential Act, the *Kyrie, eleison (Lord, have mercy)*, the *Gloria in excelsis* (*Glory to God in the highest*), and the Collect — are intended to combine to unite the priest and faithful. These rites likewise prepare for the Paschal event as it is announced in the Liturgy of the Word and realized in the Liturgy of the Eucharist. When the priest celebrant and the faithful give attention to each of the elements of the Introductory Rites, properly understood and engaged, then they come together as a communion, head and members in Christ, to encounter him in the word of God and in the Sacrifice of the Lord in a worthy manner. The Introductory Rites belong to the complete *Order of Mass*. However, they are at times omitted or amended when other liturgical actions or rites are combined with the Mass; for example, with the *Order of Celebrating Matrimony*, the *Order of Christian Funerals*, and the *Liturgy of the Hours*. In such cases, the norms for these circumstances are observed as found in the respective ritual books (see GIRM 46).

Description of the elements of the Introductory Rites

The Entrance

The celebration of the Eucharist begins with the faithful already assembled — assembled by Christ. The entrance of the priest celebrant with the Deacon, if he is assisting, and the liturgical ministers is not so much about entering into the assembly or simply moving to the altar. Rather, as they enter, they bring the assembly with them to enter into the Mystery of Christ that will unfold with this celebration of Mass. So, as the priest celebrant enters, the Entrance Chant begins. This chant has a specific purpose as the first element of the Introductory Rites: to open the celebration, to foster the unity of those who have been assembled, to introduce their thoughts to the mystery of the liturgical time or occasion, and finally to accompany the procession of the priest celebrant and the liturgical ministers to the altar (see GIRM 47). This chant does not so much gather people as much as it leads the whole liturgical assembly into the Paschal action of Christ in his word and Sacrifice.

This chant, especially since one of its purposes is to encourage unity among those assembled, is usually sung by everyone. The *General Instruction* further specifies that it may be carried out by the choir or cantor and the faithful alternately, or by the faithful alone or by the choir alone (see 48). Each of these options has value and should be considered for varying circumstances. Often, the option exercised is for the assembly alone to sing. As far as sources for the Entrance Chant, the *General Instruction* includes four principal options:

(1) the antiphon from the Missal or the antiphon with its Psalm from the *Graduale Romanum* as set to music there or in another setting;

(2) the antiphon and Psalm of the *Graduale Simplex* for the liturgical time;

(3) a chant from another collection of Psalms and anti-

> phons, approved by the Conference of Bishops or the Diocesan Bishop, including Psalms arranged in responsorial or metrical forms;
>
> (4) another liturgical chant that is suited to the sacred action, the day, or the time of year, similarly approved by the Conference of Bishops or the Diocesan Bishop. (48)

It is clear from the provided options that the content of the Entrance Chant should be above all the word of God with antiphons and psalms sung in a variety of ways, including responsorially and metrically. If for some reason the corresponding psalm is not the option chosen, then the chant that is chosen, such as a hymn, must suit the purpose of the Entrance Chant as well as the liturgical observance or time. The Entrance Chant, especially as it makes use of the word of God to lead those assembled into the Mystery of Christ, is a constitutive element of the Introductory Rites and should never be omitted. In those instances when it is not sung, the antiphon provided by the *Roman Missal* should be recited. This can be done by the body of the faithful or only a few of them, by the reader, or even by the priest celebrant. In some situations, the priest celebrant may choose to make use of the recited antiphon as part of the introduction of the Mass that follows the Greeting of the Mass (see GIRM 48 and 31). It seems more appropriate with all of these options for the recited antiphon from the *Roman Missal* that everyone reciting it together be the norm. This accords more with the stated purpose of this element of the Introductory Rites, especially to foster the unity of those assembled.

Reverence to the Altar and Greeting of the Assembled People

The altar as a sign of Christ and his saving Sacrifice on the cross is the centerpiece and focus of the whole of the celebration of the

Eucharist. As such, the altar receives its own reverence, which is a profound bow on the part of the priest celebrant, the Deacon, if he is assisting, and the liturgical ministers as they come before it in the sanctuary (see GIRM 49). If the tabernacle with the Most Blessed Sacrament is in the sanctuary, the profound bow is replaced with a genuflection on the part of all (274). The bow does not substitute for a genuflection. They each have different meanings and purposes as discussed previously in chapter two. In addition to reverencing the altar, the priest celebrant and the Deacon, if he is assisting, also venerate it with a kiss (49). This kiss should be intentional and express a true devotion to the altar Mystery. It does not matter what side of a free-standing altar is venerated; typically, this veneration by the priest celebrant takes place in the center of the altar, regardless of the side. When it is fitting, and especially for more solemn celebrations, the cross and the altar may be incensed as discussed in chapter three. The reverence and veneration of the altar, as well as the incensation, if it takes place, are part of the Entrance and therefore should be accompanied by the single Entrance Chant.

After the priest celebrant has venerated the altar and incensed it, if incensation takes place, he goes and stands at the chair. When the Entrance Chant is finished, the priest celebrant makes the Sign of the Cross, and the faithful do the same as together they give expression to the Trinitarian Faith of the Church and their baptismal privilege to give thanks and praise to God with the Eucharist. The Sign of the Cross is followed by the Greeting, which also has particular meaning at this point: "By means of the Greeting [the priest celebrant] signifies the presence of the Lord to the assembled community. By this greeting and the people's response, the mystery of the Church gathered together is made manifest" (GIRM 50).

The *General Instruction* attributes a level of theological meaning and weight to this Greeting that underscores the need that it be carried out with dignity and care and not in a perfunctory manner. The priest celebrant is at the chair, the place that signifies he is head of the assembled body of the faithful, the ordained oriented to the baptized. He makes use of the apostolic texts to greet the faithful, and they respond recognizing the spirit within him that acclaims it is truly the Lord who has assembled his Church for the celebration of his Mysteries. Following the Greeting, as discussed in chapter three, the Mass may be introduced briefly by the priest celebrant or the Deacon, if assisting, or by someone else prepared to do so (see 50). An extended Greeting on occasion can move beyond its function and actually draw attention away from the overall purpose of the Introductory Rites; for example, when a reference at this point to the biblical texts becomes more of a reflection which properly belongs to the Homily of the Mass.

The Penitential Act

The Penitential Act, with several formulae in the *Order of Mass*, follows the Sign of the Cross and the Greeting. The priest celebrant calls the faithful to take part in the Penitential Act with his invitation, which includes a pause for a brief period of silence, followed by one of the proposed forms for the Penitential Act, and then his concluding absolution. The silence that follows the invitation is a corporate act of recollection and should be consistently observed by all as a stable part of the Penitential Act. This act is not about the forgiveness of sins but rather an occasion to focus on the celebration of the Sacred Mysteries to follow without the distraction of our daily sins. Thus, the *General Instruction* gives the reminder that the absolution of the priest celebrant in this instance is not comparable to the absolution of the Sacrament of Penance (see 51).

The Kyrie, Eleison

The *Kyrie, eleison (Lord, have mercy)* usually follows the Penitential Act. However, when the *Kyrie* is part of the Penitential Act, such as in the third form presented in the *Order of Mass,*[1] then it is not repeated as an independent element of the Introductory Rites. With the *Kyrie*, the faithful acclaim that Christ is Lord and beg him to pour out his abundant mercy, and so it is typically sung by everyone with alternation between the cantor or the choir and the faithful. The *Order of Mass* provides that each "Lord, have mercy," "Christ, have mercy," and "Lord have mercy" be repeated twice.[2] However, it is also possible that each be repeated several times, depending on the language used or the musical form employed. When the *Kyrie* forms part of the Penitential Act, such as in the third form, it is preceded by an invocation or a trope (see GIRM 52).

When the Introductory Rites are replaced by another rite (for example, by a procession[3] or the Morning and Evening Prayer of the Liturgy of the Hours[4]), the *Kyrie* may still be sung or recited as an independent element.

The Gloria in Excelsis

The *Gloria in excelsis (Glory to God in the highest)* is beautifully described in the *General Instruction* as "a most ancient and venerable hymn by which the Church, gathered in the Holy Spirit, glorifies and entreats God the Father and the Lamb" (53). The Trinitarian structure of this ancient song repels any rearrangement of the text but rather recommends that it be sung or recited as composed. The *Gloria* is above all a hymn intended to be sung whenever possible, and certainly on more festive and solemn occasions. When it is sung, it is typically intoned by the priest or, if he is not able to do so, then by the cantor or the choir, and then sung by everyone. It can also be sung alternately with the choir and at times sung by the choir alone. When it is not sung, it is recited by everyone or by two groups responding one to the other (see GIRM 53). When it is sung by the choir alone, which is usually due to a complex composition, the hymn setting must allow for all to experience the worship of God and not be reduced to a performance experience.

The *Gloria* is sung or recited on Sundays, except for those in Advent and Lent, and on solemnities and feasts. It may also be sung or recited on particular occasions of a more festive or solemn character (see 53). It is required for certain Ritual Masses regardless of the liturgical time, including Advent and Lent, during which they are celebrated (see *Roman Missal*, Ritual Masses).

The *Gloria* is part of the *Order of Mass* and therefore cannot be replaced by any other hymn text (see GIRM 53). When it is recited, the rendering is often without a sense of corporate praise and sounds more like the rattling off of words. The priest celebrant can set the tone and pace for a deliberate recitation of the hymn so that even in the spoken form it receives a dignified sound. In addition, the recitation by two groups, suggested in the *General Instruction*, fosters a more careful recitation of the hymn. The use of the sung *Gloria* as an Entrance or to accompany the Sprinkling of Water is a misuse of the hymn and a misappropriation of this element of the Introductory Rites.

The Collect

The Collect, the highpoint of the Introductory Rites because it identifies the observance or character of the celebration, concludes these rites. The priest celebrant invites the faithful to pray and then together with them observes a sufficiently brief period of silence. This silence is a part of the structure of the Collect. It allows that everyone "may become aware of being in God's presence and may call to mind their intentions" (GIRM 54). Therefore, it should be sufficiently long for the gathering of intentions and not be omitted. The prayer itself follows this silence. Only a single Collect is ever prayed at Mass (see 54).

The *General Instruction* gives specific directions for the conclusion of this prayer and the faithful's Acclamation to it:

By an ancient tradition of the Church, the Collect prayer is usually addressed to God the Father, through Christ, in the Holy Spirit, and is concluded with a Trinitarian ending, or longer ending, in the following manner:

> – If the prayer is directed to the Father: Through our Lord Jesus Christ, your Son, who lives and reigns with you in the unity of the Holy Spirit, God, for ever and ever;
>
> – If it is directed to the Father, but the Son is mentioned at the end: Who lives and reigns with you in the unity of the Holy Spirit, God, for ever and ever;
>
> – If it is directed to the Son: Who live and reign with God the Father in the unity of the Holy Spirit, God, for ever and ever.
>
> The people, joining in this petition, make the prayer their own by means of the acclamation *Amen.* (54)

On the occasions when this prayer is sung, the musical notations given in the *Roman Missal* for presidential prayers for the solemn and the reciting tone are observed.[5]

Directions for the Introductory Rites

Now with each element of the Introductory Rites described liturgically and theologically, the directions to follow possess a weight that presses for their authentic and careful observance in the celebration of Mass. Oftentimes casualness accompanies these rites, which diminishes their significance to the whole of the Mystery of Christ in the celebration of the Eucharist and compromises their purpose to assist the priest celebrant and the faithful in encountering Christ in his saving work. Throughout the presentation of each of the forms of the Mass, more specific points for the *ars celebrandi* are proposed.

The Introductory Rites for Mass without a Deacon

The directions for the celebration of Mass in both the *General Instruction* and the *Order of Mass* begin with the fact that the people are already assembled.[6] The priest celebrant, as he processes to the altar, collects the assembled faithful with him as together they enter into the celebration of the Mystery of Christ. Therefore, everything that is directed for this procession is inclusive of the faithful, especially by way of the Entrance Chant, so they can be united to the priest celebrant as he moves toward the altar. The priest celebrant and the liturgical ministers wear their respective proper vestments as described in chapter three and with everything prepared for Mass as described in chapter four (see GIRM 120).

The *General Instruction* outlines the order for this procession to the altar:

> a) the thurifer carrying a smoking thurible, if incense is being used;
>
> b) ministers who carry lighted candles, and between them an acolyte or other minister with the cross;
>
> c) the acolytes and the other ministers;
>
> d) a reader, who may carry a Book of the Gospels (though not a Lectionary), slightly elevated;
>
> e) the Priest who is to celebrate the Mass.
> If incense is being used, before the procession begins, the Priest puts some into the thurible and blesses it with

the Sign of the Cross without saying anything. (120)

During the procession, as the priest celebrant and liturgical ministers move toward the altar, the Entrance Chant is sung or recited.[7] Again, one of the chief purposes of this chant is to accompany the whole of this procession (see GIRM 47). Both those in the procession and the liturgical musicians need to be mindful of the correspondence between the movement to the altar and the Entrance Chant. The order given above for the procession presumes a more solemn celebration of the Eucharist with a full complement of liturgical ministers and the use of incense. What is to be observed in this order is a universal pattern for the procession, both when all elements are in place and when only a few are in place. For example, if there is only a cross bearer and a reader along with the priest celebrant, then the order follows the above pattern, with the cross bearer first, followed by the reader and then the priest celebrant. The thurible, prepared beforehand, is smoking for the procession. The rising of the incense even at this moment indicates that the procession is an action of worship. The cross bearer is positioned between the candle bearers. The *Book of the Gospels*, but never the *Lectionary for Mass*, is carried in procession by a reader always immediately in front of the priest celebrant. The procession is not simply a practical gesture of getting from one place to another for the celebration of the Eucharist. Rather, it is a movement with theological meaning, a movement into the Mystery of Christ. So, its pace should be purposeful. Everything carried in the procession — the thurible and boat, the cross and candles, the *Book of the Gospels* — should likewise be fitting and designed for a liturgical procession. Often, non-liturgical items, such as flags and banners, are suggested for this procession. If they have meaning for those celebrating and do not distract from the purpose of this procession and the Eucharist itself, then they might be carried before the incense or cross and placed in a suitable place away from the altar, even outside of the sanctuary.

When the priest celebrant and the liturgical ministers reach the altar, they make a profound bow to it.[8] If the tabernacle with the Most Blessed Sacrament is in the sanctuary, a genuflection in adoration of the Sacrament replaces this bow. The liturgical ministers, if they are carrying something, bow their heads (see GIRM 274). If the cross has been carried in procession, it may be placed next to the altar to serve as the altar cross. If it serves as the altar cross, then it is to be the only cross in the sanctuary. For this reason, the *General Instruction* insists that this cross have a figure of the crucified Christ on it (see 308). If the cross is not going to serve as the altar cross, then it is placed out of sight in a suitable place, either hanging on a wall or in a stand and not leaning against a wall. If the candlesticks have been carried in procession, then they may be placed on the altar or near it. Otherwise, they also are placed out of sight in a suitable place. The use of the procession cross and candles for the altar cross and candles visibly unites the action of the Entrance with the celebration of the Eucharist and so should be given serious consideration, as mentioned in chapter four. The reader is to place the *Book of the Gospels* flat on the mensa of the altar itself, leaving sufficient room for the veneration of the altar by the priest celebrant. The practice of standing the *Book of the Gospels* upright on the altar draws unnecessary attention to it prior to the Gospel reading. The presence of Christ arrives when the Gospel is proclaimed, and it is for this reason the book is carried and incensed. The gesture of placing the *Book of the Gospels* on the altar makes the theological connection between the saving Mystery of Christ announced with the Gospel and the sacrament of this same Mystery that will take place at the altar.[9]

After the priest celebrant reverences the altar, he then goes up to the altar itself and venerates it with a kiss. Everything about this veneration should demonstrate a profound regard for the altar itself and the Sacrifice that will take place upon it. Therefore, in an unhurried way, with hands folded or placed upon the altar, the priest reverently kisses it. On more solemn occasions, it is appropriate that incense be used at this point. The altar cross is incensed first, and then the altar is incensed according to the pattern described in chapter three.[10]

After the altar has been venerated and, if used, the incensation completed, the priest celebrant goes to his chair, which is typically facing the faithful.[11] Thus, the position for the priest celebrant is to face the faithful throughout the Introductory Rites. This position of the priest celebrant allows for the dialogue between the ordained and baptized, the head and members of the Body of Christ, and authentically frames and forms the liturgical assembly with these rites. The liturgical ministers also take their place in the sanctuary but not next to the chair of the priest celebrant. The Entrance Chant should conclude as the priest celebrant arrives at the chair, standing along with all the faithful. It is explicitly clear from the directions found in the *General Instruction* and the *Order of Mass* that the chair is the place for the priest celebrant to carry out the Introductory Rites and not the altar. If a server is not available to minister the *Roman Missal* for the Introductory Rites, a stand may be placed at the chair for these rites, as previously mentioned. Again, one of the theological points to be grasped by the position of the priest celebrant at the chair for these rites is that he acts as head of the body of the faithful. Together, the priest and the faithful become sacramentally the whole Christ for the celebration of his Mystery that will unfold at the ambo and at the altar.

Next the priest celebrant and the faithful reverently make the Sign of the Cross. The priest celebrant, again facing the people, sings or says, without any introduction, "In the name of the Father, and of the Son, and of the Holy Spirit," to which the faithful respond, "Amen."[12] The Sign of the Cross is the first declared text of the *Order of Mass* that belongs to the priest celebrant. It is first presented with musical notations and then the spoken text follows. This pattern of first presenting the text with musical notation and then the spoken text alone is followed throughout the *Order of Mass* in the *Roman Missal.* The liturgical book itself in this way makes the point that the Roman Mass is typically sung. The musical notations found throughout the *Order of Mass* are the solemn tone. The simple tone is found in the appendix to the *Roman Missal.* When the Mass is sung, it is preferable that the same tone be used for all the parts of the Ordinary to allow for unity of musical sound throughout the course of the Eucharist.[13]

The Sign of the Cross is followed by one of three possible greetings provided in the *Order of Mass.* They can all be used equally at the choice of the priest celebrant and are carried out in the same way. Again, the priest celebrant, facing the faithful, extending and closing his hands, greets them, and they respond to any of the three greetings with "And with your spirit."[14] The *Order of Mass* provides the musical notations for each greeting and the response. The *Order of Mass* also includes the greeting that a bishop celebrant may use: "Peace be with you," in place of the greeting option "The Lord be with you."[15] Following the Greeting, the Mass of the day may be briefly introduced by the priest celebrant or someone else as described in chapter two.[16] Attentiveness to the *ars celebrandi* recognizes a link between the actions of the reverencing or greeting of the altar and the greeting of the faithful — the sign of Christ and those who belong to Christ's Body. It is not fitting to intrude on these actions with a "Good Morning" or some other pedestrian greeting at the chair. Rather, with the introduction that follows the Greeting of the Mass, a welcome can be extended, if at all necessary, to the faithful.

The Penitential Act follows the Greeting or the introduction to the Mass of the day, if this took place (see GIRM 125). The first part of the Penitential Act is the invariable introduction, which is sung according to the musical notations in the *Order of Mass* or recited by the priest celebrant. A brief pause for silence follows so that all may become recollected.[17] This silence, a corporate action, should be unhurried and serious if it is to accomplish its purpose. Three possible forms for the Penitential Act follow, which can be equally used for any celebration of Mass. The first form is the "I confess," recited by all together. There is no provision for this form to be sung. During the "I confess," all strike their breast only once during the words, "through my fault, through my fault, through my most grievous fault."[18] The second form includes a set of versicles and responses between the priest and the faithful, which can be sung according to the musical notations in the *Order of Mass* or recited.[19] The third form includes three invocations, with "Lord, have mercy" after the first; "Christ, have mercy" after the second; and "Lord, have mercy" after the third in English or Greek, sung according to the musical notations in the *Order of Mass* or recited by the priest celebrant or someone else. The *Order of Mass* provides for one set of invocations. One of the appendices to the *Roman Missal* provides for seven additional sets of invocations for this third form.[20] Invocations suitable for the liturgical observance or occasion can be composed based on the liturgical texts or the Biblical Readings, always, however, directed to the Lord Jesus. All three forms of the Penitential Act conclude with the absolution sung according to the musical notations found in the *Order of Mass* or recited by the priest celebrant.[21] Simple tones for the Penitential Act can be found in another appendix to the *Roman Missal*.[22] Neither the priest celebrant nor the faithful make the Sign of the Cross during the absolution that concludes the Penitential Act.

The *Order of Mass* indicates in a note that the Penitential Act may be replaced with the Rite for the Blessing and Sprinkling of Water occasionally on Sundays, including anticipated Masses, and especially in Easter Time as a vivid reminder of Baptism.[23] The Rite for the Blessing and Sprinkling of Water likewise follows the Sign of the Cross and Greeting at the chair. The first part of the rite includes an invitation to the faithful, a pause for a sufficiently brief period of silence for recollection, and the blessing of the fresh water to which all respond "Amen." Two options are provided for the blessing of the water, one for outside Easter Time and one for Easter Time. Additionally, a form for the blessing of salt to be added to the water is provided as an option. The priest celebrant is directed to face the people and to keep his hands joined throughout this rite, except for the gesture of blessing over the water and the mixing of the salt into the water, if this takes place. The vessel to be filled with fresh water should be dignified and suited for this rite and not a household item. Also, the vessel should be held before the priest celebrant, without blocking his view of the faithful, from the invitation through the end of the blessing. At the conclusion of the blessing, the priest celebrant takes the aspergillium (the sprinkler) and sprinkles himself, the clergy, the liturgical ministers, and the faithful. He may move through the church for the sprinkling of water if this is appropriate. The *Roman Missal* gives a series of antiphons and a hymn for Outside and During Easter Time which also may be replaced by other suitable chants. Finally, after the sprinkling, the priest celebrant returns to the chair and concludes the rite with the text provided in the *Roman Missal*, to which the people respond, "Amen." The composition of this particular text does not easily suggest the faithful respond with the "Amen," so the priest celebrant should prompt this response in the way he sings or speaks this text. According to the *Roman Missal*, the *Gloria* is sung or recited, when prescribed, following the Rite for the Blessing and Sprinkling of Water.[24]

The Penitential Act is followed by the *Kyrie* which is sung or said as indicated in the *Order of Mass*.[25] This means that the *Kyrie* always follows the first and second forms of the Penitential Act; it does not follow the third form since it is a part of it. The *Order of Mass* presents the *Kyrie* with each phrase repeated twice, in English and Greek, with musical notations followed by the spoken form.[26] When the *Kyrie* is recited, the priest celebrant typically begins the alternation with the faithful.

When the *Gloria* is prescribed as indicated in the *Roman Missal*, it follows the *Kyrie*.[27] The *Order of Mass* provides for the *Gloria* first with musical notations and then in the spoken form.[28] If it is not sung, the priest celebrant typically begins the recitation of the *Gloria* with the faithful joining him for the remainder of the hymn.

Finally, the priest celebrant prays the Collect of the Mass. With his hands joined, he invites the people to pray as he sings or says, "Let us pray," with no further elaboration. Then all pray together in silence for a while, taking their time with this silence to recall the intentions to be brought forward in this particular celebration of the Mystery of Christ. Then, with hands extended, the priest celebrant sings or says the Collect of the Mass. He joins his hands again at the end of the Collect and the people acclaim, "Amen."[29]

The Introductory Rites for Mass with a Deacon

When a Deacon is present for the celebration of Mass, he is expected to carry out his liturgical ministry, always wearing the vestments proper to a Deacon. The *General Instruction* summarizes the service of the Deacon during the course of the Eucharist. The Deacon:

> a) assists the Priest and walks at his side;
>
> b) ministers at the altar, both as regards the chalice and the book;
>
> c) proclaims the Gospel and may, at the direction of the Priest Celebrant, give the Homily (cf. no. 66);
>
> d) guides the faithful people by giving appropriate in-

structions, and announces the intentions of the Universal Prayer;

e) assists the Priest Celebrant in distributing Communion, and purifies and arranges the sacred vessels;

f) carries out the duties of other ministers himself, if necessary, when none of them is present. (171)

In general, the Deacon assists the priest celebrant with these listed duties during the celebration of Mass and directs the participation of the faithful. The specific duties during the parts of the Mass, other than during the Introductory Rites, will be presented more completely in the subsequent chapters. In every part of the Mass, the Deacon should be ready to assist the priest celebrant with setting and indicating the proper pages in the *Roman Missal* and assisting the other liturgical ministers as well. This requires the Deacon to be well versed in the *Order of Mass*, the role of the priest celebrant, his own role, the duties of the liturgical ministers, and the particular features of the celebration taking place. Deacons are intended to assist in a proactive way throughout the Mass.

During the Entrance, the Deacon processes at the side of the priest celebrant. Typically, the Deacon is to the right side. However, the *General Instruction* simply indicates that the Deacon is at the side, specifying neither the right nor left. If the *Book of the Gospels* is to be carried in procession, the Deacon carries it, elevated only slightly so people can see it, and precedes the priest celebrant in the procession to the altar.[30] Elevated slightly suggests that the book is at shoulder level and not blocking the eyes. When the Deacon, carrying the *Book of the Gospels*, arrives at the altar, he makes no reverence at all and immediately goes up to the altar and places the *Book of the Gospels* flat on the mensa of the altar, leaving sufficient room for the veneration by the priest celebrant.

The Deacon remains at the altar, having moved to the side, and then together with the priest celebrant kisses the altar (see GIRM 173). If the priest celebrant venerates the altar with hands folded, then so does the Deacon. If the priest celebrant venerates the altar with hands joined, then so does the Deacon. If the Deacon does not carry the *Book of the Gospels* in procession, then he bows profoundly or genuflects, depending on the location of the tabernacle, with the priest celebrant before the altar and then with him goes up to the altar and kisses it. On those occasions when incense is used, the Deacon assists the priest by taking the boat for the imposition of the incense. The Deacon bows to the cross with the priest celebrant for the incensation and may lead him around the altar as it is incensed (see 173).

After the veneration of the altar and, if used, the incensation, the Deacon accompanies the priest celebrant to the chair where there is also a seat for him. For the Introductory Rites the Deacon stands at the side of the priest celebrant, also facing the faithful, participating in the rites and ready to assist as needed (see GIRM 174). The Deacon may be the one to introduce the Mass of the day after the Greeting.[31] The Deacon may also announce the invocations of the third form of the Penitential Act.[32] Although it is a widespread practice, there is no indication in the *General Instruction* or the *Order of Mass* for the Deacon to lead the spoken *Kyrie, eleison.*

The Introductory Rites for Concelebrated Mass

When the faithful are gathered and everything is prepared, the procession moves to the altar. The concelebrant processes immediately ahead of the principal celebrant (see GIRM 210). In some cases, such as when there is a large number of concelebrants or a concelebrant with a disability, they may already be in place before the procession. Once the concelebrant arrives at the altar, he makes a profound bow to it or genuflects, depending on the location of the tabernacle. He then goes up to the altar and venerates it with a kiss and then moves to his designated seat. When concelebrants kiss the altar, they may venerate it two by two or even in greater numbers, if the altar allows for it, and on different sides of a free-standing altar. The concelebrant does not need to wait for the principal celebrant to reach the altar to make his reverence. In fact, he can go immediately up to the altar and venerate it and then go to his seat. This is especially the case when a Deacon is assisting and at the side of the principal celebrant. The seat for the concelebrant should be located in the sanctuary apart from the chair for the principal celebrant, as there is always only one priest who acts throughout the celebration of the Eucharist as the head of the assembled body. The seat for the concelebrant, however, should be placed so that he may easily engage the action of the priest celebrant, especially at the altar. In those circumstances where it is not possible for the concelebrants to have seats in the sanctuary, then whatever is arranged should have the concelebrants placed in such a way that their sacramental association with the priest celebrant is preserved. Under no circumstances should the concelebrants be seated among Deacons or the faithful. The principal celebrant, after he venerates the altar and, if incense is used, incenses the cross and altar, then goes to his chair (see 211).

If a Deacon is not present and the *Book of the Gospels* is carried in procession, the concelebrant does so in the same manner as a Deacon and places it flat on the mensa of the altar. If a Deacon is not present and incense is used, the concelebrant assists the principal celebrant in the same manner as a Deacon. The concelebrant may briefly introduce the Mass of the day and lead the invocations of the third form of the Penitential Act (see GIRM 208). All throughout the Introductory Rites, the concelebrant participates in each element like the faithful. If the Rite for the Blessing and Sprinkling of Water takes the place of the Penitential Act, the concelebrant is sprinkled first before the faithful.

The Introductory Rites for Mass at Which only One Minister Participates

In the celebration of Mass at Which only One Minister Participates, the Introductory Rites are carried out as directed for the Mass with the People, with the minister assisting and responding to the priest celebrant (see GIRM 252). If a Deacon is assisting, he carries out his proper duties as described above in the form of the Mass with a Deacon (253). In fact, the Mass should not be celebrated without anyone present except for a just reason,[33] as previously mentioned. When this is the case, the greetings, instructions, and the blessing are omitted (254).

The priest celebrant has two options for where the Introductory Rites take place in this form of the Mass: either at the chair or at the altar. So, the priest celebrant processes to the altar and there makes a profound bow or genuflection, depending on the location of the tabernacle. The Deacon and/or the minister does the same as the priest celebrant. Then, the priest celebrant goes up to the altar and venerates it with a kiss. At this point, he may either go to the chair or remain at the altar. If he remains at the altar, then the *Roman Missal* is placed on the altar before the celebration of Mass. Standing at the chair or at the altar, the priest celebrant recites the Entrance Antiphon from the *Roman Missal*.[34] For the Sign of the Cross and the Greeting, making use of one of the options in the *Order of Mass*, the priest celebrant faces the Deacon and/or the minister.[35] The Penitential Act without the introduction; the *Kyrie*, if not included in the Penitential Act; and the *Gloria*, if prescribed, are carried out as in the form of Mass with the People.[36] The Collect concludes the Introductory Rites as usual. The priest celebrant, with hands joined, gives the invitation, then after a brief period of silence and now with hands extended, recites the Collect. The Deacon and/or the minister at the conclusion of the prayer acclaims, "Amen."[37]

The Orations

As already stated above, there is only one Collect in any form of the Mass. The *Roman Missal* provides Collects for the Sundays and weekdays of the Liturgical Year; for solemnities, feasts, and memorials; and for various Commons, Ritual Masses, Masses for Various Needs and Occasions, Votive Masses, and Masses for the Dead. In some instances there are optional choices for the Collect as well as for the Prayer over the Offering and the Prayer after Communion that are used in conjunction with the Collect. The *General Instruction* provides assistance for these options:

> In any Mass the orations proper to that Mass are used, unless otherwise noted. On Memorials of Saints, the proper Collect is said or, if this is lacking, one from an appropriate Common. As to the Prayer over the Offerings and the Prayer after Communion, unless these are proper, they may be taken either from the Common or from the weekday of the current time of year. On the weekdays in Ordinary Time, however, besides the orations from the previous Sunday, orations from another Sunday in Ordinary Time may be used, or one of the Prayers for Various Needs provided in the Missal. However, it shall always be permissible to use from these Masses the Collect alone. In this way a richer collection of texts is provided, by which the prayer life of the faithful is more abundantly nourished. However, during the more important times of the year, provision has already been made for this by means of the orations proper to these times of the year that exist for each weekday in the Missal. (363)

The Collect establishes the proper and specific theological sentiments of the celebration of the Eucharist on every occasion. Therefore, some thought should be given to the choice of the Collect when there are options so that there is a harmony with other elements of the celebration, especially the liturgical observance and the Biblical Readings. Likewise, when there is a choice for the Collect, some additional thought should be given to the options for the Prayer over the Offerings and the Prayer after Communion to provide for a reasonable association among the orations of the Mass.

Instituted and Deputed Ministers and the Introductory Rites

Every celebration of Mass, as noted in chapter two, expects the service of a Deacon, if possible, and more specifically of liturgical minsters. For the Introductory Rites, the duties of the instituted acolyte and instituted reader are described in a general way in the *General Instruction* as they are for all parts of the Mass. In fact, the *General Instruction* offers this principle: "If at any celebration of Mass a Deacon is present, he should exercise his function. Furthermore, it is desirable that an acolyte, a reader, and a cantor should usually be there to assist the Priest Celebrant. Indeed, the rite … foresees an even greater number of ministers" (116).

Deputed servers and readers carry out similar duties to those of instituted acolytes and readers, respectively. The duties of an acolyte or server are varied, and several may serve at the same Mass. So, for the Mass with the People without and with a Deacon, and on more solemn occasions, several acolytes or servers are needed to carry out these duties. If only one instituted acolyte is present among several servers, he carries out the more significant duties and the deputed servers carry out the other duties (see GIRM 187).

For the Introductory Rites, an instituted acolyte, if he is the only one present, carries the cross in the procession as he walks between two other ministers with the lit candles. Otherwise, a deputed server carries the cross. If the cross will serve as the altar cross, the acolyte or server bows to the altar with the cross in hand and then places it near the altar. If the cross will not serve as the altar cross, the acolyte or server places it in a dignified area for the duration of the Mass. After the cross is in place, the acolyte or server assumes his place in the sanctuary (see GIRM 188). If other instituted acolytes are present for the Mass, they assist with the thurible and boat, if used, and the processional candles. Otherwise, deputed servers carry out these duties. Additionally, the duty of the acolyte or server during these rites is to assist the priest, and in some cases the Deacon, when needed, especially with the *Roman Missal*. If the Rite for the Blessing and Sprinkling of Water is used, then the acolyte or server holds the vessel with water before the priest celebrant and accompanies him as he sprinkles those assembled. The place for the instituted acolyte and deputed server is in the sanctuary where they can easily and carefully assist at the chair (see 189).

The instituted reader for the Introductory Rites may carry the *Book of the Gospels* in a slightly elevated position in the procession to the altar, if no Deacon or concelebrant is present. If this is the case, the instituted reader with the *Book of the Gospels* processes immediately in front of the priest celebrant of the Mass. If the instituted reader is not carrying the *Book of the Gospels*, he processes after the other instituted acolytes and/or deputed servers who are leading the procession (see GIRM 194). When the instituted reader reaches the altar, he makes a profound bow or genuflects depending on the location of the tabernacle. If he carried the *Book of the Gospels* in the procession, without bowing, he places it flat on the mensa of the altar, leaving sufficient room for the veneration.[38] He then assumes his place in the sanctuary (see 195). If a deputed reader carries the *Book of the Gospels* in the procession, then after placing it on the altar, he or she returns to his or her place in the nave.

Conclusion

It is worth repeating at this point the purpose of the Introductory Rites: to establish a communion within the liturgical assembly and to prepare all to hear the word of God and celebrate the Eucharist worthily (see GIRM 46). This purpose is realized, with the many elements of the Introductory Rites in each form of the Mass, with a meaningful focus on the part of the priest celebrant and the faithful throughout these rites. This includes a serious regard for each liturgical action with respect to postures and gestures, with an emphasis on the hands of the priest celebrant; to the occasions for silence; to a thoughtful choice of options for what is to be sung and spoken; and to the pacing of the rites. This meaningful focus during the first part of the Mass allows for an established *ars celebrandi*, which aids the priest and people in truly encountering Christ in their midst, and especially in his saving word and Sacrifice.

As the actual elements of the Introductory Rites prepare the ordained and baptized to enter into the liturgical celebration of the Mystery of Christ in the Eucharist, so similar moments and experiences in the Christian life, such as awareness of belonging to Christ and one another, a mindfulness of sinfulness and God's mercy, praising God, and seeking his help in prayer, lead to a deeper participation in these same rites and enrich them.

The next chapter looks at the Liturgy of the Word of the Mass with a description of the several elements and directions for their celebration for each form of the Mass.

CHAPTER SIX
The Liturgy of the Word

This chapter presents all the elements of the Liturgy of the Word. Some of these elements belong only to a Sunday or solemnity celebration of the Eucharist and others to every celebration. The announcement of the Mystery of salvation and redemption in the word of God takes place with several different ministers in the service of this Mystery and also of the liturgical assembly. Participation in this Mystery of Christ in the Liturgy of the Word, as it is oriented to the same Mystery in the Liturgy of the Eucharist, is enhanced when there is a focus on the *ars celebrandi* on the part of all the ministers for the rites that make up this part of the Mass.

The Liturgy of the Word

The Readings and explanation of the word of God is a principal element of the whole Mass. The *General Instruction of the Roman Missal* introduces this element from various theological perspectives. First, when the Sacred Scriptures are read during the course of the celebration of the Eucharist, God speaks to his people. In addition, when the Gospel is proclaimed, it is Christ himself who announces his own Gospel, for Christ is truly present in his word. Second, since the proclaiming of the biblical texts is indeed a communication of the divine word, this most important element of the Liturgy of the Word calls for a reverent attention and engagement on the part of everyone listening. Third, the Homily that follows the reading of Sacred Scripture provides for "a fuller understanding" of the texts and allows for "a greater efficaciousness of the word" as an essential part of the action of the Liturgy of the Word (see GIRM 29).

The Liturgy of the Word consists of several distinct elements: silence, the readings from Sacred Scripture, the chants that occur between the readings, the Homily, the Profession of Faith, and the Universal Prayer (see 55). Depending on the liturgical occasion, there may be only one Reading before the Gospel, and the Profession of Faith is not sung or recited. All of these parts combine to announce the saving word of the Lord.

In a densely theological manner, the *General Instruction* presents how each of these elements of the Liturgy of the Word also combines for an encounter between God himself and the assembled faithful as Christ makes known and present "the mystery of redemption and salvation" (55). God speaks to his people in the Liturgy of the Word, and this invites a response to this same Mystery on the part of the ordained and the baptized, making it their own and leading to prayer for others:

> For in the readings, as explained by the Homily, God speaks to his people, opening up to them the mystery of redemption and salvation, and offering spiritual nourishment; and Christ himself is present through his word in the midst of the faithful. By silence and by singing,

> the people make this divine word their own, and affirm their adherence to it by means of the Profession of Faith; finally, having been nourished by the divine word, the people pour out their petitions by means of the Universal Prayer for the needs of the whole Church and for the salvation of the whole world. (55)

Such a profound experience occasioned between God and his people in every celebration of the Liturgy of the Word demands an intentional regard for each element so that the theological dimensions are easily accessible and properly distinguished from typical human discourse and interaction. God is speaking! Christ is announcing his own Gospel! Redemption and salvation are taking place in the midst of the assembled faithful! Thus, the ministers of the Liturgy of the Word must have an understanding and appreciation of their role and duties in relationship to this display of revelation of the Mystery of Christ. They need to be well prepared and have the necessary skills for proclaiming, singing, and speaking the word of God. Each element of the Liturgy of the Word, as described below, in itself and related to the others, participates in the announcement of the word of God and needs to be understood first in this way. The order of the Liturgy of the Word is purposely arranged to allow for the divine dialogue that is this part of the Mass and so needs to be respected so that there is the opportunity for a response in faith to the saving voice of the Lord. Additionally, the suitability of the ambo, the vesture for the proclaimers, the *Lectionary for Mass*, the *Book of the Gospels*, the presentation of the Responsorial Psalm and the Universal Prayer, as well as the candles and thurible that may be used require deliberate attention during the Liturgy of the Word so that an artful celebration is achieved and the reverent reception of the word of God becomes the norm.

Description of the elements of the Liturgy of the Word

The elements of the Liturgy of the Word are outlined and described in the General Instruction and the General Introduction to the Lectionary, second edition.[1] These elements — Silence, the Biblical Readings, the Responsorial Psalm, the Acclamation before the Gospel, the Homily, the Profession of Faith, and the Universal Prayer — as already indicated, together make known the saving Mystery of the Lord in his word.

Silence

Today, many observe that the celebration of the Eucharist is highly verbal and lacks a sense of awe and wonder at the revelation of the Mystery of salvation that is actually taking place. The *General Instruction* identifies the theological fact that, with the proclamation of the word of God, and even with the Homily, the very Mystery of redemption and salvation is opened up to those who participate in the Liturgy of the Word. Our presence to this Mystery demands an attentiveness that can only happen with a focused silence. For this reason, the manner of celebrating the Liturgy of the Word should be such as to allow for meditation on the word of God and anything which impedes such meditation, especially racing through the readings, should be avoided (see 56). The use of brief silences during the course of the Liturgy of the Word, silence understood and observed by all in the liturgical assembly, will promote a meditative, reflective celebration of the Liturgy of the Word. The *General Instruction* further notes that the use of these brief silences allows for the Holy Spirit to act in such a way that "the Word of God may be grasped by the heart and a response through prayer may be prepared" (56). The four moments for these brief silences, consistently observed, are: before the announcement of the First Reading, after the First and Second Readings, and following the Homily (see 56). A dedicated observance of these brief silences simultaneously promotes a meditative character to the Liturgy of the Word and the *ars celebrandi* that should govern it.

The Biblical Readings

The Biblical Readings for the Liturgy of the Word are arranged in the *Lectionary for Mass*. The order of readings as found in the *Lectionary for Mass* for all occasions follows the order of the covenants: The readings from the Old Testament always precede those of the New Testament, which expresses the unity of the Testaments and of the divine plan of salvation (see GIRM 57). It is absolutely prohibited to substitute any non-biblical text for the word of God. This also includes the biblical text of the Responsorial Psalm (see 57). The dignity of the word of God and its fitting announcement requires that all the Biblical Readings be proclaimed from the ambo in Masses celebrated with the people (58).

As there is a certain hierarchy to the Biblical Readings, with the Gospel ranking above all others, so there is a corresponding ordering of sacred and liturgical ministers associated with the readings. The role of proclaiming the Biblical Reading is a ministerial function rather than a presidential function. Therefore, the Gospel is properly read by a Deacon and, if this is not possible, then by another priest. Only when these two possibilities are not present is the Gospel proclaimed by the priest celebrant himself. The other readings are proclaimed by readers. If this is not possible, then a Deacon, if he is present, may proclaim the readings. If a reader and a Deacon are not present, only then are the readings proclaimed by the priest celebrant. The one proclaiming the reading makes the Acclamation for the response of everyone else in the liturgical assembly, a response that salutes the word of God and receives it in faith and gratitude (see GIRM 59). Since the proclamation of the readings is ministerial rather than presidential in the service of the word and the assembly, the priest celebrant rarely reads the readings, including the Gospel.

The most significant Biblical Reading in the course of the Liturgy of the Word is the Gospel (see 60). As noted above, when the Gospel is proclaimed, Christ himself speaks his own word (29). The voice of the Bridegroom is heard by his Church.[2] The manner in which the Gospel is carried out affirms that it is indeed the word of the Savior announcing his own saving Mystery. The preparatory blessing or prayer that precedes the Gospel; its proclamation by the Deacon or in his absence by a priest; that it follows an Acclamation of faith in the real presence of Christ in his Gospel; and that a distinct book, the *Book of the Gospels*, is used on more solemn occasions for its proclamation — all these things together manifest to the assembled faithful that indeed it is the most significant of the Biblical Readings (see GIRM 60). The posture for the Gospel, with everyone standing to listen with reverence and to receive Christ's word with faith, is another indication of its significance. Standing for the Gospel not only distinguishes it from the other Biblical Readings but is the proper posture for the Gospel. The assembled faithful assume the posture of their communion with the Risen Lord as this same Risen Lord now addresses his Body in the Liturgy of the Word.

The Responsorial Psalm

The Responsorial Psalm is a Biblical Reading. It is considered on its own because of its function during the Liturgy of the Word. The Responsorial Psalm follows the First Reading in the order of the Liturgy of the Word, directly responding to what was just announced, and "fosters meditation on the Word of God" (GIRM 61). As with the other Biblical Readings, the Responsorial Psalm is found in the *Lectionary for Mass*.

The psalms belong to the sung prayer of the Hebrew people and entered the Christian liturgy as sung prayer as well. It is preferable that the Responsorial Psalm be sung, and in fact this should be the norm. This can be achieved in several different ways. For example, the response alone is sung, or the response is sung and the psalmist, cantor, or choir sings the verses, or the psalm is sung straight through. Responses and psalms are set aside in the *Lectionary for Mass* for the times of the Liturgical Year or certain observances that can be used with greater frequency so that the people can become quite familiar with them and sing them with ease (see GIRM 61). The participation of the faithful in the Responsorial Psalm is integral to its function as a response to the proclaimed word of God, in whatever form this participation includes.

On those occasions when the Responsorial Psalm is read by the reader, in accord with its function, it should be recited in a manner that equally fosters meditation on the word of God (see 61). The sound of the psalm should be distinct from the proclamation of a reading or an announcement. A meditative style suggests the use of a deliberate cadence following the sense lines of the psalm. Even in this instance of recitation, it is possible to make use of the given response or to read the psalm straight through. When the Responsorial Psalm is recited, there does not need to be an introduction to respond. Rather, the given response itself encourages its repetition as the response.

The *General Instruction* indicates additional options for the Responsorial Psalm other than those in the *Lectionary for Mass*. These options, although infrequently employed, deserve some attention as other possible responses to the proclaimed word of God. These include the responses found in the *Graduale Romanum* and *Graduale Simplex*, especially the Responsorial Psalm or the Alleluia Psalm in the latter hymnal. It is also possible to use other sets of psalms and antiphons, even in a metrical form, approved by the Conference of Bishops or the Diocesan Bishop as the Responsorial Psalm (see GIRM 61). The use of these options, especially in vernacular translations, emphasizes the function of this part of the Liturgy of the Word as a sung response to the First Reading. Because the Responsorial Psalm is the word of God it cannot be replaced by paraphrased texts, poems, hymns, or songs (61).

As a Biblical Reading, the Responsorial Psalm, sung or recited, takes place at the ambo, the place for the word of God. The psalmist, the cantor, or the reader arrives at the ambo just like the reader for the First Reading, for God is ready to speak to the assembled faithful as they sit and listen with reverence and faith. Another suitable place, especially if this assists the singing of the Responsorial Psalm, may be used other than the ambo (see 61). The use of another place for the Responsorial Psalm, however, should never reduce the impact that it is truly the word of God.

The Acclamation before the Gospel

The Acclamation before the Gospel is an independent rite (see GIRM 37, 62). It stands alone with its own structure but is not an essential element of the Liturgy of the Word. Its purpose, however, suggests that it happens regularly. The Acclamation before the Gospel is sung or recited immediately before the Gospel. As already mentioned above, when the Gospel is proclaimed, it is the Lord Jesus himself announcing his own word to the assembly. The Acclamation before the Gospel is directed to this announcement of Christ's word. With it everyone stands and welcomes and acknowledges the Risen Lord present in his Gospel (62).

The *General Instruction* provides clear instruction on the manner for singing this Acclamation, as well as which form is sung when, and when it is actually sung:

> It is sung by everybody, standing, and is led by the choir or a cantor, being repeated as the case requires. The

verse, on the other hand, is sung either by the choir or by a cantor.

> a) The Alleluia is sung in every time of year other than Lent. The verses are taken from the Lectionary or the Graduale.
>
> b) During Lent, instead of the Alleluia, the Verse before the Gospel as given in the Lectionary is sung. It is also possible to sing another Psalm or Tract, as found in the Graduale.

When there is only one reading before the Gospel:

> a) during a time of year when the Alleluia is prescribed, either an Alleluia Psalm or the Responsorial Psalm followed by the Alleluia with its verse may be used;
>
> b) during a time of year when the Alleluia is not foreseen, either the Psalm and the Verse before the Gospel or the Psalm alone may be used;
>
> c) the Alleluia or the Verse before the Gospel, if not sung, may be omitted. (62–63)

These instructions allow for a great deal of variety with the use of the Acclamation before the Gospel. As an independent rite it consists of two parts: the Alleluia or the verse given for Lent as found in the *Lectionary for Mass*,[3] and a verse from Sacred Scripture, typically following the Alleluia or the verse given for Lent, which is then repeated after the biblical text. It is not so much that the Alleluia or the verse given for Lent welcomes the Lord but rather the word of God, the verse from Sacred Scripture, welcomes the word of Christ that will be spoken in the Gospel. There is no provision in the liturgical books for simply singing or saying the Alleluia or the verse given for Lent; the Scripture verse is an integral element of the Acclamation before the Gospel. The Alleluia or the verse given for Lent is intended to be sung by everyone, although it may be led by a choir or cantor and repeated as necessary. The Scripture verse is typically sung by the choir or the cantor. In addition to the Acclamation before the Gospel being an independent rite, it also accompanies, as a rite, a procession: the procession of the *Book of the Gospels* to the ambo on some occasions, and always the procession of the proclaimer of the Gospel. This procession marks the coming of Christ with his Gospel.[4] As it accompanies this procession, it may be necessary to repeat the Alleluia or the verse given for Lent with additional verses from Sacred Scripture as well.

The *General Instruction* lists options for the Acclamation before the Gospel that are rarely employed but also merit some consideration. The *Graduale Romanum* provides additional sources for the biblical verses in addition to those in the *Lectionary for Mass* when the Alleluia is sung. Likewise, during Lent, the *Graduale Romanum* provides for an alternative psalm or tract to be sung instead of what is provided in the *Lectionary for Mass* as far as the verse and biblical text. One of the reasons these options are utilized so infrequently may be because of the skill needed to sing the musical forms in the *Graduale Romanum* and the lack of vernacular translations. Nonetheless, the options should not be overlooked.

Easier options to employ are those listed for the case of only one reading before the Gospel. An Alleluia psalm as found in the *Lectionary for Mass* may replace the Responsorial Psalm and the Alleluia and the Scripture verse. During Lent, when there is no Alleluia, the Responsorial Psalm alone may be used or with the verse given for Lent and biblical text. Then, there is the option all the time to omit the Acclamation before the Gospel when it is not sung. These options seem appropriate on less solemn occasions and when there is no real procession to the ambo.

In the *General Instruction*, the Sequence is mentioned with very little information about it. The Sequence precedes the Acclamation before the Gospel and is optional except on Easter Sunday and Pentecost Sunday (see GIRM 64). The *Lectionary for Mass* provides for four sequences in the course of the Liturgical Year: the two obligatory sequences for Easter and Pentecost Sundays (but not at their Vigils), the optional sequences for the Solemnity of the Most Holy Body and Blood of Christ, and for the Memorial of Our Lady of Sorrows. The Sequence allows for a lyrical announcement of the occasion celebrated and to be proclaimed in the Gospel. The Sequence when it is read and not sung should be recited with a sensitivity to the sense lines of the text.

The Homily

The *General Instruction* summarizes the Homily carefully:

> The Homily is part of the Liturgy and is highly recommended, for it is necessary for the nurturing of the Christian life. It should be an explanation of some aspect of the readings from Sacred Scripture or of another text from the Ordinary or the Proper of the Mass of the day and should take into account both the mystery being celebrated and the particular needs of the listeners. (65)

The Homily is identified as part of the Liturgy like all the other elements of the Liturgy of the Word (see also 29). Even though there is no given text and it can take many forms, depending on a variety of circumstances, it is part of the Liturgy. It is part of the announcement of the saving word of God. It is part of the saving event that is the Sacred Liturgy, the Paschal action of Christ. If this is the case, then as part of the Liturgy — as a part of the Paschal action of the Lord — it participates in the glorification of God and the holiness of the assembled faithful. The Homily is typically preached by the priest celebrant on most occasions, but it can be preached by another concelebrant and at times a Deacon. The faithful are to engage the preacher's words, participating in the Homily as they listen with reverence and faith as they did with the proclamation of Sacred Scripture. In this way the Homily is understood as "necessary for the nurturing of the Christian life." The *General Instruction* also describes the Homily as "a living commentary on the word" (see GIRM 29). Therefore, its content derives from the very texts that manifest the living presence of Christ and his Mystery in the celebration of the Eucharist, the Biblical Readings, and the prayers of the *Roman Missal*. All too often the Ordinary or Proper *Roman Missal* texts are not a source for the Homily, and yet these texts give a very helpful explanation to the faith of the Church that arises from a foundation in the word of God. The Homily, as a part of the liturgical action, with one of its purposes being to open up the Mystery of Christ according to the day or time of the Liturgical Year, aims to deepen the participation of the assembled faithful in the whole of the Eucharist.

The Homily belongs to the presidential role of the priest celebrant and therefore is typically given by him. However, on occasion it may be given by a concelebrant. For a good reason, a bishop or a priest may give the Homily when present for the Mass but not concelebrating (see GIRM 66). The Homily is rightly associated during the celebration of the Eucharist with the one who presides over the proclamation of the message of salvation (see 93). Therefore, the *General Instruction* is precise when it states that "from time to time and, if appropriate," a Deacon may give the Homily, but never a lay person (66). When someone other than the priest celebrant preaches the Homily, this should take place at the ambo.

The order of the Liturgy of the Word presumes a Homily. More specifically, the *General Instruction* states: "On Sundays and Holydays of Obligation there is to be a Homily at every Mass that is celebrated with the people attending, and it may not be omitted without a grave reason. On other days it is recommended, especially on the weekdays of Advent, Lent, and Easter Time, as well as on other festive days and occasions when the people come to church in greater numbers" (66).

The Homily is not an interruption in the course of the Liturgy of the Word, something that takes place between the Gospel and the Profession of Faith. Rather, the Homily develops what is announced and professed in the course of the Liturgy of the Word. The needed skill and understanding of this part of the Liturgy cannot be overlooked as a support for the *ars celebrandi*. Therefore, as with every other part of the celebration, the Homily requires constant review and refinement. The brief period of silence that is observed following the Homily allows for one more way for the assembled faithful to participate in it as together they reflect further on the message of salvation (see 66).

The Profession of Faith

The Profession of Faith is also called the Creed and the Symbol of Faith in the *Roman Missal*. Each of these three titles accents a certain aspect of its purpose: a confession by the Church, a rule of faith, and a witness to Tradition. More specifically, the *General Instruction* identifies the purpose of the Profession of Faith in the celebration of the Eucharist as a response of the assembled faithful to the word of God proclaimed with the Sacred Scriptures and further expressed in the Homily (67). In making this response, those assembled give voice with the Creed to a profession of the Faith that belongs to the single Body of Christ throughout the ages — *Credo* (I believe) — inclusive of the particular assembly and in communion with every assembly of the faithful. Thus, this confession of "the great mysteries of the faith," with a formula time-honored and approved by the Church, anticipates these very same mysteries to be realized in the Liturgy of the Eucharist (see 67).

The Profession of Faith is an element of the Liturgy of the Word that takes place every Sunday and solemnity, and it can also be a part of the Liturgy of the Word on more solemn occasions outside of a Sunday or a solemnity. The Creed may be sung or said by the priest celebrant with the faithful (see GIRM 68). The *General Instruction* gives a variety of ways to carry out the Creed:

> If it is sung, it is intoned by the Priest or, if appropriate, by a cantor or by the choir. It is then sung either by everybody together or by the people alternating with the choir.
>
> If it is not sung, it is to be recited by everybody together or by two choirs responding one to the other. (68)

The manner described for singing or reciting the Profession of Faith in the *General Instruction* is indicative of several things. The presentation of a sung Profession of Faith first in the *Order of Mass* not only highlights a preference but also illustrates a theological value — the importance of the articles of faith — with the sung form. In addition, if it is sung, then the priest celebrant intones it as in the first option. The priest celebrant, when he intones an element of the celebration, does so in his role as head of the Body. What follows with these directions for both singing and reciting the Profession of Faith is that it is done by everyone, priest and people, or with one part of the assembled faithful announcing the mysteries of faith to the other, as a corporate and ongoing response to the Sacred Scriptures and the Homily. When the Profession of Faith is recited, which is the more typical form, it begins without any introduction and only with the "I believe in one God" begun by the priest celebrant.

The Universal Prayer

The title of this element of the Liturgy of the Word is instructive as to its content: the Universal Prayer. *Sacrosanctum concilium* specifically legislated the restoration of this common prayer or prayer of the faithful during the Mass for all and for all needs.[5] In the tradition and as a restored element of the Liturgy of the Word, the Universal Prayer belongs uniquely to the assembled faithful as a response to the proclaimed word of God to intercede "for the salvation of all" (GIRM 69). There is no aspect to the Universal Prayer that is sentimental, individualistic, commemorative, or directional. The intentions of the Universal Prayer, also called the Prayer of the Faithful or the Bidding Prayers in the *General Instruction* and the *Order of Mass*, reflect a universal need, a need that includes all the members of the Church — all those who govern, all those weighed down by a variety of needs, for all people and their salvation (see 69).

The Universal Prayer should take place at all Sunday and weekday Masses with the people. It belongs to them as an action of their priestly participation in the Eucharist (see 69). Throughout the course of the celebration of the Mass, the assembled faithful participate as sharers in the priesthood of Christ received at baptism and unite themselves to the offering of Christ the Priest in the Holy Eucharist. There are key moments in the Eucharist when this priesthood of the baptized is especially evident, and the Universal Prayer is one of these moments. In addition to making of themselves an offering to be united with the Sacrifice of Christ, they too have the duty that also arises from baptism to make an offering for those who belong to them in the Body of Christ for whatever their needs may be. When the reader declaims the intentions of the Universal Prayer, a text is provided with the universal needs of the Body of Christ offered by the assembled faithful to be joined at the altar as the Eucharist continues. These intentions will become one with the bread and wine offered at the hands of the priest as the Liturgy of the Eucharist begins. The universal character of these intentions as the priestly offering of the baptized for all should not be restricted by sentiment or personal need and, more importantly, should not be easily omitted.

The *General Instruction* precisely orders the sequence for the intentions that form the Universal Prayer:

> a) for the needs of the Church;
>
> b) for public authorities and the salvation of the whole world;
>
> c) for those burdened by any kind of difficulty;
>
> d) for the local community.
>
> Nevertheless, in any particular celebration, such as a Confirmation, a Marriage, or at a Funeral, the series of intentions may be concerned more closely with the particular occasion. (70)

While the sequence for the intentions is clear (with particular ritual occasions allowing for an adaptation of this sequence) the intentions themselves always focus on a universal need. In one of the appendices to the *Roman Missal*, several formulae for the Universal Prayer for general use are provided for the times of the Liturgical Year, and for Masses for the Dead.[6]

As part of his presidential role in the celebration of Mass, the priest celebrant introduces the Universal Prayer and concludes it with a prayer at the priest celebrant's chair (see GIRM 71). With his introduction to the Universal Prayer, the priest celebrant, acting in the person of Christ, the Head of the Body, directs it to the assembled faithful, the Body of Christ, and not to God. "The intentions announced should be sober, be composed with a wise liberty and in few words, and they should be expressive of the prayer of the entire community" (71). Since the intentions are in some way a response to the word of God, the biblical texts proclaimed at the Mass should serve as a reference for both phrases and ideas for the composition of these intentions, expressive of the priestly offering of the faithful.

The ambo, the altar of the word of God, is the typical place for the declamation of the intentions of the Universal Prayer. This is especially the case when a Deacon presents the intentions, or when a reader or another member of the liturgical assembly carries out this duty in his absence or instead of him. When the intentions are sung by someone other than a Deacon, they can be carried out in another suitable place, such as the cantor's place in the sanctuary, which may be necessary for musical assistance (see 71). The engagement of the people with the intentions of the Universal Prayer heightens their participation and awareness of their unique priestly role in this prayer. They are standing as they make their offering in the Risen Lord and make the intentions their own with a response or with silence (71). The typical invitation today for the response of the faithful is "Let us pray to the Lord" with the reply, "Lord, hear our prayer." It is certainly acceptable to vary this invitation and response, especially seasonally. The invitation should be obvious as an invitation to prayer to those responding, and the response should not be cumbersome because of length or content. As a dialogue, this invitation and response recommends singing it even if the intentions are spoken.

Directions for the Liturgy of the Word

Now that each of the elements of the Liturgy of the Word has been more fully described, especially from a theological and liturgical perspective, the order for the Liturgy of the Word is now presented according to the directions found in the *General Instruction* and the *Order of Mass*. These directions follow, as with the Introductory Rites, for the forms of the Mass: Mass without a Deacon, Mass with a Deacon, Concelebrated Mass, and Mass at Which only One Minister Participates. Throughout the presentation of each of these forms of the Mass, more specific points for the *ars celebrandi*, an artful and careful celebration of the Eucharist, are proposed.

The Liturgy of the Word without a Deacon

The order for the Liturgy of the Word is first presented in the *General Instruction* for the form of the Mass without a Deacon. Increasingly, the more common practice is for a Deacon to assist at Mass, especially on Sundays. However, following the outline of the *General Instruction*, the Liturgy of the Word for Mass with a Deacon will be presented later in this chapter.

The Liturgy of the Word, as one of the two principal parts of the *Order of Mass*, combines with the Liturgy of the Eucharist and the Introductory and Concluding Rites for the single act of worship that is the Holy Eucharist (see GIRM 28). Before considering the directions for the Liturgy of the Word, recall the purpose of the Introductory Rites: to form a communion among the assembled faithful and to prepare them, dispose them, to listen to the word of God (46). One of the chief ways to make the transition from the Introductory Rites to the Liturgy of the Word, especially if the Introductory Rites have been carried out with care and thoughtfulness — and so have achieved their purpose — is to observe a brief period of silence before the First Reading (s56). Although this is rarely done, it will greatly help for the whole of the Liturgy of the Word to be conducted in a way "to favor meditation" (GIRM 56) and to lead everyone to celebrate the Eucharist more fully.

For the beginning of the Liturgy of the Word, after the Collect that concludes the Introductory Rites, all take their seats, including the priest celebrant at his chair. Once everyone is seated, the priest celebrant may introduce the Liturgy of the Word, following a possible brief period of silence. The *Lectionary for Mass* is already in place at the ambo. At this point it is necessary to note that the Biblical Readings are always proclaimed from the proper liturgical book. The reader, after the introduction, if it took place, goes to the ambo to proclaim the First Reading as all listen to it. At the end of the reading the reader acclaims, "The word of the Lord," and all respond, "Thanks be to God." After all have responded to the Acclamation, the reader then leaves the ambo. A brief period of silence follows the reading for all to meditate on the word of God.[7] The First Reading is followed by the Responsorial Psalm. The psalmist or the reader sings or proclaims the verses of the Responsorial Psalm with the assembled faithful responding.[8] If there is a Second Reading prior to the Gospel, it is carried out in the same way as the First Reading: at the ambo with a period of silence observed after it.[9] If the *Book of the Gospels* is used, the reader removes the *Lectionary for Mass* from the ambo prior to the Acclamation before the Gospel.[10]

At times, the Liturgy of the Word, especially the Biblical Reading(s) and Responsorial Psalm that precede the Gospel, takes place in a hurried way and with insufficient attention to the needed skills to proclaim the word of God. This easily deters the assembled faithful from engaging and listening attentively with reverence and faith. The use of the introduction to the Liturgy of the Word by the priest celebrant can assist with this, especially if it is brief and focuses the assembled faithful on the Mystery to be announced in the readings from Scripture. The ambo should be prepared for its use, as the altar would be prepared, with sufficient amplification and lighting as well as with the *Lectionary for Mass*, and nothing else, including alternative books or papers, instead of the *Lectionary for Mass*. All this needs to be prepared before Mass begins. The *Lectionary for Mass* should be closed when first placed at the ambo. It is not yet in use. It is opened by the first reader. Some may be anxious about this for fear that the first reader might not open the book to the appointed Biblical Reading. However, this detail should be expected of a reader. Those who are instituted or deputed to read the word of God should be familiar with the order of the Liturgy of the Word, have a familiarity with the different books of the Bible and with the *Lectionary for Mass*, and have the skills for speaking the word of God in the liturgical assembly. Each reading requires its own minister.[11]

Instituted readers, usually vested in an alb, have their place in the sanctuary. Deputed readers have their place among the assembly. Those entrusted to read the word of God go to the ambo without any type of procession. There is only one procession during the Liturgy of the Word, and that anticipates the Gospel. As the readers move to the ambo, it is fitting for them to bow profoundly to the altar and then move to the ambo. When the readers return to their places from the ambo, they should again bow profoundly to the altar. Again, the altar is the centerpiece of the whole Mass, and each part of the Mass looks to the Paschal action that takes place at the altar for its meaning and purpose. Posture, diction, and projection, in a way that befits the dignity of the word of God, all promote an artful and careful proclamation of the saving Mystery of the Lord in the Biblical Readings. On more solemn occasions, the readers can sing the readings and, even more often, sing the Acclamation with the faithful singing the response. The *Roman Missal* provides the form for singing these dialogues in the *Order of Mass*[12] and for the readings in its "Appendix I, Various Chants for the *Order of Mass*." The manner for carrying out the Responsorial Psalm has already been addressed. However, mention needs to be made again about making use of the additional possibilities to ensure that the response is sung rather than recited. Finally, the proposed silences that follow the First and Second Readings form a corporate response on the part of all. Most people do not know how to observe this silence. It is more than just being quiet. It is an active engagement in a few moments of reflection or meditation on the message of salvation. Some catechesis at times outside of Mass, perhaps with spoken or published announcements, on the purpose of this silence and how to participate in it will enhance its effectiveness. In addition to providing catechesis, modeling a consistent observance of this silence is also an excellent type of instruction.

At the conclusion of the Responsorial Psalm or the Second Reading, everyone stands, and the Acclamation before the Gospel is sung according to the time of the Liturgical Year.[13] If incense is used, it is placed in the thurible and blessed by the priest celebrant during the Acclamation before the Gospel. After this, the priest celebrant with hands joined bows profoundly before the center of the altar and prays quietly, "Cleanse my heart and my lips, almighty God, that I may worthily proclaim your holy Gospel."[14] This is one of the few personal prayers of the priest celebrant reminding him of his unique ministry, and is to be carried out in a devout manner. Even if the altar is not passed on the way to the ambo, it is actually significant for the priest celebrant to move before the altar to make the connection between the singularity of the action of Christ that occurs with the proclamation of the Gospel and the Eucharistic Prayer at the altar.

If the *Book of the Gospels* has already been placed upon the altar, the priest celebrant retrieves it and moves to the ambo with the book slightly elevated. Ahead of him, those with the thurible and candles move to the ambo. All present face the ambo for the proclamation of the Gospel as an expression of reverence for the presence of Christ in his Gospel (see GIRM 133).

In these directions for the procession for the Gospel, there are many parts, and each should be observed intentionally. The priest celebrant actually prepares himself before the altar with the specified prayer and not from another position facing the altar as is sometimes done. If incense is to be used, he provides for this before he moves to the altar for the preparatory prayer. The *General Instruction* and the *Order of Mass* mention incense with and without the *Book of the Gospels*. Further, the *Order of Mass* speaks of the use of incense and candles when appropriate, which suggests the *Book of the Gospels* may be used without them.[15] The number of candles is not specified, but it is typically two candles as at the Entrance. Incense may be used even if only the *Lectionary for Mass* is used for the Gospel. At the ambo, the incense is directed to Christ and his word rather than to the book itself. If the *Book of the Gospels* is used, then the incense and candles accompany the book in procession to the ambo as the priest celebrant holds it only slightly raised, avoiding any exaggerated position with it. It is presumed that the thurible and candles arrive at the ambo with the *Book of the Gospels* and remain there during the proclamation. This whole procession should be carefully choreographed so that it flows in an orderly and reverent manner and actually moves directly to the ambo. The places for those with the thurible and candles at the ambo should be determined beforehand. The server with the thurible should be near to the Gospel proclaimer.

Once the priest celebrant arrives at the ambo, he opens the book and, with his hands joined, says, "The Lord be with you." Everyone replies, "And with your spirit." Then he announces the evangelist without the title "Saint": "A reading from the holy Gospel according to N." As he says this, he also makes the Sign of the Cross with his thumb on the book itself, that is, on the text to be read,[16] and then on his forehead, mouth, and breast, as everyone else follows suit. There is no prescribed silent prayer which accompanies this action. The people acclaim the announcement of the Gospel by replying, "Glory to you, O Lord." If incense is used, the priest incenses the book and then proclaims the Gospel. At the end of the Gospel, he acclaims, "The Gospel of the Lord," and everyone responds, "Praise to you, Lord Jesus Christ." After all have responded, the priest venerates the book with a kiss and quietly says the prayer, "Through the words of the Gospel may our sins be wiped away."[17] In the instance when no readers are present, the priest himself proclaims the reading(s) and the Responsorial Psalm while standing at the ambo. Also, if incense is used in this case, the priest places incense in the thurible and blesses it at the ambo. He also then bows profoundly and prays the preparatory prayer from the ambo, facing the altar (see GIRM 135).

What has already been said about the reading skills of the reader certainly applies to the priest who proclaims the Gospel. The very manner of a clear, expressive, and easily heard proclamation is a fundamental contribution to the *ars celebrandi* of the Liturgy of the Word. When the priest arrives at the ambo, he opens the book. This presumes the use of the *Book of the Gospels*. However, the *Lectionary for Mass* may have been closed as well for the singing of the Acclamation before the Gospel or the Responsorial Psalm if there was no Second Reading or Acclamation before the Gospel. The priest keeps his hands joined like a Deacon when he introduces the Gospel with the greeting. This only reinforces that the reading of the Gospel is in all instances a ministerial duty, but one that at this point is being carried out by the same person who is also in the presidential role. The signing of the book and the priest's forehead, lips, and breast are carried out with a certain deliberateness.

If the book is to be incensed, then the pattern already described for this manifestation of the presence of Christ, as with all the other manifestations of the presence of Christ, is observed. A profound bow is made in the direction of the book before and after the incensation, which consists of three single swings of the thurible (see GIRM 277). In this case, it is one swing to the center, left, and right.[18] At the conclusion of the Gospel, the priest should first receive the response of the people ("Glory to you, O Lord") before he venerates the text of the Gospel or the book. Also, the book is not raised for this dialogue.[19] The tradition is that the text is kissed, yet the *General Instruction* and the *Order of Mass* specifically direct that the book be kissed.[20] The Gospel is the high point of the Liturgy of the Word. One of the ways, in addition to all the other signs provided, to indicate this is to sing it, especially on more solemn occasions.[21] The solemn and simple tones for singing the Gospel are found in the *Roman Missal*, Appendix I, Various Chants for the *Order of Mass*. On many more occasions, the dialogues and Acclamations that surround the Gospel can be sung according to the forms found in the *Order of Mass*.[22] The proclamation of the Gospel leads to the Homily, which extends the announcement of the message of salvation in all the Biblical Readings. Therefore, it makes no sense for any formal procession after the Gospel for those who carried the incense and the candles. Moreover, the Acclamation before the Gospel in any form would not be repeated after the Gospel. Its purpose is to announce the coming of Christ in his saving word.

It would be rare that a priest would make use of incense when other ministers are not present to read the reading(s) and the Responsorial Psalm. However, if this does take place, according to the *General Instruction*, the priest celebrant would remain at the ambo for the preparatory prayer (see 135). He would do this by turning toward the altar and then bowing profoundly for the prayer. This instance also suggests that incense, as indicated above, can be used when the *Lectionary for Mass* is used for the Gospel.

Following the Gospel, the priest celebrant gives the Homily. This can take place again in several different places, with the priest standing at the chair or at the ambo or another worthy place, especially on Sundays and holy days of obligation, but on other days as well. The Homily is followed by a period of silence.[23]

If the priest is already at the ambo to proclaim the Gospel, it makes little sense for him to return to the priest celebrant's chair to preach. However, the chair always seems the most appropriate place and is the sign indicating the role of the priest celebrant as presiding over the assembled faithful and the announcement of the message of salvation. This may account for the chair being listed first among the options for the place to give the Homily. It seems, since giving the Homily is a presidential duty, that almost any other place in the sanctuary area would also suffice. This could mean at the entrance to the sanctuary or even at the altar. The proposed silence that follows the Homily is again a corporate act — reflecting on the Mystery just explained needs to be understood by all. This silence is a key way to achieve the deeper participation of the assembled faithful in the liturgical action of the Homily.

On certain days the Creed is prescribed to follow the Homily, with the priest and people standing and singing or reciting it together. At the words, "and by the Holy Spirit … and became man," everyone makes a profound bow. At these same words on the Solemnity of the Annunciation of the Lord and the Solemnity of the Nativity of the Lord, everyone genuflects (see GIRM 68 and 137). The *Order of Mass* allows for the Apostles' Creed to be used instead of the Niceno-Constantinopolitan Creed, especially during Lent and Easter. Likewise, with the Apostles' Creed, all bow profoundly at the words, "who was conceived by the Holy Spirit, born of the Virgin Mary."[24]

The Profession of Faith, as an element of the Liturgy of the Word, needs some additional explanation. It is an act carried out by the priest (standing at his chair) and people together, whether sung or said. As a confession of the Mysteries heard in the word of God and the rule of faith of the Church, it deserves a thoughtful and careful recitation so that it is truly the priest and people together professing the Faith. When the Creed is recited on a Sunday or a solemnity, its recitation is frequently tedious and sounds like many people simply speaking at the same time without any sense of singularity to their confession of the rule of faith. The quality of its recitation deserves to be addressed — and even rehearsed — for the benefit of grasping its more profound theological meaning and that of the assembly's shared response to what was just revealed in the word of God. Just as sung parts of the Eucharist are often rehearsed prior to the celebration, in a similar way, recited parts could be rehearsed as well, achieving an awareness that the voice of many become one.

Singing the Profession of Faith, at least on more solemn occasions, should be seriously considered. The third edition of the *Roman Missal* provides for two sung forms of the Profession of Faith in the *Order of Mass*, number 18, and an alternate musical setting in Appendix I, which are rarely used. The sung Profession of Faith would greatly assist the assembled faithful to be more in communion with one another, sounding as one voice announcing the mysteries of salvation.

The Apostles' Creed is not intended to replace the Niceno-Constantinopolitan Creed. Rather, it is especially recommended for Lent and Easter due to the connection of these times of the Liturgical Year with the making and renewing of Baptismal Promises. If the choice is to use the Apostles' Creed during

Lent and Easter, it makes sense to use it on all the Sundays and solemnities of both times of the Liturgical Year.

After the Profession of Faith, or at least after the Homily when the Profession of Faith is not prescribed, the Universal Prayer takes place. Again, the priest is standing at the priest celebrant's chair and, with his hands joined, addresses the assembled faithful to be a part of the Universal Payer. The intentions follow, declaimed at the ambo or another suitable place by the cantor, the reader, or someone else. The people reply to the needs announced. The priest celebrant brings the Universal Prayer to an end as he extends his hands for the concluding prayer.[25]

The Universal Prayer should always be prepared. At times the priest celebrant may be able to introduce it and conclude it with extemporaneous texts. However, these should follow what is described above for the content of the introduction and concluding prayer. The concluding prayer, as a rule, should have the short ending, "Through Christ our Lord," and not imitate the longer conclusion of the Collect. The gestures directed for the priest celebrant as he introduces the Universal Prayer (hands joined) and for the concluding prayer (hands extended) follow the same directions for similar occasions elsewhere in the *General Instruction* and the *Order of Mass*. Whether the intentions are read by the cantor, reader, or another reader, this person should be at the ambo for the introduction and remain for the concluding prayer. The Universal Prayer is a single element of the Liturgy of the Word in three parts. Those who will be declaiming the intentions should bow profoundly to the altar as they move to and away from the ambo. The texts for the Universal Prayer, the introduction, the intentions and the concluding prayer, should be suitable in composition and content for the celebration of the Eucharist and for the offering of prayers to Almighty God for the salvation of all.

The Liturgy of the Word for Mass with a Deacon

As with every part of the Mass, in the Liturgy of the Word the role of the Deacon is ministerial. The Deacon ministers to the priest and people as he carries out his unique functions. In the Liturgy of the Word his functions include the proclamation of the Gospel and the declamation of the intentions of the Universal Prayer. In the absence of other ministers, the Deacon carries out their roles as well.

Throughout the Liturgy of the Word, the Deacon typically assumes his place to the side of the priest celebrant, standing and sitting when appropriate. As the Acclamation before the Gospel is sung, if incense is used, he stands to the side of the priest celebrant and assists him as incense is placed in the thurible (see GIRM 175). This means that the Deacon typically takes the boat of incense into his hand so the priest celebrant, standing as well, can fill the thurible with the incense. At times the Deacon may also need to assist the person with the thurible to raise it to a convenient height for the priest celebrant. After this, and also when incense is not used, the Deacon as he bows profoundly asks the priest celebrant in a low voice for the blessing to proclaim the Gospel. The text for the Deacon is always the same, regardless of whether a bishop or priest gives the blessing: "Your blessing, Father." In a low voice, the priest blesses the Deacon with these words: "May the Lord be in your heart and on your lips, that you may proclaim his Gospel worthily and well, in the name of the Father and of the Son ✠ and of the Holy Spirit." The Deacon blesses himself and responds, "Amen."[26] All of this takes place at the priest celebrant's chair. The priest blesses the Deacon, so the gesture of blessing corresponds to the words of the Sign of the Cross over the Deacon's bowed head. At this point, it is inappropriate to introduce other gestures that have a significantly different meaning than the Sign of the Cross, such as an imposition of hands.

The *General Instruction* at this point presumes the use of the *Book of the Gospels* for the Deacon to proclaim the Gospel, so it carefully describes the Deacon's use of this book. Sundays and solemn occasions suggest the use of the *Book of the Gospels* (in other words, occasions when the actual Gospel text to be proclaimed is in the *Book of the Gospels*). When the *Book of the Gospels* is used, it will have already been placed on the altar by the Deacon at the conclusion of the Entrance. After the Deacon asks for and receives the blessing from the priest celebrant, he goes to the altar and first bows to it. The Deacon then lifts the *Book of the Gospels* from the mensa of the altar and begins to process to the ambo. He carries the *Book of the Gospel* only in a slightly elevated way. The Deacon, at least in this description of the use of the *Book of the Gospels*, is preceded by the thurifer with the smoking thurible and by additional ministers with lighted candles. The *Order of Mass*, however, mentions the use of incense and candles when appropriate.[27]

There are many theological points being expressed in these actions on the part of the priest celebrant and the Deacon. The blessing given by the priest to the Deacon indicates that the priest celebrant does indeed preside over the announcement of the whole word of salvation during the Liturgy of the Word, even if he himself does not speak a word of the Sacred Scriptures. The Deacon receives the blessing as someone delegated by the presider over the word to announce the word, the Gospel of the Lord, and is blessed as the proper minister of this Gospel announcement. The bowing to the altar indicates that the altar is always reverenced as the sign of Christ and his Mystery, the centerpiece even of the Liturgy of the Word. For the Deacon to process to the ambo with the *Book of the Gospels* only slightly raised dignifies the bearing of the book as the vessel of Christ's words. Christ is truly present with the proclamation of the Gospel. For a Deacon to bear the book in an exaggerated way really has no meaning, but becomes simply awkward. The use of the smoking incense and lighted candles brings forward to the proclamation of the Gospel the same meaning that incense and candles have throughout the celebration of the Eucharist: reverence, worship, and the real presence of Christ.

Once the Deacon reaches the ambo, he places the *Book of the Gospels* upon it and opens to the text to be proclaimed. This means that the *Lectionary* previously used to proclaim a reading or the text for the sung Acclamation before the Gospel has been removed by the reader or cantor.[28] As the thurifer arrives at the ambo, this person should be so placed as not to impede the Deacon from going directly to the ambo to place the *Book of the Gospels* on it and should also be ready for the book to be incensed. As the lighted candles arrive at the ambo, they also should be placed so as not to impede the Deacon. At this point these candles should flank the ambo, as with the altar, for the proclamation of the Gospel.

When all is ready, and the Acclamation before the Gospel is concluded with the Deacon singing it as well, he greets the people with his hands joined, saying, "The Lord be with you." The people respond, "And with your spirit." Then the Deacon identifies the Evangelist without the title "Saint": "A reading from the Holy Gospel according to N." The *General Instruction* indicates that the Deacon should make the Sign of the Cross on the book, that is on the text itself, precisely at the words, "A reading from the Holy Gospel."[29] He then makes the Sign of the Cross on his forehead, lips, and breast. The people respond, "Glory to you, O Lord." Then he incenses the *Book of the Gospels*, if incense is used, and proclaims the Gospel.[30]

A great deal is taking place in succession at this moment. The Deacon participates in the procession to the ambo as he sings the Acclamation with everyone else who is waiting for the Lord to speak his own word. His gestures are to be carried out with care, demonstrating the meaning they have for him, for the assembly, and in themselves. Many reasons are offered as to why the Deacon does not extend his hands for the greeting prior to the Gospel. The fact that he is instructed not to extend his hands with this greeting, when at other moments during the Eucharist this same greeting is accompanied by extended hands, suggests some additional meaning here. It seems that the Deacon greets with the same words and hears the same response as at other times to express that this is an action of Christ acting in the Deacon to prepare everyone for Christ to speak his own word. However, hands joined with this greeting suggests that the Deacon acts not as the priest presiding as head of the Body as with the Introductory Rites or at the beginning of the Eucharistic Prayer, but more so as the minster of the servant Christ. As when the priest proclaims the Gospel, the Signs of the Cross, imitated by everyone else in the assembly as directed in the *General Instruction* (see 134), ought to be carried out with care. If the book is to be incensed, then the pattern already described for this manifestation of the presence of Christ should be observed. A profound bow is made in the direction of the book before and after the incensation, which consists of three swings of the thurible (see 277). In this case, it is one swing to the center, left, and right.[31]

When the proclamation of the Gospel is concluded, the Deacon acclaims, "The Gospel of the Lord," and everyone responds, "Praise to you, Lord Jesus Christ."[32] Again, the book is not raised for this dialogue.[33] Only after the people have responded does the Deacon then venerate the book with a kiss. It is important for the Deacon to receive the response of the people to the Acclamation before he venerates the book. As with the veneration of the altar, so this intimate gesture should be carried out with intention, reverence, and care. As the Deacon kisses the book, he says quietly (that is, for no one else to hear), "Through the words of the Gospel may our sins be wiped away." After this, the

Deacon returns to his place at the side of the priest celebrant.[34]

It is a bad habit, although not intended for the most part, that the response of the faithful to a greeting or an Acclamation is frequently poorly received by the one greeting or announcing the Acclamation. The Gospel Acclamation is a fine example of this. The people have just heard the Deacon declare that it is indeed Jesus Christ himself who has spoken his Gospel to us. Their response is actually a statement of praise to their Lord: "Praise to you, Lord Jesus Christ." All too often the response of the faithful is directed to the top of the head of the Deacon as he is already bent over to venerate the *Book of the Gospels*. An attentiveness to the value of each of these actions demonstrates a regard for both those responding and the *Book of the Gospels*. The *General Instruction* and the *Order of Mass* simply direct the Deacon to kiss the book.[35] Presumably, the actual text proclaimed is venerated, which accords with the tradition. However, the closed book might conceivably be venerated as well. While this is not addressed in the directions for the celebration of Mass, it seems obvious that the book should remain open at the ambo if the Homily will take place there, as the Homily is derived from the readings of Sacred Scripture (see GIRM 65) and is a continued announcement of the word of God (29). And likewise, the book would be closed at the conclusion of the Homily.

The *General Instruction* makes a ceremonial point for when a bishop is the principal celebrant and the Deacon proclaims the Gospel. After the Deacon concludes the proclamation of the Gospel at the ambo, he does not venerate it. Rather, he carries the book (the *General Instruction* presumes the *Book of the Gospels*) in the same manner as to the ambo but now to the bishop at his chair for him to venerate it and to say quietly, "Through the words of the Gospel may our sins be wiped away." Depending on circumstances, the Deacon may venerate the book at the ambo even when a bishop is the celebrant. It seems logistics alone would dictate the choice for this and thus require a previous settlement on this option. After the bishop venerates the *Book of the Gospels* — again open to the proclaimed text or simply the book itself — he may, depending on the solemnity of the occasion, bless the people with the *Book of the Gospels*. After the bishop venerates it, and also blesses the faithful with it, the book should be carried by the Deacon to a side table or another place appropriate for the *Book of the Gospels*.[36] Anything like putting the book on the floor next to the chair of the Deacon is abhorrent. A similar case could be made when the book remains at the ambo after the proclamation of the Gospel. When the Deacon arrives at the ambo for the Universal Prayer, there should be a suitable place for the book so that it is not simply shelved for the announcement of the intentions.

In addition to proclaiming the Gospel, the Deacon typically declaims the intentions of the Universal Prayer, which follow the introduction by the priest celebrant. The proper place for a Deacon to do this is at the ambo (see GIRM 177). In some places a custom has developed of the Deacon remaining at the side of the priest celebrant for the intentions. Such an approach diminishes both the role of the Deacon and the relationship of these intentions to the word of God. The ambo is the principal place from which the Deacon ministers to the assembled faithful. It is from the ambo that he sings the Easter announcement of the Risen Lord (see 309) and proclaims the Gospel. The intentions of the Universal Prayer, the common prayer for the needs of all, arrive from a response to the Gospel and find their shape according to the word of God (69).

Finally, when a Deacon is present and there is no one to carry out the duties of the reader, the Deacon also reads the other readings and the Responsorial Psalm (see 176). In this instance, the Deacon, after going to receive the blessing of the priest celebrant, also proclaims the Gospel and reads the intentions of the

Universal Prayer as usual.

The Liturgy of the Word for Concelebrated Mass

For a Concelebrated Mass, the concelebrants follow the posture of the principal celebrant during the course of the Liturgy of the Word. As the principal celebrant is seated for the Biblical Readings and Responsorial Psalm prior to the Gospel, so the concelebrants are seated at their places. As the principal celebrant stands for the Gospel, so the concelebrants stand at their places. The concelebrants stand with the celebrant when the Acclamation before the Gospel begins. This means that all stand at the same time when the chant begins. An exception to this is when a bishop is the principal celebrant and incense is used. In this case, all the concelebrants stand when the chant begins except for the bishop, who remains seated to impose incense and then blesses the Deacon to proclaim the Gospel.[37] In the absence of a Deacon, a concelebrant steps forward to receive the blessing of the bishop to proclaim the Gospel (see GIRM 212). The text for the concelebrant in this circumstance is the same as that of a Deacon: "Your blessing, Father." During the proclamation of the Gospel, all turn and face the one proclaiming the Gospel (133). Again, the concelebrants stand along with the principal celebrant as he stands for the Profession of Faith and the Universal Prayer.

In a Concelebrated Mass where the principal celebrant is a priest and no Deacon is present, one of the concelebrants always proclaims the Gospel but does not ask for a blessing (see 212). Rather, the concelebrating priest bows before the center of the altar and prays the preparation prayer to proclaim the Gospel. The proclamation of the Gospel, which properly belongs to the Deacon, is always considered a ministerial and not a presidential function. So, it is improper for a bishop or principal priest celebrant for the Concelebrated Mass, when no Deacon is present, to assume this ministerial function as well. If the *Book of the Gospels* is used for a Concelebrated Mass, then the concelebrant who will proclaim the Gospel follows the same pattern for the use of this book as when there is a Deacon (see GIRM 175).

In a Concelebrated Mass, the Homily is given by the principal celebrant or by one of the concelebrants (see 213). The Homily, as mentioned previously, is the duty of the one who presides over the whole of the Liturgy of the Word, the principal celebrant of the Mass. So, although permissible, this duty should not be easily abdicated simply because there are concelebrants. The Homily, as with every form of the Mass, may take place at the priest celebrant's chair, at the ambo, or another suitable place (see 136). If the Homily is given by a concelebrant, obviously it is given either at the ambo or perhaps at the entrance to the sanctuary. All concelebrants, seated for the Homily, should be considered when the place for the Homily is determined so that the one who is giving the Homily is in their view.

The Liturgy of the Word for Mass at Which only One Minister Participates

The Liturgy of the Word is integral to every celebration of the Eucharist, and this is expressed both in the manner in which it is carried out and the place for it. One of the first directives given for the Liturgy of the Word for Mass at Which only One Minister Participates is that the readings from Sacred Scripture, if at all possible, should be proclaimed from the ambo or a least a lectern (see GIRM 260). This directive is more than an effort to protect the rite. Rather, it is a conscious application of all that has been already said about the word of God in the celebration of the Eucharist, regardless of the form of the Mass. Thus, in this form of the Mass, the altar should not double as the ambo or lectern.

The Liturgy of the Word follows the pattern outlined in the *Order of Mass* for the minister and the priest celebrant. The minister carries out the duties of the reader, reading the readings, the Responsorial Psalm, and the Acclamation before the Gospel.[38] In this form of the celebration, with only one minister participating, the introductions and Acclamations that are part of the proclamation of the word of God are maintained. Likewise, the periods of silence should be observed. If for some serious reason there is not a minister participating and the priest is alone for the celebration, then he assumes the duties of the reader.[39] The priest celebrant carries out the rites that belong to the proclamation of the Gospel in the usual way. He bows profoundly before the center of the altar and quietly says the prayer, "Cleanse my heart and my lips, almighty God, that I may worthily proclaim your holy Gospel." Then he reads the Gospel. At the conclusion of the proclamation of the Gospel, the priest says, "The Gospel of the Lord," with the minister responding, "Praise to you, Lord Jesus Christ." The priest then venerates the book with a kiss and quietly says, "Through the words of the Gospel may our sins be wiped away."[40] Neither the *General Instruction* nor the *Order of Mass with the Participation of a Single Minister* suggest a Homily in this form of the Mass. However, with a minister present, there is nothing that prevents a brief commentary on the word of God.

Both the *General Instruction* and the *Order of Mass with the Participation of a Single Minister* direct that, following the Gospel, the priest celebrant and minister recite, when prescribed, the Profession of Faith.[41] As with the other forms of the Mass, even in this form, the Universal Prayer may follow. The priest celebrant introduces and concludes the Universal Prayer as usual, and the minister declaims the intentions.[42]

Perhaps of all the forms of the Mass, Mass at Which only One Minister Participates may be the form that needs to be carried out with greater consciousness of the theological meaning of the various elements of the Liturgy of the Word to ensure a careful manner for celebrating it.

Instituted and Deputed Ministers and the Liturgy of the Word

The celebration of the Eucharist in all its forms anticipates the presence of a reader to proclaim the Biblical Readings that precede the Gospel. The reader may be instituted by a special rite for this service to the word of God, or may be someone, properly prepared, who has been deputed without institution to read the readings at Mass (see GIRM 99 and 101). The duties of the reader, in addition to proclaiming the Biblical Readings, may include the reading of the intentions of the Universal Prayer and, if there is no psalmist, the reading of the Responsorial Psalm. The specific duties of the reader are proper to the person designated to carry them out (see 99).

As noted above, when the Sacred Scriptures are read during the course of the celebration of the Eucharist, God himself is speaking. The reader who assumes this role becomes the voice for the divine word. The reader does not merely read a prescribed text but animates the very word of God by reading it. Again, this requires that readers understand their role, develop proclamation skills, and maintain a genuine sense of service to the word and to those who will hear it. A well-prepared and articulate reader significantly contributes to the artful celebration of the Eucharist. It is this type of proclamation that allows the listeners to nurture "in their hearts a sweet and living affection for Sacred Scripture" (GIRM 101).

All of the readings should be read from the ambo, including the Responsorial Psalm (which is read by the reader if there is no psalmist). If no Deacon is present, the reader also reads the intentions of the Universal Prayer from the ambo. For Mass, when the Entrance and Communion Chants are not sung, the reader reads the given respective antiphons for the celebration (see 196–198). These antiphons are typically texts from the Sacred Scripture and as such can also be recited at the ambo. Again, as far as the number of readers needed for the celebration of Mass, there should be one different reader for each Biblical Reading.[43]

On those occasions when a procession accompanies the *Book of the Gospels* to the ambo, the acolytes or servers should be ready to present the boat with incense at the priest celebrant's chair, and to follow the thurifer with the candles to the ambo. The pattern for the servers to begin, process, and arrive at the ambo depends on the arrangement of the sanctuary. At the ambo, the servers with candles stand on either side of the Deacon or priest proclaiming the Gospel.[44] The acolyte or server is needed to minister to the priest celebrant at his chair with the texts for the Profession of Faith and the Universal Prayer.

Conclusion

The Liturgy of the Word in all its elements announces the saving Mystery of Christ and looks forward to this same Mystery fully revealed in the action at the altar. Although the Gospel is the most significant of the Biblical Readings, each element combines with it for God to speak to his people and for them to respond. When one element receives greater weight or expectation, such as the Homily, it keeps the whole of the Liturgy of the Word from being engaged as the announcement of the Mystery of salvation and redemption.

The divine dialogue that is the Liturgy of the Word is enhanced when each minister assumes the responsibility of proclaiming fully and well the word of God with faith and conviction. The genuine response on the part of all to this dialogue is enriched when the Liturgy of the Word is not robbed of reflective silence. The highly verbal content of the Liturgy of the Word requires a disciplined *ars celebrandi* throughout, so the words become worship and form the hearers to unite with the offering of Christ that follows with the Liturgy of the Eucharist.

The reception of the word of God during the Liturgy of the

Word demands a previous encounter with this same word outside of the liturgical celebration through reading, prayer, and study. It is always helpful for the ordained and the baptized to be acquainted with the Biblical Readings prior to hearing them in the celebration so they can engage them more fully. This type of engagement then allows for the word of God to be "living and effective, sharper than any two-edged sword, penetrating even between soul and spirit, joints and marrow, and able to discern reflections and thoughts of the heart" (Heb 4:12). In this way, the saving word of God spoken during the Eucharist finds expression in the Christian life.

The next chapter looks at the Preparation of the Gifts during the Liturgy of the Eucharist of the Mass with a description of its several elements and directions for each form of the Mass.

CHAPTER SEVEN

The Liturgy of the Eucharist and the Preparation of the Gifts

There are three parts to the Liturgy of the Eucharist: the Preparation of the Gifts, the Eucharistic Prayer, and the Communion Rite. This chapter will look only at the first part, the Preparation of the Gifts, as the prelude to the Eucharistic Prayer. The Preparation of the Gifts includes two significant elements: the actual preparation itself and the Prayer over the Offerings. The description of the Preparation of the Gifts in the *General Instruction of the Roman Missal* and the directions for how to carry out this rite in the *General Instruction* and the *Order of Mass* repeat important information for emphasis. In this chapter, the directions for the Preparation of the Gifts are described in detail for each form of the celebration of Mass. Everyone, both the ordained and the baptized, should be attentive to how each aspect of this part of the Liturgy of the Eucharist is observed, allowing for a more conscious and authentic participation in the Eucharistic Prayer to follow. The *ars celebrandi* of the Preparation of the Gifts arrives from a true grasp of the elements, and consistent practice of the directions for the rite prevents this moment in the Eucharist from becoming simply functional, as is often the case.

The Liturgy of the Eucharist

The *General Instruction*, as with the Introductory Rites and the Liturgy of the Word, offers a sound theological purpose for this part of the Mass:

> At the Last Supper Christ instituted the Paschal Sacrifice and banquet, by which the Sacrifice of the Cross is continuously made present in the Church whenever the Priest, representing Christ the Lord, carries out what the Lord himself did and handed over to his disciples to be done in his memory.
>
> For Christ took the bread and the chalice, gave thanks, broke the bread and gave it to his disciples, saying: Take, eat and drink: this is my Body; this is the chalice of my Blood. Do this in memory of me. (72)

This text clearly presents the traditional faith of the Church that Christ himself at the Last Supper gave the enduring form for his Pascal Sacrifice on the cross. The second and related point in this text is especially significant for this presentation of the *ars celebrandi* and the celebration of the Eucharist. The Paschal Sacrifice of Christ on the cross actually takes place when the priest, representing Christ the Lord, does what the Lord himself did and also handed on to his Apostles to do in his memory. This "doing" is not simply a matter of function and imitation; even more, it is a sacramental correspondence that allows for what the priest does to be exactly the same thing that the Lord himself did. Therefore, in the whole of the celebration of the Mass, and especially in the Liturgy of the Eucharist, great care should be exercised by the priest celebrant, the Deacon, the liturgical ministers, and the faithful in carrying out the rites of each part of the Liturgy of the Eucharist as described and directed by the Church to achieve both the full meaning of these rites and the greatest participation possible in the Mystery they celebrate.

The *General Instruction* further states that the Church has structured the whole of the Liturgy of the Eucharist in three parts to correspond precisely to the words and actions of the Lord at the Last Supper:

> a) At the Preparation of the Gifts, bread and wine with water are brought to the altar, the same elements, that is to say, which Christ took into his hands.
>
> b) In the Eucharistic Prayer, thanks is given to God for the whole work of salvation, and the offerings become the Body and Blood of Christ.
>
> c) Through the fraction and through Communion, the faithful, though many, receive from the one bread the Lord's Body and from the one chalice the Lord's Blood in the same way that the Apostles received them from the hands of Christ himself. (72)

The Preparation of the Gifts, as the first of these three parts in the Liturgy of the Eucharist, focuses on the bread and wine and how they are set apart for the Sacrifice of the Lord. This Sacrifice will then unfold with the Eucharistic Prayer and then with complete participation in it with Holy Communion. Paying attention to the detail of this first part of the Liturgy of the Eucharist, mindful of the *ars celebrandi*, focusing on the same elements that Christ himself took into his hands, allows for an ever deepening of the meaning of his Sacrifice and our Communion from that Sacrifice.

Description of the elements of the Preparation of the Gifts

Two elements of the Preparation of the Gifts are presented in the *General Instruction*, namely, the actual preparation of the gifts of bread and wine and the prayer that concludes it, the Prayer over the Offerings. The description of these elements at different points includes some directional guidance. The inclusion of rubrical items in the description emphasizes especially the theological points and highlights the need for a careful carrying out of the rite.

The Preparation of the Gifts

At this point, the altar is already covered with a white cloth and appointed with lit candles and a cross with the image of the crucified Lord on or near it. From the beginning of Mass to this point, there has been nothing else on the altar, except perhaps the *Book of the Gospels*. Yet everything that has taken place thus far in the celebration has pointed to the altar and the Liturgy of the Eucharist as the realization of the saving event of Christ in the Eucharistic Prayer. The assembling of the faithful and the announcement of the message of salvation with the Liturgy of the Word now allows for a more immediate preparation for the Eucharistic Prayer with the Preparation of the Gifts.

The whole of the Liturgy of the Eucharist begins with the gifts of bread and wine — the gifts that will become the holy Body and Blood of Christ — being brought to the altar (see

GIRM 73). The altar is made ready for the Sacrifice. The altar is at the center; it is the focus in a more explicit manner of the whole of the Liturgy of the Eucharist. To prepare the altar for the offering of the Lord, it is necessary before the bread and wine are placed upon it that a corporal be placed on it, as well as the purificator, the *Roman Missal*, and the chalice. The chalice is brought to the altar if it will be prepared at the altar. It is also possible for the chalice to be prepared at the credence table. Now the altar is ready to receive the gifts of bread and wine. The offerings are brought forward, usually by members of the faithful. The priest or the Deacon accepts the gifts and then carries them to the altar. At this time, other gifts, such as money for the poor or for the Church, can be brought forward. Since their use is not so much for the Sacrifice about to take place, although certainly associated with it, these gifts are placed away from the altar and in the sanctuary. In fact, only gifts that will in some way be consumed or used for another purpose — in a manner like the bread and wine — are permitted for this procession. Other things of a more thematic or symbolic nature are out of place with the procession of the gifts and therefore should not be included.

This element of the Preparation of the Gifts, generally described above, is actually further described in a more complete way in the *General Instruction* in two stages: the preparation of the altar itself and then the preparation of the actual gifts, which indicates a significance to each stage. The prepared altar receives the gifts to be prepared.

The details of this first stage include the actual preparation of the altar with the corporal, the purificator, the *Roman Missal*, and the chalice. The *General Instruction* at this point establishes a principle for the preparation of the altar for the celebration of Mass for all sizes of congregations (see 73). Regardless of the size of the congregation, the items and pattern of preparation of the altar are typically the same. Nothing is said of the size or color of the corporal. It is traditionally white in color like the altar cloth, and should be a sufficient size for one chalice and one paten. On occasions when there is the need for additional sacred vessels for Communion of large congregations and a great number of concelebrants, the corporal should be large enough so that all the vessels may be set upon it, even if it covers the entire mensa. There is no mention of an additional corporal or several corporals for a large number of sacred vessels. Such a practice introduces unnecessary distinctions among the sacred vessels. The *General Instruction* only states that the corporal is placed on the altar. So, more needs to be said about this action. Typically the corporal is folded in such a way that it has the shape of a square. Regardless of how it is folded, it should be placed flat on the altar center and unfolded from its place on the altar. It is not a secondary altar cloth, and so it is not spread like a tablecloth. Rather, it is typically opened from side to side and then top to bottom. Once it is unfolded on the altar, it should not require any further positioning or smoothing.

Before any of the gifts are brought to the altar, its preparation should be complete with the purificator or purificators set upon it, usually to the side of the corporal. The *Roman Missal* is typically set to the left of the center of the altar so that it can be read easily. Often, for ease of reading, the *Roman Missal* is on a book stand or pillow to give it a comfortable angle and height. The *Roman Missal* should be opened to the proper section in the *Order of Mass*. Sometimes, the *Roman Missal* is placed directly in front of the priest celebrant or centered on the altar beyond the gifts. In both instances, the *Roman Missal* is given a primary place more than the gifts whose place is at the center of the altar.

The details for the second stage consider bringing forward the gifts. This includes both the bringing forth of the offerings from among the people or from a side table in the sanctuary. This second stage is all too easily missed when the gifts come from the side table in the sanctuary. The *General Instruction* reminds us of the praiseworthy practice of the presentation of the gifts, the bread and wine, by the faithful: "Even though the faithful no longer bring from their own possessions the bread and wine intended for the liturgy as was once the case, nevertheless the rite of carrying up the offerings still keeps its spiritual efficacy and significance" (73). When the faithful bring forward the bread and wine, they arrive with these gifts and all their baptismal priestly offerings associated with them that will also be united to the Sacrifice of the Lord at the altar. Nothing is said of quantity here, but the principle is identified. If the bread and wine are to be brought forward from among the people, then all the bread and wine needed for consecration should be brought forward.

The action of the procession of the gifts takes place with an accompanying chant, the Offertory Chant, which should last at least until the gifts are placed on the altar (see GIRM 74). The *General Instruction* directs that the Offertory Chant follow the patterns indicated for the Entrance Chant. Unlike with the Entrance Chant with the description of its content, coming from the Church's hymnals and the psalmody, there is nothing prescribed as far as the source or content of the Offertory Chant. By reference to the Entrance Chant, the Church's hymnals and the psalmody would also be a preference. However, this is also the place when the liturgical time or occasion might be highlighted with an appropriate hymn. Since a chant is not required at this point, either silence or instrumental music may also be fitting. The *General Instruction* further notes that the Offertory Chant can take place even when there is no procession with the bread and wine (see 74).

Once the bread and wine are brought forth, the priest is the one who places the elements on the altar (see 75). This placement of the paten with the bread and the chalice with the wine on the corporal is an act of great significance. It is what sets the bread and wine apart for the Sacrifice of Christ. Sometimes there is an unnecessary lifting up, placing down, and rearranging of the sacred vessels on the altar, thereby diminishing this action of the placement on the altar and its meaning. This placement of the sacred vessels on the altar is to be accompanied by the given formula in the *Roman Missal.* The praying of this formula for the bread and wine is secondary to the placement of the bread and wine on the altar of Sacrifice.

Once the gifts have been placed on the altar, when it is opportune and especially on more solemn occasions, these same gifts may be incensed, followed by the cross and the altar. The *General Instruction* describes this incensation as signifying "the Church's offering and prayer rising like incense in the sight of God" (75). Following this incensation, the priest and people may be incensed as sharers in the priesthood of Christ, although in distinct manners — the ministerial priesthood and baptismal priesthood, respectively — and as those who now offer, again in a distinct manner, the saving Sacrifice of Christ. The use of incense during the Preparation of the Gifts is optional. The *General Instruction* does not indicate that there is an option as to what is incensed at this point. Rather, what is identified for the incensation — the gifts, the cross, the altar, the priest, and the people — link what is to be offered, the signs of the offering, and those who make the offering in anticipation of the actual Sacrifice of Christ with the Eucharistic Prayer.

The priest, after having set the gifts aside for the Sacrifice of the Lord, and having possibly incensed them, washes his hands at the side of the altar. This rite takes place at the side of the altar intentionally because it is not central to the action of the preparation, which took place at the center of the altar, and its meaning, a desire for interior purification, is personal to the priest (see 76).

The Prayer over the Offerings

This prayer is one of the principal presidential prayers of the Mass and brings to a conclusion the Preparation of the Gifts. First, the priest invites the faithful to prayer and then prays the Prayer over the Offerings, which looks to the Eucharistic Prayer, the second part of the Liturgy of the Eucharist (see GIRM 77). As with the Collect, the *General Instruction* gives specific directions for the conclusion of this prayer and the faithful's Acclamation:

> At Mass, a single Prayer over the Offerings is said, and it ends with the shorter conclusion, that is: *Through Christ our Lord.* If, however, the Son is mentioned at the end of this prayer, the conclusion is: *Who lives and reigns forever and ever.*
>
> The people, joining in this petition, make the prayer their own by means of the acclamation *Amen.* (77)

Directions for the Preparation of the Gifts

The description of the Preparation of the Gifts and the Prayer over the Offerings gives a general indication of how each is carried out at this point in the celebration of the Eucharist. The directions from both the *General Instruction* and the *Order of Mass* are more precise for each form of the Mass. These directions require study and an understanding of the theological values inherent in them regarding the Preparation of the Gifts and its relationship to the whole of the *Order of Mass*. The combination of knowing the directions, understanding their meaning, and carrying them out with reverence and care allows for an *ars celebrandi* that calls forth a more authentic and focused participation in the Mystery of Christ on the part of all.

The Preparation of the Gifts for Mass without a Deacon

It is very common today to speak of the parts of the Mass, especially the Liturgy of the Word and the Liturgy of the Eucharist, as if they were units within the whole of the celebration. It is more precise to see all the parts of the Mass, as presented earlier, as combining to form a single act of worship of Almighty God. This is especially clear with the directions for the Preparation of the Gifts as given in the *General Instruction* and the *Order of Mass*. In both instances, the Universal Prayer, which is the final element of the Liturgy of the Word, turns over without interruption into the Offertory Chant, which is designed to accompany the presentation of the gifts.[1] With the Universal Prayer the baptized expressed their own priesthood which now, with the Preparation of the Gifts, is more completely joined to the work of the priest celebrant. The priest unites the faithful to himself as together they uniquely and distinctly prepare to offer the Sacrifice of Christ.

The acolyte, or in most cases the deputed server, assists the priest celebrant in the celebration of Mass without a Deacon. It is the proper role of the acolyte or server, once the Universal Prayer is completed, to prepare the altar for the gifts. The acolyte or server brings from a side table the corporal, the purificator, the chalice, and the *Roman Missal* to be placed upon the altar.[2] If an acolyte or deputed server is unavailable, then the duties proper to this role are assumed by the priest celebrant. The directions given in the *General Instruction* and the *Order of Mass* for the element of the Preparation of the Gifts describe a celebration with a limited number. Depending on the number of priests and people, the size of the corporal varies for the number of sacred vessels needed for the bread and wine, and the number of purificators depends on the number of chalices required for the Communion of all. Following the order of the items to be brought to the altar is reasonable and recommended. The altar has nothing on it at this point, except perhaps the candles and a crucifix if they are not positioned elsewhere near the altar. First, the corporal is spread on the altar. The placement of the purificator (or purificators) depends on their use. If only one chalice is to be used, the purificator is placed to the right of the side of the altar where its preparation may take place. If several purificators will be needed, they can be placed on the altar at this same time near the other chalices, or these purificators can be brought to the altar during the Communion Rite. The chalice and the pall are brought to the altar and placed on the right side for preparation. The use of the pall is optional yet practical. It only makes sense to bring the pall to the altar if it will be used. As far as the use of the pall, it covers the chalice after it has been presented during the Preparation of the Gifts and is in use in this way until the reception of Communion (see GIRM 142). However, the pall is removed prior to the epiclesis through the showing of the Blood of Christ after the consecration, and then for the Doxology, for the Fraction of the Bread, and if the chalice is used for the invitation to Holy Communion.

As the *General Instructions* indicates, it is a praiseworthy practice to veil the chalice for the celebration of Mass (see 118). However, the veil should be removed before it is brought to the altar. Finally, once the linens and the chalice are in place, the *Roman Missal* is brought to the altar. The *Roman Missal*, once it is placed on the altar, should be opened to the Liturgy of the Eucharist. It is always possible for more than one acolyte or server to assist with the preparation of the altar and to bring these items to the altar.

What needs to be impressed upon the faithful as they sit while the altar and gifts are prepared is that their posture is not indicative of a passive participation but of their actual participation: interior participation in the rite. In fact, the *General Instruction* and the *Order of Mass* echo what has already been described for the Preparation of the Gifts when both sources give directions for this part of the Liturgy of the Eucharist. A connection is made between the actual participation of the faithful in the offering of the Eucharist and their bringing forth the bread and wine for the Eucharist.[3] In a similar way, their participation is enhanced when, along with the bread and wine, other gifts for the benefit of the Church and the poor are likewise brought forward.[4] As mentioned above with the description of this element of the Preparation of the Gifts, the desirable practice of bringing forward the gifts links in a tangible way the interior participation of the faithful in offering themselves with the offering of the bread and wine that takes place at the altar.

In this form of the Mass (without the assistance of a Deacon), the acolyte or a deputed server assists the priest celebrant as he receives the gifts. The acceptance of the gifts can take place in a variety of ways. The acolyte or deputed server can receive them and bring them to the priest celebrant at the altar, or the priest celebrant can receive them directly. They can be received at the entrance to the sanctuary area or at the altar itself. The gifts that are intended for the needs of the Church and the poor are accepted after the bread and wine and are placed in the sanctuary apart from the altar (see GIRM 140 and 73). It seems reasonable for these additional gifts to be retained in the sanctuary as an indication that they are associated with the offering that is taking place on the altar.

After the altar has been prepared, if the gifts are to be brought forward, the priest celebrant goes to the entrance to the sanctuary or to the altar to receive the gifts. As in every circumstance when the priest celebrant arrives to the altar, he bows and then begins the liturgical action. Now at the prepared altar, he accepts the paten with the bread. A careful reading of the *General Instruction* and the *Order of Mass* at this point indicates a single vessel for the bread. Presumably, this vessel would have bread sufficient for all who will receive Communion. In circumstances when additional patens or ciboria are needed for the

Communion of all, they should be placed on the altar by the priest or the acolyte or the deputed server before the priest celebrant accepts the principal paten to be presented. All the bread to be consecrated for the Communion of all should be placed on the altar during the Preparation of the Gifts. The priest celebrant, standing at the center of the altar, accepts the bread with both hands and holds it slightly raised above the altar.[5] This is not an elevation. This is to emphasize that the bread accepted is set aside for the Sacrifice of the Lord as it is placed by the priest celebrant on the altar. As the priest is holding the paten with the bread slightly raised, he quietly or in a low voice says the prayer, "Blessed are you, Lord God of all creation ..." Once the prayer is completed, he places the sacred vessel on the corporal.[6] There is a tendency among some priest celebrants to begin the prayer as they are accepting the paten and to conclude it as they are placing it on the altar. There should be a deliberateness associated with this action to give equal emphasis to the action of presenting the bread which will "become for us the bread of life" with the prescribed prayer and the setting aside of the offering for the sacrifice. So, the prayer begins as the paten is held slightly raised and concludes before it is placed on the altar.

The *Order of Mass* gives an additional direction at this point, that the prayers for the presenting of the bread and wine may also be said aloud if the Offertory Chant is not sung or if there is no instrumental music. If this is the case, these prayers of the priest celebrant are followed by the people's Acclamation, "Blessed be God for ever."[7] There is no requirement to speak these prayers aloud if there is no chant or even instrumental music at this point. The option remains for the priest celebrant to recite them quietly. Even when these prayers are said by the priest in a low voice without song or music accompanying the liturgical action, the faithful should still engage in the action at the altar. They are engaged not so much in the immediate presentation of the bread and wine at the altar for the Sacrifice to follow but in the presentation of themselves along with the bread and wine for the offering of themselves in the Eucharistic Prayer. This understanding recommends that these prayers be recited quietly with some regularity even when there is no song or music.

Once the paten with bread has been presented, the chalice is prepared to be presented as well. In most circumstances, the chalice in a celebration without a Deacon is prepared not at the center of the altar but rather at its side. The priest moves to the side of the altar, typically the right side, and he receives the cruets of wine and water from the acolyte or the deputed server. The preparation of the chalice includes pouring wine and water into it. Only one chalice is indicated at this point in the *General Instruction* and the *Order of Mass*. This vessel as well should have wine sufficient for all who will receive Communion. In circumstances when additional chalices are needed for the Communion of all, they should be placed on the altar by the priest or the acolyte or the deputed server before the priest celebrant accepts the paten to be presented. All the wine to be consecrated for the Communion of all should be placed on the altar during the Preparation of the Gifts. At the side of the altar, the priest celebrant first takes the cruet with wine and fills the chalice as needed. Then, as he adds a little bit of water into the wine in the chalice, he says quietly or in low voice the prayer, "By the mystery of this water …"[8] Water may be added to the additional chalices as well at this time. The preparation of the chalice is not central to its presentation for the offering of Christ and so it does not take place at the center of the altar.

Once the chalice is prepared, the priest celebrant moves again to the center of the altar, raises the chalice with both hands only slightly above the altar, and says quietly the prayer, "Blessed are you, Lord God of all creation …" At the conclusion of the prayer, the chalice is placed upon the corporal on the altar.[9] The same deliberateness mentioned above with the presentation of the paten should mark the presentation of the chalice and for the same reason, as this wine "will become our spiritual drink." The *General Instruction* mentions that the pall to cover the chalice may be employed once the chalice is placed upon the altar (see 142). The pall carries out a practical purpose: to prevent anything, especially bugs, from flying into the wine. If the pall is to be used, it does not make sense that only the chalice presented has a pall placed on it. If a pall is used for one chalice, then it should be employed for all chalices. If the pall is used at this point, for one or several chalices, then it should be employed throughout the Liturgy of the Eucharist as directed by the *General Instruction.*

Once the chalice is placed upon the altar, the priest celebrant, remaining at the center of the altar, bows profoundly and says quietly the prayer, "With humble spirit ..."[10] Again there is the tendency among some priest celebrants to begin the prayer as they are bowing and conclude it as they are again standing erect. The posture of the profound bow gives expression to the text of the prayer "with humble spirit and contrite heart," and therefore should be the posture throughout the whole of the prayer.

The Preparation of the Gifts may include the use of incense, if appropriate to the celebration and/or the occasion. After the prayer "With humble spirit ..." the priest celebrant places some incense in the thurible, and as usual blesses it without saying anything. The offerings are incensed with three single swings of the thurible or a Sign of the Cross over them, then the cross and the altar. The acolyte or deputed server stands at the side of the altar and incenses the priest celebrant and then goes to a convenient place to incense the faithful.[11] The priest celebrant does not bow before he incenses the offerings, as they are not yet signs of Christ. Rather, he takes the thurible and begins immediately incensing the offerings either with three single swings or with the Sign of the Cross. Then he bows to the altar cross if it is in front of him and incenses it with three single swings of the thurible and bows afterward again. If it is not in front of him, he incenses it in the same way as he passes it. The altar is incensed without a bow before or after and with single swings of the thurible. The movement of the thurible should indicate that the whole of the altar is incensed, mensa as well as base. The priest and the faithful are incensed with three single swings of the thurible with a bow before and after the incensation (see GIRM 277).

After the prayer "With humble spirit ..." or after the incensations, the priest celebrant, again at the side of the altar, washes his hands. As the acolyte or the deputed server pours the water over his hands, he says quietly the prayer, "Wash me, O Lord ..." This gesture appears useless to many, and the lack of practical need often leads to the rite being carried out in a hasty way, with little regard for its meaning and the engagement of the persons carrying it out. While the rite should not be accorded any increased significance in the overall plan of the Preparation of the Gifts, it should be carried out with care. Today, the rite is a sign of the priest's desire for interior purification, and it should be carried out with a carefulness that suggests respect for the action of another person willingly ministering to the priest celebrant, pouring water over his hands and then handing him a towel to dry them. The care and respect at this point is an overarching indication of the same care and respect for every other action and engagement of persons in the celebration of the Mystery of Christ in the Eucharist. There is no provision for the priest celebrant to simply dip his fingers in a bowl of water and then dry them. Rather, he is to wash them with water poured over them.

The first element of the Preparation of the Gifts comes to

an end with the washing of the hands, and now the second element unfolds with the greeting and the Prayer over the Offerings. The priest celebrant returns to the center of the altar and, as the *General Instruction* and the *Order of Mass* indicate, he faces the people.[12] The practice throughout most of the world with the Roman Rite for the Liturgy of the Eucharist is that it is to be carried out at a freestanding altar with the priest celebrant facing the people all throughout this part of the Mass. Yet the *General Instruction* and the *Order of Mass* indicate the *ad orientem* posture. Still, at this point and all throughout the Liturgy of the Eucharist, the typical posture is *ad populum*. With the greeting, the dialogue that introduces the Prayer over the Offerings, the priest celebrant extends and then joins his hands as he invites the people to pray as they respond to his invitation, "Pray, brethren …" The people, who up to this point have been seated, rise and respond, "May the Lord accept the sacrifice …"[13] The people rise as an expression of their more active engagement with their response, praying that what they have to offer will indeed be accepted along with the bread and wine for the glory of God and the benefit of the whole Church. This greeting, this dialogue, as with all others in the celebration of the Mass, is intended above all to be sung. The priest and people form the whole Christ who worships the Father. With the gifts prepared, they are now prepared to enter into the Eucharistic Prayer, where this worship reaches its peak in the Sacrifice of Christ. Thus, the *Order of Mass* provides the sung form for this greeting first, followed by the recited text.

The Prayer over the Offerings follows the greeting just described, and not with the usual invitation to pray. The priest extends his hands and prays aloud the prescribed Prayer over the Offerings. He brings his hands together at the simple conclusion, "Through Christ our Lord." The faithful acclaim "Amen" at the end of the prayer.[14] On the occasions when this prayer is sung, the musical notation given in the *Roman Missal* for the presidential prayers for the solemn tone and the reciting tone is observed. When the Eucharistic Prayer is sung according to the tone provided in the *Roman Missal*, the solemn tone is always used for the Prayer over the Offerings.[15]

The Preparation of the Gifts for Mass with a Deacon

When a Deacon assists the priest celebrant at Mass, his duties are specified for the Preparation of the Gifts. Typically, the Deacon will have declaimed the intentions of the Universal Prayer. So, after the "Amen" concluding the Universal Prayer, the Deacon moves to the altar from the ambo and bows profoundly before the altar. The priest celebrant remains at the chair. The acolyte or deputed server assists the Deacon in preparing the altar with the corporal, purificator, and *Roman Missal*. It is uniquely the role of the Deacon to take care of the sacred vessels, specifically their preparation and placement on the altar, except for those to be set upon the altar by the priest celebrant. The Deacon accompanies the priest celebrant as he receives the gifts from the faithful. The Deacon, at the altar, is the one to hand to the priest celebrant the paten with bread. At the side of the altar, he prepares the chalice with the wine and a little water, while in a quiet voice making use of the accompanying prayer, "By the mystery of this water …" The Deacon then presents the prepared chalice to the priest celebrant. The Deacon may prepare the chalice at the credence table and bring it to the priest at the altar. If incense is used, the Deacon assists the priest. He or the acolyte or the deputed server holds the boat for the priest celebrant. The Deacon may accompany the celebrant for the incensations of the offerings, the cross, and the altar, bowing with him and leading him around the altar. The Deacon or the acolyte or the deputed server then incenses the priest celebrant and the faithful.[16]

The Preparation of the Gifts for Concelebrated Mass

The principal celebrant carries out the Preparation of the Gifts as described above in the form for the Mass without a Deacon or with a Deacon. The concelebrants remain seated at their places during this first part of the Liturgy of the Eucharist (see GIRM 214). Concelebrants are expected to join in the Offertory Chant, if there is one. Otherwise, they are focused on the action at the altar, uniting themselves in the course of the Preparation of the Gifts with the elements for the Sacrifice that will soon occur with the Eucharistic Prayer to which they will be intimately associated with the priest celebrant.

The Preparation of the Gifts for Mass at Which only One Minister Participates

The Preparation of the Gifts is carried out in the very same way as Mass with the People (see GIRM 265). If a Deacon is present, he carries out his proper diaconal roles. In the Order of Mass for this form, it is possible for the Roman Missal already to be at the altar from the Introductory Rites. Therefore, moving it would not be part of the Preparation of the Gifts.[17] It is possible that the corporal, purificator, and chalice may have already been placed on the altar at the beginning of Mass.[18]

Instituted and Deputed Ministers and the Preparation of the Gifts

The celebration of the Eucharist in all its forms anticipates the presence of an acolyte or deputed server. For more solemn occasions, several acolytes or deputed servers may share duties. For the reverent and careful celebration of the Mass, and especially for the Preparation of the Gifts, those who assist as acolytes and servers should be well-informed of their duties and practiced in how to carry them out, according to what is directed by the *General Instruction* and the *Order of Mass*. Certain duties, such as the preparation and placement of the sacred vessels, are the prerogative of the Deacon and should not be usurped by the server. The priest alone should place the paten with bread on the altar, and no one else. It is not uncommon for a server, and at times a Deacon, to place this paten to the side of the altar and even in the center only for the priest to pick it up to place it again. This should not happen.

The specific duties of the acolyte or deputed server include, when a Deacon is not present, assisting with the preparation of the altar. With the priest celebrant remaining at his chair, the acolyte or the deputed server spreads the corporal on the altar, then brings the purificator, chalice, and pall, along with the *Roman Missal*, to the altar as described above. The acolyte or deputed server assists the priest as he receives the gifts, handing them to the priest at the altar. The acolyte or deputed server likewise assists with the incensation of the offerings, the cross, and the altar and finally incenses the priest and the people (see GIRM 190). The acolyte or deputed server also assists the priest celebrant with the washing of his hands.

Conclusion

This first part of the Liturgy of the Eucharist, the Preparation of the Gifts, can frequently be carried out with little attention to its detail. However, it is in its detail that the theological and liturgical dimensions of the rite become clearly manifest: the offering of the people with the offering of the bread and wine; the relationship of the altar to the gifts as they are placed upon it; the personal preparation of the priest celebrant; and the movement of this rite toward the Sacrifice that actually occurs with the Eucharistic Prayer. The *ars celebrandi*, a careful and attentive approach to these details, on the part of both the ordained and the baptized, allows for a meaningful correspondence between exterior participation and interior participation throughout the

Preparation of the Gifts.

The Christian life consists of preparation for a daily joining of ourselves to the offering of Christ that takes place with the Eucharist. This preparation that is the routine of the Christian life reaches a peak when it is ritualized with the Preparation of the Gifts and leads to this true union in the Eucharistic Sacrifice. Likewise, conscious participation in the Preparation of the Gifts guides the daily orientation of the Christian "to offer [themselves] as a living sacrifice, holy and pleasing to God, [their] spiritual worship" (Rom 12:1) outside of the celebration of the Mass.

The next chapter looks at the Eucharistic Prayer, during the Liturgy of the Eucharist of the Mass, with a description of its several elements and directions for each form of the Mass.

CHAPTER EIGHT
The Liturgy of the Eucharist and the Eucharistic Prayer

This chapter reviews the second part of the Liturgy of the Eucharist: the Eucharistic Prayer. The Eucharistic Prayer is the centerpiece of the celebration of Mass and the moment when the Paschal Mystery of the Lord becomes most perfectly present to us as it takes place eternally at the right hand of the Father in heaven. The *General Instruction of the Roman Missal* and the *Order of Mass* describe and direct the Eucharistic Prayer in such a way that it has its own integrity and singularity of purpose and expression in proclaiming and making present the Mystery of Faith. The Eucharistic Prayer in all forms of the celebration of Mass requires a focused *ars celebrandi* to ensure that it is carried out with the dignity it is to be accorded. An artful and careful proclamation of the Eucharistic Prayer fosters the greatest possibility of participation on the part of the priest and the faithful for their unique roles in the offering of the Sacrifice of Christ.

Description of the Eucharistic Prayer

Every part of the Mass in its own way announces the Paschal Mystery of Christ. The Introductory Rites prepare us to encounter the Sacred Mysteries. The Liturgy of the Word proclaims the Mystery of Christ. The Preparation of the Gifts immediately readies us to enter into the Christian Mystery that will fully unfold with the Eucharistic Prayer. The Communion Rite reveals many dimensions of the Mystery of Faith. The Concluding Rites send us forth to live the Mystery that we have encountered, shared, and received in so many ways in the celebration of Mass. The Eucharistic Prayer, though, is "the center and high point of the entire celebration" (GIRM 78). The Eucharistic Prayer in every celebration of the Mass is the most excellent manifestation of the actual saving death and resurrection of Christ. This is the Mystery of Faith. This is the fullness of the announcement of salvation and of our worship of Almighty God.

With the proclamation of the Eucharistic Prayer, the purpose of the Sacred Liturgy becomes truly evident. This is the moment when the divine reality of Christ's death and rising actually occurs, God the Father is glorified, and all assembled share in the holiness of God. The proclamation of the Eucharistic Prayer includes the priest celebrant and the faithful taking distinct and complementary roles as it is carried out:

> The Priest calls upon the people to lift up their hearts towards the Lord in prayer and thanksgiving; he associates the people with himself in the Prayer that he addresses in the name of the entire community to God the Father through Jesus Christ in the Holy Spirit. Furthermore, the

> meaning of this Prayer is that the whole congregation of the faithful joins with Christ in confessing the great deeds of God and in the offering of Sacrifice. (GIRM 78)

The faithful enter into the action of the Eucharistic Prayer as they listen with attentiveness to its content, a listening that allows them to participate interiorly with the offering that is occurring — an offering of themselves with the offering of the Lord, "with reverence and in silence" (78).

In the current edition of the *Roman Missal*, there are ten Eucharistic Prayers that may be used, some of them at any time and others on certain occasions. These ten Eucharistic Prayers include prayers that are ancient and others that are recently composed. The *General Instruction* outlines the main elements of Eucharistic Prayers prayed in the modern Roman Rite. Each of the elements, although distinguishable, form an integrated whole for the proclamation and manifestation of the Paschal Mystery with each Eucharistic Prayer. These elements are:

> a) The thanksgiving (expressed especially in the Preface), in which the Priest, in the name of the whole of the holy people, glorifies God the Father and gives thanks to him for the whole work of salvation or for some particular aspect of it, according to the varying day, festivity, or time of year.
>
> b) The acclamation, by which the whole congregation, joining with the heavenly powers, sings the Sanctus (Holy, Holy, Holy). This acclamation, which constitutes part of the Eucharistic Prayer itself, is pronounced by all the people with the Priest.
>
> c) The epiclesis, in which, by means of particular in-

vocations, the Church implores the power of the Holy Spirit that the gifts offered by human hands be consecrated, that is, become Christ's Body and Blood, and that the unblemished sacrificial Victim to be consumed in Communion may be for the salvation of those who will partake of it.

d) The institution narrative and Consecration, by which, by means of the words and actions of Christ, that Sacrifice is effected which Christ himself instituted during the Last Supper, when he offered his Body and Blood under the species of bread and wine, gave them to the Apostles to eat and drink, and leaving with the latter the command to perpetuate this same mystery.

e) The anamnesis, by which the Church, fulfilling the command that she received from Christ the Lord through the Apostles, celebrates the memorial of Christ, recalling especially his blessed Passion, glorious Resurrection, and Ascension into heaven.

f) The oblation, by which, in this very memorial, the Church, in particular that gathered here and now, offers the unblemished sacrificial Victim in the Holy Spirit to the Father. The Church's intention, indeed, is that the faithful not only offer this unblemished sacrificial Victim but also learn to offer their very selves, and so day by day to be brought, through the mediation of Christ, into unity with God and with each other, so that God may at last be all in all.

g) The intercessions, by which expression is given to the fact that the Eucharist is celebrated in communion with

> the whole Church, of both heaven and of earth, and that the oblation is made for her and for all her members, living and dead, who are called to participate in the redemption and salvation purchased by the Body and Blood of Christ.
>
> h) The concluding doxology, by which the glorification of God is expressed and which is affirmed and concluded by the people's acclamation *Amen.* (79)

It becomes very clear just what happens with the Eucharistic Prayer when these several elements are studied as part of its description. The priest celebrant and the faithful each have a role and part in the Eucharistic Prayer as they distinctly and uniquely participate in the Sacrifice of the Lord. The Eucharistic Prayer is directed to the praise of the Father, as the Holy Spirit and the Church cooperate to bring about a real encounter with the death and rising of Jesus, by whom "the Sacrifice is effected" (GIRM 79). The Memorial of the Lord is recalled and made present with the Eucharistic Prayer, so that it is the offering of the unblemished sacrificial Victim on the part of the priest celebrant to which the faithful unite their very lives. This Eucharistic Prayer brings together heaven and earth as it is an action of the whole Church and for the whole Church united to Christ in glory.

Directions for the Eucharistic Prayer

The directions for the Eucharistic Prayer, as found in the *General Instruction* and the *Order of Mass*, are quite clear and promote its central place in the celebration of Mass. The liturgical and theological weight of the Eucharistic Prayer, as well as its pastoral effectiveness, demand that it be proclaimed with the greatest care and reverence and that the rubrics be followed precisely. The Eucharistic Prayer requires an *ars celebrandi* par excellence, both out of regard for the divine event that occurs with this prayer and for the authentic engagement of the priest celebrant and the faithful in it.

The Eucharistic Prayer for Mass without a Deacon

The priest celebrant has just prayed the Prayer over the Offerings and so is standing at the center of the altar to begin the Eucharistic Prayer. The choice for the Eucharistic Prayer (which includes the Preface) should be made before the actual celebration of Mass, and this choice is based on the values to be presented later in this chapter. In other words, the choice is not arbitrary, nor should the priest celebrant pray the same Eucharistic Prayer all the time, regardless of the day or the occasion. The proclamation of the Eucharistic Prayer belongs only to the priest celebrant.[1] By virtue of his ordination, only he can pronounce the words of the Lord of the institution narrative and consecration as well as pray for the whole Church and in the name of the Church with the Eucharistic Prayer (see GIRM 147). Although the priest celebrant alone proclaims the Eucharistic Prayer, the faithful are associated with him throughout it, even though they are silent for most of it. The faithful unite themselves interiorly to the offering of Christ, respond to the introductory dialogues of the Preface, to the Mystery of Faith with one of the prescribed Acclamations, and with the concluding "Amen" to the doxology. The priest celebrant and the faithful pray together as they sing or recite the "Holy, Holy, Holy" (see 147 and 151).

The priest celebrant may sing the Eucharistic Prayer, especially the principal parts,[2] when the solemnity of the occasion suggests this. The *Roman Missal* provides for singing Eucharistic Prayers I through IV. For Eucharistic Prayer I (the Roman Canon), a simple and a solemn chant form are given. Only one chant form is provided for the others.[3] When the Eucharistic Prayer is sung, the notation to be used is that found in the *Roman Missal.*

As far as the choice to sing only the principal parts, these parts are not identified specifically in either the *General Instruction* or the *Order of Mass*. However, an argument could be made that these include, in addition to the preface, the epiclesis, the institution narrative and consecration, and the anamnesis. These are the three parts that concelebrants must pray along with the priest celebrant in a Concelebrated Mass. Although the singing of the Eucharistic Prayer is possible in all Masses, at the very least on days of greater festivity, the dialogues — during the preface, the Mystery of Faith, and the doxology with the "Amen" — and the preface itself should typically be sung. The musical notations for these are found in the *Order of Mass*.

The priest celebrant begins every Eucharistic Prayer following the same pattern of gestures. First, he extends his hands for the greeting and without closing them sings or says, "The Lord be with you." The faithful respond, "And with your spirit." Next, he raises his hands and continues, "Lift up your hearts," but still does not close his hands. The faithful respond, "We lift them up to the Lord." Then he brings his hands again to the position of the initial greeting and continues, "Let us give thanks to the Lord our God," again without closing his hands. The people respond, "It is right and just." The priest celebrant then continues with the preface with his hands extended until the end, then joins his hands as he sings or recites the "Holy, Holy, Holy" together with the faithful.[4]

Following the preface, the priest celebrant continues to proclaim the Eucharistic Prayer, observing carefully the rubrics in place (see GIRM 149). Throughout most of the Eucharistic Prayer, the priest celebrant prays with his hands extended. The rubrics direct when his hands are to be joined. There are three occasions in each Eucharistic Prayer where the gestures vary, and the rubrics are the same for each of these three occasions, namely, the epiclesis, the institution narrative and consecration, and the doxology.

For the epiclesis, as that part of the Eucharistic Prayer begins, the priest celebrant, first joining his hands, extends both hands, presumably together, over the offerings. Before he makes the Sign of the Cross over the offerings, he joins his hands. He then makes the Sign of the Cross once over the bread and wine, and then joins his hands again. These two gestures should happen with deliberateness and in such a way that all can easily observe them. If the pall is in use, then it is removed from the chalice prior to the epiclesis. Likewise, the lids to any ciboria are removed at the same time.[5]

For the institution narrative and consecration, the priest celebrant begins with his hands joined. Only when he speaks of the Lord taking the bread does he raise the host slightly above the altar. Before he begins to speak the words of the Lord, he bows slightly for the entirety of the words of the consecration of the bread. With the conclusion of these words, he stands erect and shows the Body of the Lord to the faithful. In order to do this, he needs to raise the now consecrated Host for the faithful to see it. After this, he replaces the Body of the Lord on the paten, and then he genuflects. Likewise, the same pattern is followed for the chalice. The priest celebrant begins with his hands joined. Only when he speaks of the Lord taking the chalice does he raise the chalice slightly above the altar. Before he begins to speak the words of the Lord, he bows slightly for the entirety of the words of the consecration of the wine. With the conclusion of these words, he stands erect and shows the Blood of the Lord to the faithful. In order to do this, he needs to raise the chalice for the faithful to see it. After this, he replaces the chalice with the Blood of the Lord on the corporal, and then he genuflects. If the pall is in use, he replaces it on the chalice after the showing of the Blood of Christ. Likewise, the lids to any ciboria are replaced at the same time.[6]

For the words of consecration, each of the Eucharistic Prayers directs that "the words of the Lord should be pronounced clearly and distinctly, as the nature of these words requires."[7] These rubrics for the institution narrative and consecration frame this part of the Eucharistic Prayer as distinct from the other parts, especially with the direction on how to speak the words of the Lord. While these rubrics do not propose anything dramatic, they do ensure a focus and reverence for the very words of the Lord, the very Sacrifice of Jesus, which occurs in our time and place for us and our salvation. A practice that is counterintuitive during this part of the Eucharistic Prayer is for the priest celebrant to direct the words of the narrative to the faithful with the host and chalice in hand. With the priest and people typically facing one another for the Eucharistic Prayer, there is a natural pull on the part of the priest celebrant and the faithful to look at one another as if in conversation. A careful and reverent observance of these directions allows for the divine event itself to become the focus rather than those praying the Eucharistic Prayer.

Before the priest celebrant begins to sing or say the doxology, he picks up the paten and chalice and raises them both at the same time and then continues, "Through him, and with him, and in him ..." He keeps both raised until the faithful acclaim the doxology with their "Amen" and then replaces them on the corporal.[8] Of all the times that the priest celebrant takes a sacred vessel in his hands during the Preparation of the Gifts and the Eucharistic Prayer, this is the only time that the verb "to raise" without any adverb is used. In each of the other times, the rubrics direct him to hold the vessel slightly above the altar or to raise it slightly or to show it. There is significance in the gesture that corresponds to the action of the doxology. The glorification of the Father reaches a climax with the event of the Paschal Mystery of Christ with the Eucharistic Prayer. So with the conclusion of the Eucharistic Prayer, the elements of this glorification are significantly raised up to the "glory and honor" of the Father "for ever and ever." It is equally important that the faithful acclaim with their "Amen" the raised elements and the announcement of this same glory. It makes little sense for the priest celebrant to replace the chalice and paten before the faithful have the opportunity to acclaim "Amen." In some cases, the priest celebrant will hold the Host over the chalice for the doxology. This is a gesture of showing for adoration or an invitation, as with the invitation to Communion, which is counter-indicative to the raising of the sacred vessels with the Body and Blood of the Lord for the praise and glory of the Father.

In Eucharistic Prayer I or the Roman Canon, the Sign of the Cross over the offerings takes place in the early part of the Prayer after the preface and is not a part of the epiclesis. Following the anamnesis, the priest celebrant is directed to bow with his hands joined for the section, "In humble prayer we ask you, almighty God …" After the words "the most holy Body and Blood of your Son," he is directed to stand erect and make the Sign of the Cross as he continues, "may be filled with every grace and heavenly blessing," after which he joins his hands. All throughout Eucharistic Prayer I, the bracketed words may be omitted.[9]

Each of the Eucharistic Prayers mentions the bishop of the local Church. When the bishop himself is the celebrant of the Mass, the *General Instruction* and the *Order of Mass* give directions for how to adjust the Eucharistic Prayer. The *General Instruction* states:

> If the celebrant is a Bishop, in the Prayers, after the words *N., our Pope,* he adds, *and me, your unworthy servant.* If, however, the Bishop is celebrating outside his own diocese, after the words *with … N., our Pope,* he adds, *my brother N., the Bishop of this Church, and me, your unworthy servant*; or after the words *especially … N., our*

> *Pope,* he adds, *my brother N., the Bishop of this Church, and me, your unworthy servant.*
>
> The Diocesan Bishop, or one who is equivalent to the Diocesan Bishop in law, must be mentioned by means of this formula: *together with your servant N., our Pope, and N., our Bishop (or Vicar, Prelate, Prefect, Abbot).*
>
> It is permitted to mention Coadjutor Bishop and Auxiliary Bishops in the Eucharistic Prayer, but not other Bishops who happen to be present. When several are to be mentioned, this is done with the collective formula: *N., our Bishop and his assistant Bishops.*
>
> In each of the Eucharistic Prayers, these formulas are to be adapted according to the requirements of grammar. (149 and OM EP I, 84)

In the *Order of Mass*, Eucharistic Prayer I or the Roman Canon is presented with a number of proper forms for the *Communicantes* and an additional *Hanc igitur* prior to the epiclesis. For this Eucharistic Prayer and for the others, additional interpolations are found in the *Roman Missal*, especially when ritual Masses are celebrated. They should not be overlooked but included at their proper place in the Eucharistic Prayer for these occasions.

As the Eucharistic Prayer is prayed, a bell may be rung as an indication to the faithful of what is taking place shortly before the consecration and when the Body and Blood of the Lord is shown to the faithful by the priest celebrant. The bell before the consecration is typically rung at the time of the epiclesis. Also, on those occasions when incense is used, as the Body and Blood are shown to the faithful, each may be incensed with three single swings of the thurible (see GIRM 150).

The Eucharistic Prayer for Mass with a Deacon

The priest celebrant stands at the center of the altar as he prays the Eucharistic Prayer. When a Deacon assists at Mass, his place is not next to the priest celebrant like that of a concelebrant. In fact, this position should always be avoided. Even though the Deacon is distinguished by vesture from the priest celebrant, his position makes a stronger statement about his proper role at this point in the Mass. Therefore, the Deacon stands near the priest celebrant but somewhat behind him so as to be ready to assist when needed (see GIRM 179). The Deacon may assist during the Eucharistic Prayer with the pages of the *Roman Missal* as the priest celebrant continues praying. If the pall is used, the Deacon removes it from the chalice(s) before the epiclesis and returns it after the showing of the Blood of Christ. He also removes it before the doxology and returns it after the "Amen." Likewise, if any ciboria are covered, the Deacon removes the lids before the epiclesis and recovers them after the showing of the Blood of Christ.[10] The Deacon also assists with the chalice (see 179). In fact, during the doxology, it is the proper duty of the Deacon to hold the chalice with the Blood of Christ elevated with both hands as the priest celebrant elevates the paten with the Body of Christ until the faithful have acclaimed "Amen." The Deacon stands next to the priest celebrant, usually to his right, for the doxology (180). The Deacon may be handed the chalice for the elevation, or he may take it himself.

The placement and posture of the Deacon should be carefully observed so that his role of assisting is not ambivalent. In addition to assuming a place slightly behind the priest celebrant from which he can assist when needed, he also assumes a posture of example to the faithful. The Deacon typically kneels from the epiclesis until after the priest celebrant shows the chalice with the Blood of Christ to all. On occasions when incense is used, and if another Deacon is present, the other Deacon may prepare the thurible and then from a place in front of the altar incense, according to the usual pattern, the Body and the Blood of the Lord as they are shown for adoration (see GIRM 179). It makes sense that this Deacon is in place from the beginning to the end of the Eucharistic Prayer, which further points to the unity of the Prayer.

The Eucharistic Prayer for Concelebrated Mass

Throughout the celebration of the Eucharist, the concelebrant or concelebrants should exercise a disciplined attentiveness to the liturgical action that is taking place. This is especially so with the Eucharistic Prayer in the Concelebrated Mass. During the Eucharistic Prayer, perhaps more than any other part of the Mass, the concelebrant is united to the person and actions of the principal celebrant in a most intimate way, as ministerial priests united one to the other and to Christ the Priest for the offering of his Sacrifice.

Up until this point in the Mass, the concelebrant has remained at his place distinct from that of the principal celebrant. For the Eucharistic Prayer, the concelebrant takes his place at the altar along with the priest celebrant. Once the priest celebrant concludes the Prayer over the Offerings, the concelebrant moves to the altar so he is in place for the dialogue that begins the Eucharistic Prayer. The position of the concelebrant at the altar should be such that he does not impede the actions of the principal celebrant — his gestures and genuflections — and also that the faithful may clearly observe what is taking place at the altar (see GIRM 215). Only when this is not possible for legitimate reasons (such as the number of concelebrants or the disability of a concelebrant) does the concelebrant remain in place. Even in this case, the concelebrant or concelebrants should turn to the altar itself.

If a Deacon assists at this Mass, the position of the concelebrant should allow for the Deacon to be near the altar and to assist the celebrant with the *Roman Missal*, the pall, if needed, and with the chalice for the doxology. The Deacon needs to be careful not to stand among concelebrants. Rather, as with the form of the Mass with a Deacon described above, his position during the Eucharistic Prayer is behind the concelebrant who is near the principal celebrant (see GIRM 215). In this case, the Deacon might position himself to the right of the concelebrant so that he can easily assist when needed and kneel when prescribed.

The Manner of Pronouncing the Eucharistic Prayer

A concelebrant is oriented to the liturgical action of the Eucharistic Prayer at the altar and to the role of the principal celebrant in this action. He also participates intimately in it. Adjustments are made by the concelebrant as to how to do this that are distinct from how the principal celebrant carries out his role. Chief among these adjustments is the manner of speaking or pronouncing the Eucharistic Prayer. The *General Instruction* gives clear directions on the way a concelebrant is to speak the Eucharistic Prayer:

> The Preface is sung or said by the principal Priest Celebrant alone; but the Sanctus (Holy, Holy, Holy) is sung or recited by all the concelebrants, together with the people and the choir.
>
> After the Sanctus (Holy, Holy, Holy), the concelebrating Priests continue the Eucharistic Prayer in the way described below. Only the principal celebrant makes the gestures, unless other indications are given.
>
> The parts pronounced by all the concelebrants together and especially the words of Consecration, which all are obliged to say, are to be recited in such a manner that the concelebrants speak them in a low voice and that the principal celebrant's voice is heard clearly. In this way the words can be more easily understood by

> the people.
>
> It is a praiseworthy practice for the parts that are to be said by all the concelebrants together and for which musical notation is provided in the Missal to be sung. (216–218)

During the Eucharistic Prayer in a Concelebrated Mass, the voice of the principal celebrant should be clearly heard over the concelebrant. Only when a concelebrant takes an intercession in one of the Eucharistic Prayers and speaks alone does his voice take the tone of the principal celebrant. The singularity of the voice of the principal celebrant highlights the integrity of the Eucharistic Prayer as a single prayer and action. This also allows the faithful to follow and participate in the Eucharistic Prayer more easily. The concelebrant becomes one voice with the principal celebrant and the faithful as all sing or say the "Holy, Holy, Holy." The concelebrant is one with the faithful in acclaiming the Mystery of Faith and responding to the doxology with the "Amen," if he has not sung or spoken the doxology. Each of the Eucharistic Prayers is outlined in the *Roman Missal* as well, with directions for concelebration with regard to possible individual parts. Only the principal celebrant makes the Sign of the Cross over the bread and wine. The concelebrant extends his hands only when he is praying aloud with the principal celebrant or alone.

One of the more difficult challenges with the fitting manner of pronouncing the Eucharistic Prayer in the Concelebrated Mass is the competition of voices during those parts that must be said by the concelebrant with the principal celebrant. The *General Instruction* clearly explains that the concelebrant is to say the words of the epiclesis, the institution narrative and consecration, and the anamnesis with the principal celebrant (see 218, 219–234). The rule is that the voice of the principal celebrant is to be heard above every other voice, yet he should not have to shout or speak in any different way than when he prays the Eucharistic Prayer alone. The concelebrant who actually speaks the parts shared with the principal celebrant does so in a low voice that only he hears. There is a discipline to this practice, which ensures the beauty of the proclamation of the Eucharistic Prayer as a single action with a single voice. The principal celebrant should be mindful of his pacing while speaking so that the concelebrants can pray the words along with him. The parts that the principal celebrant and concelebrant share (the epiclesis, the institution narrative and consecration, the anamnesis, and the doxology), when appropriate to the occasion, may be sung according to the notation in the *Roman Missal*. This requires that those singing these parts are aware of doing so ahead of time and can do so in a way that enhances the dignity and beauty of the Eucharistic Prayer. When singing the Eucharistic Prayer, the voice of the principal celebrant should stand out above the others.

Praying the Eucharistic Prayers

In every form of the Mass, and particularly in a Concelebrated Mass, the Eucharistic Prayer must stand out as "the center and high point of the celebration." There are several points to consider with the Concelebrated Mass for this to occur. One of these points is posture and placement. Often, the principal celebrant begins the introductory dialogue to the Eucharistic Prayer before the concelebrant takes his place with him at the altar. The concelebrant is united to the priest celebrant throughout the celebration of Mass, but especially so as they share the Eucharistic Prayer. Therefore, it is important that the concelebrant be in place and ready to join in the Eucharistic Prayer before the principal celebrant sings or says, "The Lord be with you." If the concelebrant is at the altar with the priest celebrant, which is always preferred, his placement should demonstrate his association with the principal proclaimer of the Eucharistic Prayer; he is not simply haphazardly positioned near him. When there are only a few concelebrants, they can take their places on either side of the principal celebrant. If there are too many to do this, they can form an arc behind him, even standing on the sides of the altar. While the order of concelebrants is not mentioned in the *General Instruction* or the *Order of Mass*, the Roman practice is for the concelebrant to the right of the principal celebrant to take the first part designated for a concelebrant, then the concelebrant to the left takes the second part (if there is a second concelebrant). If there are several concelebrants, and the Eucharistic Prayer has three or four intercessions, then the order would move for all parts from right to left. When concelebrants pray a part of the Eucharistic Prayer, they do so from their place and do not assume the center position of the priest celebrant at the altar. The careful placement of the concelebrant contributes to the *ars celebrandi* of praying the Eucharistic Prayer with the Concelebrated Mass.

Another consideration is the use of aids to pray the Eucharistic Prayer. Often it is not possible for a concelebrant to read the *Roman Missal* easily from his place near the altar. The use of an aid for the Eucharistic Prayer is helpful, and the aid itself should be fitting for the Eucharistic Prayer. Finally, if the Eucharistic Prayer is to be prayed in parts, with the concelebrants taking the parts indicated, then this should be determined beforehand and not at the altar. The amplification of the concelebrant should not be overlooked.

Additionally, the *General Instruction* outlines how to pray each of the four Eucharistic Prayers with concelebrants:

> **Eucharistic Prayer I, or the Roman Canon:**
> In Eucharistic Prayer I, or the Roman Canon, the *Te igitur* (To you, therefore, most merciful Father) is said by the principal celebrant alone, with hands extended.
>
> It is appropriate that the commemoration (Memen-

to) of the living and the Communicantes (In communion with those) be assigned to one or other of the concelebrating Priests, who then pronounces these prayers alone, with hands extended, and in a loud voice.

The *Hanc igitur* (Therefore, Lord, we pray) is said once again by the principal celebrant alone, with hands extended.

From the *Quam oblationem* (Be pleased, O God, we pray) up to and including the Supplices (In humble prayer we ask you, almighty God), the principal celebrant alone makes the gestures, while all the concelebrants pronounce everything together, in this manner:

a) the *Quam oblationem* (Be pleased, O God, we pray) with hands extended toward the offerings;

b) the *Qui pridie* (On the day before he was to suffer) and the *Simili modo* (In a similar way) with hands joined;

c) the words of the Lord, with each extending his right hand toward the bread and toward the chalice, if this seems appropriate; and at the elevation looking toward them and after this bowing profoundly;

d) the *Unde et memores* (Therefore, O Lord, as we celebrate the memorial) and the *Supra quae* (Be pleased to look upon) with hands extended;

e) for the Supplices (In humble prayer we ask you, almighty God) up to and including the words *through this participation at the altar,*

> bowing with hands joined; then standing upright and crossing themselves at the words *may be filled with every grace and heavenly blessing.*

It is appropriate that the commemoration (Memento) of the dead and the *Nobis quoque peccatoribus* (To us, also, your servants) be assigned to one or other of the concelebrants, who pronounces them alone, with hands extended, and in a loud voice.

At the words *To us, also, your servants, who though sinners*, of the *Nobis quoque peccatoribus*, all the concelebrants strike their breast.

The *Per quem haec omnia* (Through whom you continue) is said by the principal celebrant alone.

Eucharistic Prayer II

In Eucharistic Prayer II, the part *You are indeed Holy, O Lord* is pronounced by the principal celebrant alone, with hands extended.

In the parts from *Make holy, therefore, these gifts* to the end of *Humbly we pray*, all the concelebrants pronounce everything together as follows:

> a) the part *Make holy, therefore, these gifts*, with hands extended toward the offerings;

> b) the parts *At the time he was betrayed* and *In a similar way* with hands joined;

> c) the words of the Lord, with each extending his right hand toward the bread and toward the chalice, if this seems appropriate; and at the elevation looking toward them and after this bow-

ing profoundly;

d) the parts *Therefore, as we celebrate* and *Humbly we pray* with hands extended.

It is appropriate that the intercessions for the living, *Remember, Lord, your Church*, and for the dead, *Remember also our brothers and sisters*, be assigned to one or other of the concelebrants, who pronounces them alone, with hands extended, and in a loud voice.

Eucharistic Prayer III

In Eucharistic Prayer III, the part *You are indeed Holy, O Lord* is pronounced by the principal celebrant alone, with hands extended.

In the parts from *Therefore, O Lord, we humbly implore you* to the end of *Look, we pray upon the oblation*, all the concelebrants pronounce everything together as follows:

a) the part *Therefore, O Lord, we humbly implore you* with hands extended toward the offerings;

b) the parts *For on the night he was betrayed* and *In a similar way* with hands joined;

c) the words of the Lord, with each extending his right hand toward the bread and toward the chalice, if this seems appropriate; and at the elevation looking toward them and after this bowing profoundly;

d) the parts *Therefore, O Lord, as we celebrate*

the memorial and *Look, we pray, upon the oblation* with hands extended.

It is appropriate that the intercessions *May he make of us an eternal offering to you*, and *May this Sacrifice of our reconciliation*, and *To our departed brothers and sisters* be assigned to one or other of the concelebrants, who pronounces them alone, with hands extended, and in a loud voice.

Eucharistic Prayer IV

In Eucharistic Prayer IV, the part *We give you praise, Father most holy* up to and including the words *he might sanctify creation to the full* is pronounced by the principal celebrant alone, with hands extended.

In the parts from *Therefore, O Lord, we pray* to the end of *Look, O Lord, upon the Sacrifice*, all the concelebrants pronounce everything together as follows:

a) the part *Therefore, O Lord, we pray* with hands extended toward the offerings;

b) the parts *For when the hour had come* and *In a similar way* with hands joined;

c) the words of the Lord, with each extending his right hand toward the bread and toward the chalice, if this seems appropriate; and at the elevation looking toward them and after this bowing profoundly;

d) the parts *Therefore, O Lord, as we now celebrate* and *Look, O Lord, upon the Sacrifice* with hands extended.

> It is appropriate that the intercessions *Therefore, Lord, remember now* and *To all of us, your children* be assigned to one or other of the concelebrants, who pronounces them alone, with hands extended, and in a loud voice. (219–234)

All the Eucharistic Prayers follow the same gesture pattern with regard to how they are prayed by the principal celebrant with a concelebrant or concelebrants. Generally, when the principal celebrant is praying aloud (alone or with a concelebrant) and, likewise, when a concelebrant is praying aloud (alone or with the principal celebrant), the hands are extended. A concelebrant should not extend his hands in such a way that it distracts from this gesture carried out by the principal celebrant or other concelebrants. Like the principal celebrant, at the appointed time in each prayer, the concelebrant extends both hands toward the offerings for the epiclesis. In Eucharistic Prayers II, III, and IV, the concelebrant extends his hands through the Sign of the Cross at the epiclesis. For the institution narrative and consecration, the concelebrant extends his right hand sideways in the direction of the bread and the chalice for the words of the Lord. If it is not opportune for the concelebrant to extend his right hand (for example, if he is behind several concelebrants), then he keeps his hands joined for the words of the Lord. It makes little sense for a concelebrant to be gesturing to someone's back. As the principal celebrant shows the Body and Blood of the Lord, the concelebrant looks toward them. As the principal celebrant genuflects, the concelebrant bows profoundly. In Eucharistic Prayer I or the Roman Canon there are additional gestures. From the words "In humble prayer we ask you, almighty God" to the words "this participation at the altar," the concelebrant bows with hands joined. He then stands erect and makes the Sign of the Cross at the words "may be filled with every grace and heavenly blessing." And, at the words "To us, also, your servants, who though sinners" the concelebrant strikes his breast. As for the other Eucharistic Prayers in the *Roman Missal*, the directions for concelebrants are similar to those of the four described above (see GIRM 235).

In addition to the dialogues that introduce the Eucharistic Prayer, there are two other dialogues in the course of the Prayer: the Mystery of Faith and the doxology. In the Concelebrated Mass, the principal celebrant alone sings or says, "The Mystery of Faith." The concelebrant and not the principal celebrant continues to acclaim this Mystery with one of the three possibilities provided in the *Order of Mass*. The principal celebrant does not respond to his own invitation at this point. The doxology is sung or said in the Concelebrated Mass by the principal celebrant alone and, if desired, with the concelebrant joining him. The faithful never join in saying or singing the doxology (see GIRM 236). Likewise, the principal celebrant does not respond to the doxology with the "Amen." The concelebrant does not respond to the doxology either, if he has joined in singing it with the principal celebrant. Remember, this is a dialogue. Often when a concelebrant joins the principal celebrant for the doxology, it is after it has already begun. Thus, it seems more fitting for the integrity of the doxology itself for the principal celebrant to sing or say the doxology by himself with the concelebrant and the faithful responding with the "Amen."

The Eucharistic Prayer for Mass at Which only One Minister Participates

In the celebration of Mass at Which only One Minister Participates, the Eucharistic Prayer is carried out in the same way as Mass with the People (see GIRM 265). If a Deacon assists at this

Mass, then he carries out his role as in Mass with a Deacon. Even in this form of the Mass, the Eucharistic Prayer is proclaimed aloud with the dignity and reverence accorded it as in every other form of celebration.

Choice of Eucharistic Prayer

The Eucharistic Prayer, as the principal presidential prayer in the celebration of Mass, holds the "prime place" in relationship to the other presidential prayers (see GIRM 30). As the Eucharistic Prayer is the chief moment of thanksgiving and sanctification, when the divine event of redemption and salvation occurs, the choice for which of the options in the *Roman Missal* to use in a particular Mass should be marked by thoughtfulness and reasonableness. The first part of the Eucharistic Prayer, the preface, is found typically in the *Order of Mass* according to the liturgical time, common, and votive celebrations, as well as Masses for the Dead. Prefaces for specific commemorations and Ritual Masses are found with the other texts for the Mass appointed for these occasions in the *Roman Missal*. The current edition of the *Roman Missal* includes the availability of a large number of prefaces, highlighting the act of thanksgiving that takes place with the Eucharistic Prayer. Additionally, with the prefaces for individual circumstances, different aspects of the work of salvation are more fully presented (see GIRM 364).

The *Roman Missal* is clear when it directs that certain prefaces are to be used for a liturgical time. For example, there are two prefaces for Advent: Preface I of Advent and Preface II of Advent.[11] Preface I of Advent is used from the First Sunday of Advent through December 16. Preface II of Advent is used from December 17 through December 24. Advent takes a turn in focus on the coming of the Lord with the nearness of Christmas with the Mass and Biblical Readings beginning on December 17.[12] Preface II of Advent incorporates this focus. During Lent,

Preface I of the Passion of the Lord and Preface II of the Passion of the Lord[13] are prescribed for the Fifth Week of Lent and the days of Holy Week, respectively. The choice of the prefaces for these days corresponds to a more immediate preparation to enter into the Passion of Jesus with Palm Sunday of the Passion of the Lord and the Sacred Paschal Triduum. Preface I of Easter,[14] with the mention of different times such as "on this night" and "on this day," is especially fitting for Easter Sunday and the Octave of Easter. Of the two prefaces of the Blessed Virgin Mary, Preface I of the Blessed Virgin Mary[15] is more appropriate when a particular celebration in her honor is mentioned in the preface itself.

Likewise, the *Roman Missal* is clear when a proper preface is the choice for a particular commemoration, such as the Solemnity of the Immaculate Conception of the Blessed Virgin Mary (December 8). The preface points to the mystery of Mary and the Church as rooted in the theological understanding of this celebration in the overall plan of salvation. Prefaces associated with Ritual Masses are also clearly indicated and are in the *Roman Missal* with the other texts for the Mass. For example, in the section of the *Roman Missal* for Ritual Masses, there are two prefaces for the Masses for the Conferral of Holy Orders. For the Ordination of one Bishop or Priest (or of several Bishops or Priests), the preface is the same one used for the Chrism Mass. This preface speaks of the priesthood of Christ and the ministry of priests in the Church. For the Ordination of one or several Deacons, a preface is given that is not found in any other part of the *Roman Missal*, which focuses on Christ as the source of all ministry in the Church.

Some of the Eucharistic Prayers themselves have their own prefaces, such as Eucharistic Prayer II, which is variable; Eucharistic Prayer IV, which is invariable; the Eucharistic Prayers for Reconciliation, which are variable; and the Eucharistic Prayer for Use in Masses for Various Needs, which vary according to the use of this particular Eucharistic Prayer.

The choice for the Eucharistic Prayers found in the *Order of Mass*, Eucharistic Prayers I, II, III, and IV, is guided by the norms outlined in the *General Instruction*:

> a) Eucharistic Prayer I, or the Roman Canon, which may always be used, is especially suited for use on days to which a proper text for the Communicantes (In communion with those whose memory we venerate) is assigned or in Masses endowed with a proper form of the Hanc igitur (Therefore, Lord, we pray) and also in the celebrations of the Apostles and of the Saints mentioned in the Prayer itself; likewise it is especially suited for use on Sundays, unless for pastoral reasons Eucharistic Prayer III is preferred.
>
> b) Eucharistic Prayer II, on account of its particular features, is more appropriately used on weekdays or in special circumstances. Although it is provided with its own Preface, it may also be used with other Prefaces, especially those that sum up the mystery of salvation, for example, the Common Prefaces. When Mass is celebrated for a particular deceased person, the special formula given may be used at the proper point, namely, before the part *Remember also our brothers and sisters.*
>
> c) Eucharistic Prayer III may be said with any Preface. Its use should be preferred on Sundays and festive days. If, however, this Eucharistic Prayer is used in Masses for the Dead, the special formula for a deceased person may be used, to be included at the proper place, namely after the words: *in your compassion, O merciful Father, gather to*

yourself all your children scattered throughout the world.

> d) Eucharistic Prayer IV has an invariable Preface and gives a fuller summary of salvation history. It may be used when a Mass has no Preface of its own and on Sundays in Ordinary Time. On account of its structure, no special formula for a deceased person may be inserted into this prayer. (365)

These norms allow for the Eucharistic Prayers in the *Order of Mass* to be used with greater frequency in the course of the Liturgical Year. In many instances the choice is unfortunately limited in typical practice to two or even only one of the four Eucharistic Prayers. A renewed consideration should be given to the above norms so that Eucharistic Prayer I is used on Sundays and especially those occasions when the Prayer calls for a particular *Communicantes* and *Hanc igitur*, which highlight the liturgical occasion or ritual celebration. Also, it should be considered on the days that commemorate the saints listed in it. In fact, this Eucharistic Prayer can always be used. It is significant that it is printed completely with the *Communicantes*, *Hanc igitur*, and specific text for the institution narrative and consecration with the texts for Thursday of the Lord's Supper at the Evening Mass during the Sacred Paschal Triduum.[16] The *Roman Missal*, with the inclusion of Eucharistic Prayer I for Holy Thursday, recognizes a venerable association of this Prayer with the Eucharistic Mystery.

Eucharistic Prayers II and III are perhaps the most frequently chosen for the Eucharistic Prayer. Nonetheless, the norms indicate when they are most fitting for use. Eucharistic Prayer II is an apt choice for weekday celebrations, and Eucharistic Prayer III for Sundays. The choice of Eucharistic Prayer II on a Sunday when the Mass is offered for a deceased person allows for the person's name to be included in the Prayer. This is an option that is rarely employed. The choice for Eucharistic Prayer IV is the most restricted of the four. It is always to be prayed with its given preface and therefore cannot be used with a Mass that requires a certain or proper preface. Yet it can be used on any Sunday in Ordinary Time.

The *Appendix to the Order of Mass* in the *Roman Missal* includes the Eucharistic Prayer for Reconciliation I and II as well as the Eucharistic Prayer for Various Needs. The plan for the use of these prayers in a Concelebrated Mass as well as for singing them is provided with the introduction to these Prayers. The Eucharistic Prayers for Reconciliation may be used with any of the Masses in the *Roman Missal* that convey the mystery of reconciliation, even with Masses during Lent. In the case of Lent, the prefaces of Lent may replace the preface of the Eucharistic Prayers for Reconciliation. The Eucharistic Prayer for Various Needs has four forms: The Church on the Path of Unity; God Guides His Church along the Way of Salvation; Jesus, the Way to the Father; and Jesus, Who Went about Doing Good. One of these four forms may be an appropriate choice for one of the Masses and Prayers for Various Needs and Occasions found in the *Roman Missal*. Each of the four forms of the Eucharistic Prayer for Various Needs is introduced with a list of which Masses and Prayers for Various Needs and Occasions fittingly correspond.

The Eucharistic Prayers for Masses with Children for use with the third edition of the *Roman Missal* are among the possible choices for the Eucharistic Prayer. These three Prayers are found in a supplement to the *Roman Missal* and are strictly intended only for Masses with children.[17] The choice of this prayer limits concelebration[18] and can only be used on liturgical days that do not have a proper preface.

Instituted and Deputed Ministers and the Eucharistic Prayer

During the course of the Eucharistic Prayer, the acolyte or deputed server assumes a place in the sanctuary where it is convenient to kneel and participate in the Eucharistic Prayer in the manner of the faithful. The acolyte or deputed server rings the bell and, if an additional Deacon is not present, incenses the Body and Blood of the Lord as the principal celebrant shows them for adoration after the consecration when this is appropriate to the occasion.

Conclusion

The Eucharistic Prayer in all its dimensions — with each of its elements, the required postures and gestures, the manner of reciting or singing it, and the choice for the most fitting one — defers to the *ars celebrandi* for a reverent, dignified, and vivid proclamation of the Mystery of Faith. This type of proclamation calls for a regular review on the part of the priest celebrant to maintain a conscious regard for everything associated with the Eucharistic Prayer.

The divine event that takes place with the Eucharistic Prayer is displayed in the Gospel of John with Jesus washing the feet of his disciples at the Last Supper (see Jn 13:1–20). When the *ars celebrandi* of the Eucharistic Prayer is such that it allows for the fullest encounter with the Paschal Mystery, then this encounter truly animates the Christian to imitate the same self-offering of Christ in the Christian life. When Jesus completed the task of washing the feet, an act of such humble self-offering, he stated, "I have given you a model to follow, so that as I have done for you, you should also do" (Jn 13:15). This is a grace that comes from the Eucharistic Prayer well prayed, well proclaimed, for the ordained and the baptized.

The next chapter looks at the Communion Rite during the

Liturgy of the Eucharist of the Mass with a description of its several elements and directions for each form of the Mass.

CHAPTER NINE

The Liturgy of the Eucharist and the Communion Rite

This chapter addresses the Communion Rite of the Mass, the third of the three parts of the Liturgy of the Eucharist. Three of the four elements that make up the Communion Rite (the Rite of Peace, the Fraction of the Bread, and the Communion) engage many members of the liturgical assembly, include several actions and options, and require planning and choices to be made prior to the celebration of Mass. All of this requires a particular attentiveness to the *ars celebrandi* so that a true reverence and dignity underscore the Communion Rite. Thus, this chapter describes the four elements of the Communion Rite and then provides directions for the Communion Rite for each form of the Mass. The chapter also presents norms for purification and Holy

Communion under both kinds from the *General Instruction of the Roman Missal*. Finally, it describes the duties of the liturgical ministers for the Communion Rite.

The Communion Rite

The Communion Rite of the Mass with its various elements unfolds the divine event of the Eucharistic Prayer. Each element successively deepens the experience of communion with the Paschal Mystery of the Lord realized in the Eucharistic Prayer. The Communion Rite is the principal manner of encountering the Eucharist as the Paschal Banquet. At the Last Supper the Lord himself commanded that his Body and Blood be eaten and drunk, and so the faithful, properly prepared and disposed, are intended to receive them as true spiritual food during the Communion Rite. The Lord's Prayer, the Rite of Peace, and the Fraction of the Bread all lead to an intimacy with Christ and one another for those receiving Holy Communion (see GIRM 80).

Description of the Elements of the Communion Rite

The four elements of the Communion Rite are the Lord's Prayer, the Rite of Peace, the Fraction of the Bread, and the Communion. The *General Instruction* describes each of these elements as they stand alone within the Communion Rite and also relate to the experience of Communion on many levels, reaching a climax with the reception of Communion in the Body and Blood of the Lord.

The Lord's Prayer

The Lord's Prayer belongs to those who are indeed brothers and sisters of the Lord because of their baptism and are renewed in this relationship with the Paschal event of the Eucharistic Prayer. United with Christ in his saving Sacrifice, those assembled for the Eucharist can cry out, "Father." The Lord's Prayer as it begins the Communion Rite begs for the daily bread of the Eucharist and at the same time begs for the forgiveness of sins "so that what is holy may in truth be given to the holy" (GIRM 81).

The priest celebrant invites all to pray the Lord's Prayer with the invariable introduction, "At the Savior's command and formed by divine teaching,"[1] recalling the Gospel instruction of Jesus to the Apostles. Then all pray together the Our Father. The petitions of the Lord's Prayer are elaborated by the priest celebrant, especially with the plea to be delivered from evil until the coming again of the Savior. The embolism that follows concludes with the doxology on the part of the faithful. All four parts of the Lord's Prayer — the invitation, the Our Father, the embolism, and the doxology — may be sung when not recited (see 81). The *Order of Mass* provides the musical notation for these parts, including the musical notation for the Lord's Prayer itself in Latin before it provides the same texts without music. Once again, this order suggests a preference for singing when it is fitting.[2] An appendix to the *Roman Missal* offers additional musical settings for the invitation and the Our Father: Tone B, a Mozarabic tone, and Tone C, a Solemn Anaphora tone.[3]

The Rite of Peace

As the Lord's Prayer gives expression to our communion with Christ and his Father and our Father, so also the Rite of Peace manifests the communion that is ours from the reconciling act of Christ in the Eucharistic Prayer. The Rite of Peace further asks the Lord Jesus to bring his peace and unity to the whole Church. It also provides the occasion for an immediate expression of this peace and unity among those assembled for the Eucharist in anticipation of Holy Communion (see GIRM 82).

The *General Instruction* further indicates that the manner of the sign of peace is established by the Conference of Bishops, taking into consideration local culture and customs (see 82 and 390). Although the United States Conference of Catholic Bishops to date has not determined a precise form for the actual sign of peace, the typical form is a handshake. Certainly, the traditional Roman *pax* (extending a more formal embrace) among sacred ministers is acceptable. The sign of peace expresses the peace of Christ among us with our participation in the Eucharistic Prayer, so we acknowledge this peace with those nearest and in a manner that suggests this peace, this deepening of communion (see 83). It is not uncommon today to see people, and even the priest celebrant, waving to one another at a distance from each other, blowing kisses, and making the two-finger peace signs. All of this is counter-indicative to the meaning of the Rite of Peace as the sharing of Christ's peace and its role in preparation for Holy Communion.[4]

The Fraction of the Bread

The Fraction or the Breaking of the Bread makes present an action of Christ himself at the Last Supper with his disciples at the Communion Rite of the Mass. In fact, the Christians in the Acts of the Apostles called the celebration of the Eucharist "the breaking of the bread" (2:42). With the Fraction of the Bread, the one Bread that is Christ himself is broken to be shared with the many so that they may become one in him and with one another. The Fraction of the Bread furthers the deepening of an experience of communion that began with the Lord's Prayer and the Rite of Peace.

The Fraction of the Bread, which follows the Rite of Peace, belongs to the priest celebrant alone, although he may be assisted if needed by a Deacon or another priest. The Bread that is broken is intended to be shared with the faithful (see GIRM 321). All too often, the Fraction of the Bread is begun while some are still engaged in the exchange of the sign of peace. Only after all have completed this exchange should the priest celebrant lift the Host and begin to break it carefully and reverently and without any exaggerated gesture. During the Breaking of the Bread, the priest celebrant takes a piece of it and places it in the chalice "to signify the unity of the Body and Blood of the Lord in the work of salvation, namely, of the Body of Jesus Christ, living and glorious" (83). As the priest celebrant is breaking the Bread, the "Lamb of God" is sung either by the choir, by the cantor and congregation, or by all. If it is not sung, then it is recited by all. The "Lamb of God" gives further meaning to the action of the breaking of the Bread — Christ, the Lamb, giving his life for all — as it recalls the Eucharistic Prayer and anticipates Holy Communion. It can be repeated as often as needed while the Bread is broken, with the conclusion always being "grant us peace" (83).

Communion

The Communion of the Mass begins with the priest celebrant praying quietly to prepare to receive the Holy Body and Blood of the Lord. As the priest celebrant prays with a text from the *Order of Mass*, the faithful pray silently as well. After this, the priest celebrant shows in one of two ways the Body of the Lord to those who will receive it. He may hold the broken Host over the paten or over the chalice. As he does this, he gives the invitation to the Supper of the Lamb, and all respond with the words inspired by the centurion in the Gospel (see GIRM 84).

During the Preparation of the Gifts, all the hosts and wine needed for the Communion of the priest celebrant and all the faithful were placed on the altar for the Eucharistic Sacrifice. This is what the *General Instruction* and the *Order of Mass* presume. Yet, this is not the common practice, especially on Sundays and other major feasts. In too many instances, the practice is to set only a limited number of hosts on the altar during the Preparation of the Gifts and at Communion to bring the additional consecrated Hosts needed from the tabernacle. The invitation that the priest celebrant gives is to the Supper of the Lamb — to receive the Body and Blood of the Lord from the Sacrifice of the Lord as it actually took place with the Eucharistic Prayer. Thus, the *General Instruction* declares: "It is most desirable that the faithful, just as the Priest himself is bound to do, receive the Lord's Body from hosts consecrated at the same Mass and that, in the cases where this is foreseen, they partake of the chalice, so that even by means of the signs Communion may stand out more clearly as a participation in the sacrifice actually being celebrated" (85).

There are many reasons why the consecration of sufficient hosts at Mass for all who will receive does not take place. The most unfortunate reason is a lack of awareness of the intimate relationship between the reception of Communion and the divine event that takes place with the Eucharistic Prayer. When Communion is received, it is not only the reception of the Body and Blood of the Lord but also the eating and drinking of the death and resurrection of the Lord in which all participated with the Eucharistic Prayer. Other reasons for not consecrating sufficient hosts at Mass include a fear of not having the sufficient number needed, the habit of old practices, and an impoverished understanding of Communion. Whatever the reasons for not doing so, the obligation of the priest celebrant to receive the Body and Blood of the Lord from the Mass celebrated underscores the same theological foundation as to why the baptized should not be deprived of doing the same. If it is necessary, for legitimate reasons, to go to the tabernacle for additional hosts, the appropriate time is not during the Fraction Rite, which has its own meaning, but at the time of Communion, before or after the invitation.

The Communion Chant begins as the priest celebrant receives the Body of the Lord. The chant belongs to the whole action of Communion, from that of the priest celebrant to the Communion of all who receive. As with the Entrance Chant, which had a specific purpose associated with the Introductory Rites of the Mass, the Communion Chant likewise has a specific purpose associated with the Communion Rite of the Mass. Its purpose is "to express the spiritual union of the communicants by means of the unity of their voices, to show gladness of heart, and to bring out more clearly the 'communitarian' character of the procession to receive the Eucharist" (GIRM 86). Whenever possible, the distribution of Holy Communion to everyone, including those who are assisting with singing the Communion Chant, takes place at the same time (see 86).

The singing of the Communion Chant follows the same pattern as indicated for the singing of the Entrance Chant. It is sung by the choir alone or by the choir or a cantor with the people (see 87). The sources for the Communion Chant are likewise similar to the sources for the Entrance Chant:

> In the Dioceses of the United States of America, there are four options for singing at Communion: (1) the antiphon from the Missal or the antiphon with its Psalm from the Graduale Romanum, as set to music there or in another musical setting; (2) the antiphon with Psalm from the Graduale Simplex of the liturgical time; (3) a chant from another collection of Psalms and antiphons, approved by the Conference of Bishops or the Diocesan Bishop, including Psalms arranged in responsorial or metrical forms; (4) some other suitable liturgical chant approved by the Conference of Bishops or the Diocesan Bishop. (87)

As with the content for the Entrance Chant, the word of God, especially with the use of the psalms, is the preference. The singing of the psalms also allows for an easy accompaniment of the procession to Holy Communion. If something other than a psalm is used, then it should be inspired by the proposed chant or the experience of Communion. If there is no singing during the distribution of Holy Communion, then the antiphon given in the *Roman Missal* is recited in a number of ways. It may be recited by a member of the faithful or by some of them or by a reader as the priest celebrant receives the Body of Christ. If this does not happen, the priest celebrant himself recites it after he has received the Body and Blood of Christ and before he distributes Holy Communion (see GIRM 87).

Once the distribution of Holy Communion is completed, the priest celebrant and the faithful, if opportune, pray together silently for some time. On some occasions, in place of the common silence, a psalm or canticle or hymn may be sung by everyone (see 88). Just as the silence is a corporate act following the reception of Holy Communion, so, when singing is the choice, first consideration should be given to everyone singing. Certainly, people can participate in the song sung by another person or by the choir. However, what is sung should always allow for a meditation on the Mystery just received. Certainly, this is not an appropriate place for a Marian hymn, such as the *Ave Maria*, which is a popular practice. If there is to be a song after Holy Communion, it should begin only after the distribution of Holy Communion and the accompanying Communion Chant (86).

The Communion Rite ends with the Prayer after Communion. With this prayer, the priest celebrant prays for the benefits that come from communion with Christ and one another with the participation in the Body and Blood of the Lord. At Mass, there is only one Prayer after Communion (see 89). As with the Collect and the Prayer over the Offerings, the *General Instruction* is quite specific about the conclusion of the Prayer after Communion:

It ends with the shorter conclusion; that is:

– if the prayer is directed to the Father: Through Christ our Lord;

– if it is directed to the Father, but the Son is mentioned at the end: Who lives and reigns for ever and ever;

– if it is directed to the Son: Who live and reign forever and ever. (89)

As with the other presidential prayers, the Prayer after Communion ends with the faithful acclaiming "Amen" (89). On the occasions when this prayer is sung, the musical notation given in the *Roman Missal* for the presidential prayers for the solemn tone and the reciting tone is observed.[5]

Directions for the Communion Rite

The directions for the Communion Rite of the Mass as found in the *General Instruction* and the *Order of Mass* differ considerably depending on the form of the Mass. This is especially so with the Communion for the Concelebrated Mass, and also if Holy Communion is distributed under both kinds. Again, these directions require study and an understanding of the theological and liturgical values that underscore them, especially in relationship to what occurred with the Eucharistic Prayer. A grasp of these values aids a faith-filled *ars celebrandi* that leads to a more complete participation in communion with the Mystery of Christ on the part of everyone in the liturgical assembly.

The Communion Rite for Mass without a Deacon

The priest celebrant, having set the paten and chalice on the corporal on the altar, with hands joined, gives the introduction to the Lord's Prayer. The *Order of Mass* provides for only one form for this introduction and so does not allow for it to be put aside in favor of another or for an extemporaneous introduction. After the introduction, the priest celebrant extends his hands and begins the Lord's Prayer with the faithful.[6] Once the Lord's Prayer is concluded, the priest celebrant continues with the embolism, "Deliver us, Lord …" He does not join his hands at the conclusion of the Lord's Prayer; rather, he continues with hands extended as the petitions of the Our Father continue with the petitions of the embolism. At the end of the embolism, the priest celebrant joins his hands, and the faithful make their acclamation with the doxology, "For the kingdom …"[7] The *Order of Mass* provides the musical notation for the introduction to the Lord's Prayer, the Our Father, the embolism, and the doxology for when the Lord's Prayer is sung. As already noted, additional tones are found in an appendix of the *Roman Missal*. When the Lord's Prayer is sung, all its parts are to be sung as indicative of the unity of these several parts.

The Rite of Peace begins as the priest celebrant again extends his hands and says the prayer, "Lord Jesus Christ, who said to your Apostles …" and then joins his hands, as indicated within the prayer itself, before he concludes with the "Who live and reign for ever and ever." The faithful respond, "Amen." This prayer is directed to the Lord Jesus and not to the assembly, so the priest celebrant needs to be mindful that he is not directing the text to the faithful when he is facing them, especially with the words, "Peace I leave you, my peace I give you." This prayer is followed by the priest celebrant giving the greeting, "The peace of the Lord be with you always," extending and joining his hands as he does so. The people respond as usual with "And with your spirit." This greeting is another point in the *General Instruction* and the *Order of Mass* when the priest celebrant is directed to turn toward the people. As previously indicated, this direction follows from the rubrics for the Liturgy of the Eucharist, which have the priest and people *ad orientem* together for this part of the Mass. Even though the rubrics indicate the *ad orientem* posture, at this point and all throughout the Communion Rite, the typical posture is *ad populum*. If it is opportune, then the priest celebrant gives the invitation, which is invariable, for the exchange of the sign of peace, "Let us offer each other the sign of peace." The exchange of the sign of peace is always optional and it actually makes little sense if people are not seated near to one another to exchange it. The *General Instruction* and the *Order of Mass* direct the exchange of the sign of peace for the priest celebrant. He gives the sign of peace to the liturgical ministers near to him but does not leave the sanctuary so as not to unnecessarily exaggerate the action nor interrupt the flow of the elements of the Communion Rite. For the dioceses of the United States, the *General Instruction* is adapted at this point. On certain occasions, such as a funeral, a wedding, or when a civic leader may be present, the priest celebrant may extend the sign of peace to those near to the sanctuary, if this seems reasonable. All exchange the sign of peace mindful that it is an expression of peace, communion, and charity in Christ. The *General Instruction* provides a dialogue for the exchange of the sign of peace that is not yet a common practice. When the sign of peace is extended, the person says, "The peace of the Lord be with you always," and the other person responds, "Amen." The consistent use of this dialogue will greatly assure the deepening of the meaning and decorum that should be a part of this element of the Communion Rite.[8] The *Order of Mass* provides the musical notation for the singing of the Rite of Peace when it is sung.

Once the exchange of the sign of peace is completed, if it has taken place, then the priest celebrant picks up the Host from the paten and begins to break it over the paten carefully and reverently, with the intention for some of the faithful to receive from the broken pieces. As he breaks the Host, he places a small piece in the chalice as he quietly says the prayer, "May this mingling …" As the priest is breaking the Host, the "Lamb of God" is sung or recited by the choir and by the faithful. Neither the *General Instruction* nor the *Order of Mass* indicates that the priest celebrant joins with the "Lamb of God." Once the priest celebrant has mingled the Body and Blood of the Lord with the accompanying prayer, it seems fitting for him to join in the singing or reciting of the "Lamb of God." The *Order of Mass* provides the musical notation for the "Lamb of God" in English and Latin and also gives the reminder that the invocations may be repeated as needed for the fraction, with the final invocation concluding with "grant us peace."[9]

Next, the priest celebrant, standing erect with his hands joined, says quietly his prayer of preparation for Holy Communion. Many priests bow to say this prayer as with the prayer, "With humble spirit," during the Preparation of the Gifts. This prayer before Communion is one of preparation and does not carry the sense of humility that a bow suggests. The *Order of Mass* gives two equal options for the priest for this prayer of preparation: "Lord Jesus Christ, Son of the living God …" or "May the receiving of your Body and Blood …"[10]

When the priest celebrant concludes his prayer of preparation, he genuflects with his hands joined or placed on the altar. Then he takes into his hand a piece of the broken Host consecrated at the Mass just celebrated. He does not rebuild the broken Host as if to suggest the fraction did not take place. He raises the Host only slightly, either over the paten or over the chalice. Here in the *General Instruction* and the *Order of Mass*, the priest is directed to face the people, again presuming the rubrics for the Liturgy of the Eucharist which have the priest and people *ad orientem* together for this part of the Mass. With the broken piece of the Host over the sacred vessel, together raised to a sufficient height for all to see, the priest celebrant gives the invitation, "Behold the Lamb of God ..." and together the faithful along with the priest respond one time, "Lord, I am not worthy ..."[11] The *Order of Mass* provides the musical notation for when this dialogue is sung.

The *General Instruction* and the *Order of Mass* describe the priest celebrant receiving Communion facing the altar. Again, these rubrics indicate the celebration of Mass *ad orientem*, which has already been addressed above. After the invitation and the response to Holy Communion, the priest celebrant continues to hold the paten or the chalice and reverently consumes the Body of the Lord. As he does so, he says quietly, "May the Body of Christ keep me safe for everlasting life." Then, if he held the Host over the paten, he places the paten back on the corporal and then picks up the chalice and consumes the Blood of the Lord. As he does so, he says quietly, "May the Blood of Christ keep me safe for everlasting life." If he held the Host over the chalice, after consuming the Body of the Lord, he then consumes the Blood of the Lord. After drinking from the chalice, he wipes the rim of the chalice with the purificator.[12] As the priest celebrant receives the Body of the Lord, the Communion Chant begins.[13]

After the priest celebrant receives Holy Communion, he then takes the paten or ciborium with consecrated Hosts from the altar and goes to those who are in procession to receive as well.[14] Those approaching Holy Communion are to receive from the Communion minister:

> It is not permitted for the faithful to take the consecrated Bread or the sacred chalice by themselves and, still less, to hand them on from one to another among themselves. The norm established for the Dioceses of the United States of America is that Holy Communion is to be received standing, unless an individual mem-

> ber of the faithful wishes to receive Communion while kneeling (Congregation for Divine Worship and the Discipline of the Sacraments, Instruction, *Redemptionis Sacramentum*, March 25, 2004, no. 91).
>
> When receiving Holy Communion, the communicant bows his or her head before the Sacrament as a gesture of reverence and receives the Body of the Lord from the minister. The consecrated host may be received either on the tongue or in the hand, at the discretion of each communicant. When Holy Communion is received under both kinds, the sign of reverence is also made before receiving the Precious Blood. (GIRM 160)

There are many aspects to this moment in the Communion Rite that require particular attention on the part of the priest celebrant and the faithful to ensure a careful and reverent encounter with Holy Communion. The priest, having just given the invitation to "Behold the Lamb of God … Blessed are those called to the Supper of the Lamb," goes to meet those who responded with him to this invitation. This means that there is a station for the distribution of Holy Communion, a station that is related to the altar and requires the people to move toward the altar. It seems best that the typical station would be the sanctuary step at the center. In this way, those receiving are able to process as one, only to become more so with their Communion, which is in Christ and with everyone else who receives. The typical posture of standing, a posture of communion with the Risen Lord to receive the Risen Lord, is another dimension of unity, of oneness at this moment, without prejudice to those who have another preference. Communicants arrive to the station to receive, to be fed by the Lamb, for the Body of Christ gives the Body of Christ to the Body of Christ. They do not take; they receive either on the tongue or in the hand. The bow before the Lord, the same gesture on the part of all, manifests a corporate reverence that arises from the shared faith of the Church that this is truly the Lamb of God, he "who takes away the sins of the world." For someone to enter the Communion procession, or to be encouraged to enter the Communion procession, without the intention of saying "Amen" to the reception of the Lord is counter-indicative to this moment and is to be strictly avoided.

For the actual distribution of Holy Communion, the dialogue is rather noble and straightforward and should be carried out with a certain deliberateness to avoid routine and indifference on the part of the priest celebrant, the Communion minister, and the communicant. For the Body of the Lord, the priest or Communion minister raises the Host slightly, showing it to the communicant, and then acclaims, "The Body of Christ." No name or other formula is added or used. Rather, the Body of Christ is the title of everyone receiving without distinction. The communicant responds, "Amen." As noted above, the communicant may receive on the tongue and, in the dioceses of the United States, in the hand. The choice belongs to the communicant. When Communion is received in the hand, the Host is placed in hands raised like a throne and is consumed completely and immediately.[15] The communion plate for the Communion of the faithful should be used.[16] It may be held by the deputed server or any member of the assembly.

More communicants today require a low-gluten host to receive the Body of Christ. This host should be brought to the altar with the other breads in a separate sacred vessel for this purpose during the Preparation of the Gifts. At the time for the distribution of Holy Communion, this communicant should not be separated out from the Communion procession but rather be communicated in the usual way and know at what station he or she will receive Holy Communion. The Blood of Christ should always be available to those who have wheat allergies. The rite for the distribution of the Blood of Christ will be discussed below.

The priest celebrant may be assisted with the distribution of Holy Communion by other priests who are available to do so. In this case, if they are not concelebrants, they are vested in a surplice or an alb with a stole the color of the day or white. They approach the altar after the invitation to Holy Communion, genuflect, and then take the sacred vessel with the Body of Christ to a Communion station where the people process toward the altar and distribute Communion in the manner just described (see GIRM 162).

In those instances when other priests are not available and there is a genuine need for assistance, Extraordinary Ministers of Holy Communion may assist. These include an instituted acolyte and members of the faithful commissioned for this purpose. The faithful are commissioned for this role according to the rite found in the *Book of Blessings*, Chapter 63. In the case of real necessity, the priest celebrant may depute a member of the faithful to assist for a single occasion according to the rite found in the *Roman Missal*, Appendix III. Extraordinary Ministers of Holy Communion, with their places in the nave, enter the sanctuary after the priest celebrant receives Holy Communion, bow to the altar, and then go near to the altar (on the sides or in front but not behind it) to receive Holy Communion themselves. After they have received Holy Communion, the priest celebrant himself hands the sacred vessel with the Hosts to them for the distribution of Holy Communion in the same manner as described above (see GIRM 162).

When the distribution of Holy Communion is completed, the priest celebrant returns to the altar, places the sacred vessel with any remaining Hosts on the corporal, and immediately consumes any of the Precious Blood that may be in the chalice. All others assisting with the distribution of Holy Communion also return the sacred vessels with the remaining Hosts to the altar. As for the remaining Hosts, the priest celebrant may consume them at the altar or take them to the tabernacle (see GIRM 163). At the tabernacle, the priest first places the sacred vessel inside it, genuflects, and then closes the door. If Holy Communion is to be taken to the sick and homebound, the most appropriate time for this to happen is from the Communion Rite of the Mass. Prior to the remaining Hosts being consumed or taken to the tabernacle after the distribution of Holy Communion, those taking Holy Communion from Mass to the homebound should approach the altar. They bow to it and then at the side of the altar receive from the priest celebrant the needed Hosts in a pyx. Either at this point or after the Prayer after Communion, those taking Holy Communion from Mass depart, without any blessing or dismissal, to carry out the proper rite with the sick and the homebound.[17]

At the altar, after the reservation of the Body of the Lord, the priest celebrant carefully collects any fragments or particles of the Body of the Lord from the corporal. While standing at the altar or at the credence table, he wipes the paten and/or ciborium with the purificator into the chalice and purifies the chalice as he prays quietly, "What has passed our lips …" The chalice is then dried with the purificator. The purification of the sacred vessels will be described more fully below. When the purification takes place at the altar, the purified sacred vessels are then taken by the acolyte or the deputed server to the credence table. It is also permitted, and recommended, when there are a large number of sacred vessels to be purified, that they be purified after Mass. In this case, they either remain on a corporal on the altar or on the credence table covered with a cloth, presumably another corporal. They are purified immediately after Mass at the altar or at the credence table.[18]

When all is completed with the reservation of the Body of

the Lord, if this takes place, and the purification of the sacred vessels, the priest celebrant may return to his chair and is seated for a period of sacred silence. The *General Instruction* and the *Order of Mass* direct that this silence be observed "for some time" and "for a while," respectively. In other words, this is a significant but not exaggerated period of corporate meditation on the reception of the Body and Blood of the Lord, carried out by all. It is also possible that, in place of silence, a psalm or canticle of praise or hymn to assist with this meditation may be sung.[19]

Following the period of silence after Holy Communion or the purification of the sacred vessels, or right after the purification if there was no period of silence, the priest celebrant from the chair or the altar prays the Prayer after Communion. At the chair, the priest celebrant, standing and facing the people, with hands joined says, "Let us pray," and then extends his hands to pray the Prayer after Communion. If the period of silence was not previously observed after the reception of Holy Communion, then there may be a brief period of silence following the "Let us pray" and before the prayer itself. The faithful conclude the prayer acclaiming, "Amen." If this prayer takes place at the altar, it is carried out in the same manner.[20] On the occasions when this prayer is sung, the musical notation given in the *Roman Missal* for the presidential prayers for the solemn tone and the reciting tone is observed.[21]

The Communion Rite for Mass with a Deacon

After the Deacon replaces the chalice on the corporal after the "Amen" of the faithful to the doxology of the Eucharistic Prayer, he continues to remain at the side of the priest celebrant for the Communion Rite. During the Rite of Peace, after the prayer and greeting by the priest celebrant, the Deacon, if it is opportune, gives the invitation to exchange the sign of peace. With his hands joined, facing the people, the Deacon announces the invariable formula, "Let us offer each other the sign of peace." The Deacon then receives the sign of peace from the priest celebrant. In turn, the Deacon may offer the sign of peace to the liturgical ministers nearest to him. The Deacon, like the priest celebrant, does not leave the sanctuary to exchange the sign of peace. The invitation of the Deacon and his accepting and giving of the sign of peace should carry the meaning of the action, expressing peace, communion, and charity.[22] If the Rite of Peace has been sung by the principal celebrant, then the Deacon should sing the invitation according to the musical notation in the *Order of Mass*.

The Deacon may assist with the Fraction of the Bread if necessary. He would also break the Hosts over a sacred vessel. After the priest celebrant has received Holy Communion, he then gives the Body and Blood of Christ to the Deacon in the usual manner. The Deacon retains the chalice, if the Body and Blood of Christ is to be given to the liturgical ministers in the sanctuary. Otherwise, after the Deacon receives Holy Communion under both kinds, he then takes a sacred vessel with consecrated Hosts to assist the priest celebrant with the distribution of the Body of Christ to the faithful. When Holy Communion is distributed under both kinds, it is the proper role of the Deacon to distribute the Blood of Christ. In this instance, when the distribution is concluded, the Deacon, standing at the altar, immediately and reverently consumes the Blood of Christ that remains in the chalice. Others who are distributing the Blood of Christ follow the same pattern. Those who are consuming the Blood of Christ at the altar after Holy Communion can assist one another, if needed.[23] As the Body of Christ is returned to the altar for its consumption or reservation, so also the Blood of Christ is returned to the altar for its consumption. The Blood of Christ must be consumed during the Communion Rite.

Following the distribution of Holy Communion, the priest celebrant and Deacon return to the altar with their sacred vessels. The Deacon may assist with consuming the Body of the Lord or taking the Body of the Lord to the tabernacle for reservation, if necessary. The priest celebrant goes to his chair. The Deacon collects any fragments or particles that may be on the paten or corporal and then takes all the sacred vessels, including the chalice, to the credence table to purify them as described above. A Deacon does not purify at the altar; rather he carries out the purification at the credence table and arranges the sacred vessels in a fitting manner. When a Deacon assists at Mass, it is also permitted for the sacred vessels to be purified after Mass. In this case, they remain on a corporal on the credence table covered with a cloth and then are purified immediately after Mass by the vested Deacon.[24] According to the *Order of Mass*, only the priest prays "What has passed our lips" during the purification of the sacred vessels.[25]

The Communion Rite for Concelebrated Mass

The principal celebrant with hands joined gives the introduction to the Lord's Prayer. Then he extends his hands as usual, and the concelebrant does the same as they pray together the Lord's Prayer with the faithful (see GIRM 237). The "Deliver us" follows as usual, prayed by the principal celebrant with hands extended. The concelebrant, together with the faithful, acclaims after the embolism the doxology, "For the kingdom" (see 238). For the Rite of Peace, the invitation, "Let us offer each other the sign of peace," is given by the Deacon. However, if there is no Deacon, then the concelebrant gives the invitation from his place at the altar, or he may move to a suitable place for amplification. The concelebrant receives the sign of peace from the principal celebrant before the Deacon receives it, if he is present (239). During the Fraction of the Bread, the concelebrant and the Deacon, if present, may assist the principal celebrant with the breaking of Hosts for a large number of concelebrants and the faithful (240).

The concelebrant and the Deacon break the Hosts over a sacred vessel. The principal celebrant carries out the commingling as usual. He alone, with hands joined, prays quietly one of the two preparation prayers for Holy Communion: "Lord Jesus Christ, Son of the living God ..." or "May the receiving of your Body and Blood ..." (see 241).

A concelebrant must receive the Body and Blood of the Lord consecrated at the Mass he is concelebrating. The *General Instruction* outlines several ways for the concelebrant (or concelebrants) to receive Holy Communion. In each of the possible ways outlined, the reception of Holy Communion by a concelebrant maintains the theological and liturgical foundation of the Concelebrated Mass. The concelebrant is uniquely united to the role of the principal celebrant who offers the Sacrifice in the person of Christ (see 93). The concelebrant receives Holy Communion when the principal celebrant receives, in the same manner, near or at the altar, before the faithful receive.

The first way presented in the *General Instruction* is the most common and seems most suitable when there are one or a few concelebrants surrounding the altar. After this, if a Deacon is present, the principal celebrant gives him the Body and Blood of Christ:

> Once the prayer for Communion has been said, the principal celebrant genuflects and steps back a little. Then one after another the concelebrants come to the middle of the altar, genuflect, and reverently take the Body of Christ from the altar. Then holding it in their right hand, with the left hand placed underneath, they return to their places. However, the concelebrants may remain in their places and take the Body of Christ from the paten held for them by the principal celebrant or held by one or more of the concelebrants passing in

> front of them, or they may do so by handing the paten one to another, and so to the last of them.
>
> Then the principal celebrant takes a host consecrated in the same Mass, holds it slightly raised above the paten or the chalice, and, facing the people, says the *Ecce Agnus Dei* (Behold the Lamb of God). With the concelebrants and the people he continues, saying the *Domine, non sum dignus* (Lord, I am not worthy).
>
> Then the principal celebrant, facing the altar, says quietly, *Corpus Christi custodiat me in vitam aeternam* (May the Body of Christ keep me safe for eternal life), and reverently receives the Body of Christ. The concelebrants do likewise, giving themselves Communion. After them the Deacon receives the Body and Blood of the Lord from the principal celebrant. (242–244)

Before the principal celebrant gives the invitation to Holy Communion, the concelebrant comes to the altar and reverently takes the Host from the paten. Or, the principal celebrant or another concelebrant, but not the Deacon, may present the paten with Hosts, or the paten may be passed among them. If the concelebrant approaches the altar, he genuflects first. The concelebrant does not show his Host in the manner of the principal celebrant for the invitation to follow. Rather, the concelebrant holds the Host in his right hand, with his left hand under his right hand. The concelebrant consumes the Host as the principal celebrant does. After this, if a Deacon is present, the principal celebrant gives him the Body and Blood of Christ. The manner for the reception of the Body of the Lord by concelebrants should be determined beforehand and not be decided during the Communion Rite.

The reception of the Blood of Christ for the concelebrant, which must take place, may happen in four possible ways: drinking directly from the chalice, intinction, with a tube, or with a spoon (see 245). The use of a tube or spoon is rare in the dioceses of the United States. The more common form is for the concelebrant to drink directly from the chalice. There are three procedures that may be followed when the concelebrant drinks directly from the chalice:

> a) The principal celebrant, standing at the middle of the altar, takes the chalice and says quietly, *Sanguis Christi custodiat me in vitam aeternam* (May the Blood of Christ keep me safe for eternal life). He consumes a little of the Blood of Christ and hands the chalice to the Deacon or a concelebrant. He then distributes Communion to the faithful (cf. nos. 160-162).
>
> The concelebrants approach the altar one after another or, if two chalices are used, two by two. They genuflect, partake of the Blood of Christ, wipe the rim of the chalice, and return to their seats.
>
> b) The principal celebrant consumes the Blood of the Lord standing as usual at the middle of the altar.
>
> The concelebrants, however, may partake of the Blood of the Lord while remaining in their places and drinking from the chalice presented to them by the Deacon or by one of the concelebrants, or even passed from one to the other. The chalice is always wiped either by the one who drinks from it or by the one who presents it. After each has communicated, he returns to his seat.
>
> The Deacon reverently drinks at the altar all of the Blood of Christ that remains, assisted, if the case requires, by some of the concelebrants. He then carries the chalice

> to the credence table and there he or a duly instituted acolyte purifies it, wipes it, and arranges it as usual (cf. no. 183). (GIRM 246–247)

The concelebrant, after the Communion of the principal celebrant, approaches the altar, genuflects, and reverently consumes the Blood of Christ. The Blood of Christ may also be brought to the concelebrant in his place by the Deacon or another concelebrant, or the chalice may be passed like the paten among concelebrants. The chalice rim is always wiped with the purificator, either by the one who drinks from it or the one who presents it. After the concelebrant receives the Blood of Christ, unless he is assisting with the Communion of the faithful, he returns to his place. The Deacon, or if he is not assisting at Mass then a concelebrant, consumes all of the Precious Blood that remains at the altar. The Deacon, or if he is not assisting at Mass then a concelebrant, then carries out the purification of the sacred vessels at the credence table as described above. All concelebrants should observe the same form for the reception of the Blood of Christ. The manner for the reception of the Blood of the Lord by concelebrants should be determined beforehand and not be decided during the Communion Rite.

When there is a large number of concelebrants, they can receive the Body and Blood together at the altar:

> The Communion of the concelebrants may also be arranged in such a way that each communicates from the Body of the Lord at the altar and, immediately afterwards, from the Blood of the Lord.
>
> In this case the principal celebrant receives Communion under both kinds in the usual way (cf. no. 158), observing, however, the rite chosen in each particular instance for Communion from the chalice; and the oth-

> er concelebrants should do the same.
>
> After the principal celebrant's Communion, the chalice is placed at the side of the altar on another corporal. The concelebrants approach the middle of the altar one by one, genuflect, and communicate from the Body of the Lord; then they move to the side of the altar and partake of the Blood of the Lord, following the rite chosen for Communion from the chalice, as has been remarked above.
>
> The Communion of the Deacon and the purification of the chalice take place as described above. (GIRM 248)

The sacred vessels need to be arranged for the Communion of the concelebrants by a Deacon or, if he is not assisting, by a concelebrant. This takes place after the Communion of the principal celebrant. The vessels with the Body of Christ are placed in the center of the altar and the chalices with the Blood of Christ are placed on the side of the altar on an additional corporal, if needed. The concelebrants first approach the Body of Christ, genuflect, and then consume the Host. After this, they approach the Blood of Christ and consume it. The *General Instruction* indicates that the manner of consumption of the Blood should be the same for all, including the principal celebrant. The Communion of the Deacons and the purification of the sacred vessels is as already described.

Communion of the concelebrants may also take place by intinction:

> If the concelebrants' Communion is by intinction, the principal celebrant partakes of the Body and Blood of the Lord in the usual way, but making sure that enough of the precious Blood remains in the chalice for the

> Communion of the concelebrants. Then the Deacon, or one of the concelebrants, arranges the chalice together with the paten containing particles of the host, if appropriate, either in the center of the altar or at the side on another corporal.
>
> The concelebrants approach the altar one by one, genuflect, and take a particle, intinct it partly into the chalice, and, holding a purificator under their mouth, consume the intincted particle. They then return to their places as at the beginning of Mass.
>
> The Deacon also receives Communion by intinction and to the concelebrant's words, *Corpus et Sanguis Christi* (The Body and Blood of Christ) replies, Amen. Moreover, the Deacon consumes at the altar all that remains of the Precious Blood, assisted, if the case requires, by some of the concelebrants. He carries the chalice to the credence table and there he or a duly instituted acolyte purifies it, wipes it, and arranges it as usual. (249)

In this instance as well, the sacred vessels need to be arranged for the Communion of the concelebrants by a Deacon, or if he is not assisting then a concelebrant, at the center or at the side of the altar on another corporal, if needed. This takes place after the Communion of the principal celebrant. A sufficient amount of Precious Blood needs to remain in the chalice for the Communion of the concelebrants. The concelebrants approach the altar, genuflect, and then intinct the Host into the chalice. They consume the Body and Blood of the Lord with the purificator under their mouth and then return to their seats. The Deacon also receives Holy Communion by intinction and afterward consumes the Blood of Christ that remains at the altar and carries out the purification of the sacred vessels as already described.

The Communion Rite for Mass at Which only One Minister Participates

For the most part the Communion Rite for Mass at which Only One Minister Participates follows the pattern described above for the Mass with the People. Once again, the directions in the General Instruction and the Order of Mass with the Participation of a Single Minister presume an ad orientem posture for the priest celebrant and the minister, even though this is usually not the case. During the Rite of Peace, the priest celebrant faces the minister and, extending and joining his hands, says, "The peace of the Lord be with you always," and the minister responds, "And with your spirit." Then without the invitation, if opportune, the priest celebrant extends to the minister the sign of peace.[26] As the priest celebrant recites the "Lamb of God" with the minister, he breaks the Host over the paten. After the "Lamb of God" is completed, the priest celebrant commingles the Body of Christ with the Blood of Christ in the chalice, saying quietly, "May this mingling ..."[27]

After the commingling, the priest celebrant continues as usual with one of the two preparation prayers for Holy Communion: "Lord Jesus Christ, Son of the living God ..." or "May the receiving of your Body and Blood ..." After this, he genuflects, takes the Host, holds it over the paten or the chalice, and faces the minister (if the minister is to go to Holy Communion) and gives the invitation, "Behold the Lamb of God." Together the priest with the minister says, "Lord, I am not worthy ..." The priest turns again to the altar and reverently receives the Body of Christ, saying, "May the Body of Christ keep me safe for everlasting life." He does the same with the Blood of Christ, saying, "May the Blood of Christ keep me safe for everlasting life." If the minister is not receiving Holy Communion, the priest celebrant, after genuflecting, takes the Host, holds it over the paten or the chalice, and says immediately, without the invitation, "Lord, I am not worthy ..." and then receives Holy Communion.[28] As the priest celebrant is receiving Holy Communion, the minister recites the Communion antiphon. After this, the priest celebrant, if the minister is to receive Holy Communion, goes to the minister with the paten and distributes Holy Communion in the usual way.[29]

After Holy Communion, the priest celebrant purifies the paten over the chalice and the chalice itself at the altar or at the credence table. The priest prays quietly, "What has passed our lips ..." as he carries out the purification. If the purification takes place at the altar, the minister carries the sacred vessels, including the corporal and purificator, to the credence table, or the sacred vessels may be arranged in a fitting manner at the side of the altar. Following the purification of the sacred vessels, sacred silence may be observed for a while. The Prayer after Communion takes place in the usual manner with a brief period of silence after the "Let us pray" if this did not take place previously.[30]

The Purification

The norms for purification as given in the *General Instruction* are rooted in the faith of the Church in the real Presence of Christ in his Body and Blood. These norms recognize that the purification of the sacred vessels is part of the Communion Rite of the Mass and not simply a matter of practicality or function. The norms address the reverent care to be shown to particles of the Host, the actual purification of the sacred vessels, and accidents with the Body and Blood of Christ during distribution:

> Whenever a fragment of the host adheres to his fingers, especially after the fraction or after the Communion of the faithful, the Priest should wipe his fingers over the paten or, if necessary, wash them. Likewise, he should also gather any fragments that may have fallen outside the paten.

> The sacred vessels are purified by the Priest, the Deacon, or an instituted acolyte after Communion or after Mass, in so far as possible at the credence table. The purification of the chalice is done with water alone or with wine and water, which is then consumed by whoever does the purification. The paten is wiped clean as usual with the purificator.
>
> Care is to be taken that whatever may remain of the Blood of Christ after the distribution of Communion is consumed immediately and completely at the altar.
>
> If a host or any particle should fall, it is to be picked up reverently; and if any of the Precious Blood is spilled, the area where the spill occurred should be washed with water, and this water should then be poured into the sacrarium in the sacristy. (278–280)

Only water should be used by the priest celebrant, the Deacon, and anyone who assists with the Body of the Lord to purify fingers during the Communion Rite. Hand sanitizers do not substitute for water and may be used outside of Mass after a hand-washing. Reverence and care should accompany the purification of the sacred vessels during the Communion Rite and outside of Mass. In both cases, the purification is a liturgical action. The response to accidents with the Body and Blood of Christ manifests the faith of the Church in the enduring Real Presence. As with every aspect of the celebration of the Eucharist, the purification of the sacred vessels points to the Mystery of Christ celebrated with them. Thus, the purification of the sacred vessels, whether it takes place within or outside of Mass, should be carried out with a reverence that belongs to the Eucharistic Mystery of Christ.

Communion under Both Kinds

The *General Instruction* provides a clear theological rationale for the distribution of Holy Communion under both kinds. Additionally, it presents the teaching of the Church that the whole Christ is received with one kind, and that the Church has the authority to determine the administration of the Body and Blood of Christ:

> Holy Communion has a fuller form as a sign when it takes place under both kinds. For in this form the sign of the Eucharistic banquet is more clearly evident and clearer expression is given to the divine will by which the new and eternal Covenant is ratified in the Blood of the Lord, as also the connection between the Eucharistic banquet and the eschatological banquet in the Kingdom of the Father.
>
> Sacred pastors should take care to ensure that the faithful who participate in the rite or are present at it, are made aware by the most suitable means possible of the Catholic teaching on the form of Holy Communion as laid down by the Ecumenical Council of Trent. Above all, they should instruct the Christian faithful that the Catholic faith teaches that Christ, whole and entire, and the true Sacrament, is received even under only one species, and hence that as regards the resulting fruits, those who receive under only one species are not deprived of any grace that is necessary for salvation.
>
> Furthermore, they should teach that the Church, in her administration of the Sacraments, has the power to lay down or alter whatever provisions, apart from the substance of the Sacraments, that she judges to be more readily conducive to reverence for the Sacraments and the good of the recipients, in view of changing condi-

> tions, times, and places. However, at the same time the faithful should be instructed to participate more readily in this sacred rite, by which the sign of the Eucharistic banquet is made more fully evident. (282)

With these theological points, the *General Instruction* further identifies the occasions, in addition to what is found in separate ritual books, for the possible distribution of Holy Communion under both kinds. This distribution is permissible for:

> a) Priests who are not able to celebrate or concelebrate Mass;
>
> b) the Deacon and others who perform some duty at the Mass;
>
> c) members of communities at the Conventual Mass or the "community" Mass, along with seminarians, and all those engaged in a retreat or taking part in a spiritual or pastoral gathering. (283)

In general, it belongs to the authority of the diocesan bishops to establish norms and to give the faculty to permit Holy Communion under both kinds. Proper catechesis, reverence for the Blood of Christ, and practical possibility underlie the decision for the reception of Communion under both kinds (see GIRM 283). In March 2002 the United States Conference of Catholic Bishops published a particular law for the dioceses of the United States titled, *Norms for the Distribution and Reception of Holy Communion under Both Kinds in the Dioceses of the United States of America*. These Norms are in two parts. The first part gives a theological presentation on "Holy Communion: The Body and Blood of the Lord Jesus." The second part lists the "Norms for the Distribution of Holy Communion under Both Kinds." These same norms are inserted as additional front matter in the third edition of the *Roman Missal.*

These norms confirm the manner for the distribution of Holy Communion as found in the *General Instruction*:

> When Communion is distributed under both kinds:
>
> > a) the chalice is usually administered by a Deacon or, in the absence of a Deacon, by a Priest, or even by a duly instituted acolyte or another extraordinary minister of Holy Communion, or by one of the faithful who, in a case of necessity, has been entrusted with this duty for a single occasion;
> >
> > b) whatever may remain of the Blood of Christ is consumed at the altar by the Priest or the Deacon or the duly instituted acolyte who ministered the chalice. The same then purifies, wipes, and arranges the sacred vessels in the usual way.
>
> Any of the faithful who wish to receive Holy Communion under the species of bread alone should be given Communion in this form.
>
> For Communion under both kinds the following should be prepared:
>
> a) If Communion from the chalice is done by drinking directly from the chalice, a chalice of a sufficiently large size or several chalices are prepared. However, care should be taken lest beyond what is needed of the Blood of Christ remains to be consumed at the end of the cel-

ebration.

b) If Communion from the chalice is done by intinction, the hosts should be neither too thin nor too small, but rather a little thicker than usual, so that after being intincted partly into the Blood of Christ they can still be easily distributed. (GIRM 284 and 285)

If Communion of the Blood of Christ is carried out by communicants' drinking from the chalice, each communicant, after receiving the Body of Christ, moves to the minister of the chalice and stands facing him. The minister says, *The Blood of Christ*, the communicant replies, *Amen*, and the minister hands over the chalice, which the communicant raises to his or her mouth. Each communicant drinks a little from the chalice, hands it back to the minister, and then withdraws; the minister wipes the rim of the chalice with the purificator.

If Communion from the chalice is carried out by intinction, each communicant, holding a Communion-plate under the mouth, approaches the Priest who holds a vessel with the sacred particles, with a minister standing at his side and holding the chalice. The Priest takes a host, intincts it partly in the chalice and, showing it, says, *The Body and Blood of Christ.* The communicant replies, *Amen*, receives the Sacrament in the mouth from the Priest, and then withdraws. (284–287)

When Holy Communion is distributed under both kinds and a Deacon is assisting, the Blood of Christ is distributed by the Deacon. As in all other circumstances, the Blood of Christ is to be consumed reverently and entirely during the Communion Rite at the altar itself. The Communion ministers need not stand behind the altar to do this but rather can be at the sides or in front of the altar, similar to the places where they receive Holy Communion. The Blood of Christ can never be poured into the ground or a sacrarium.[31] The purification of the many chalices is carried out as is that of a single chalice. When several chalices are used for Holy Communion under both kinds, the main chalice should be larger than the other chalices.[32] This main chalice may always be used for the distribution of Holy Communion as well. The manner of the distribution of the Blood of Christ follows the manner of the distribution of the Body of Christ. In this case, the purification of the chalice after each communicant is not to be overlooked. The manner of the distribution of the Blood of Christ with intinction makes use of a different form: The priest says, "The Body and Blood of Christ," with the communicant possibly holding a communion paten under the mouth. The priest celebrant holds the sacred vessel with the Body of Christ and another minister holds the chalice to his side for distribution by intinction.

Instituted and Deputed Ministers and the Communion Rite

If needed, the instituted acolyte, who is an extraordinary minister of Holy Communion, may assist the priest celebrant with the distribution of Holy Communion to the faithful. After the acolyte receives the Body and Blood of Christ, the priest celebrant hands him the sacred vessel with the consecrated Hosts. The acolyte goes to the station where the faithful process toward the altar and distributes the Body of Christ in the manner described above. If Holy Communion is distributed under both kinds, and in the absence of a Deacon, the acolyte may distribute the Blood of Christ in the manner described above. An acolyte may also hold the chalice with the Precious Blood next to the priest celebrant or Deacon if Holy Communion is distributed by intinction (see GIRM 191). When the distribution of the Body of Christ is completed, the acolyte returns the sacred vessel to the corporal on the altar. When the distribution of the Blood of Christ is completed, the acolyte goes and stands near the altar and consumes immediately any of the Precious Blood that remains. The empty chalice may be placed on the corporal on the altar or on the corporal on the credence table where the purification of the sacred vessels will take place (see 192).

The acolyte or deputed server assists with the purification of the sacred vessels in different ways, when the distribution of Holy Communion is completed. In the absence of a Deacon, the acolyte may take the sacred vessels from the altar to the credence table and purify them in the manner described above, making sure to wipe them clean of any particles and then to arrange them in a fitting manner. The acolyte may also purify the sacred vessels immediately after Mass. In this case, he carries them from the altar to the credence table, places them on a corporal, and covers them with a cloth until they are purified. The deputed server may bring the water and wine, if used, to the altar for the priest celebrant to purify the sacred vessels or may carry the sacred vessels to the credence table for purification by the priest immediately after Mass. In the latter case, the deputed server places the sacred vessels on a corporal and covers them. If the vessels are purified during Mass, the server arranges them in a fitting manner on the credence table (see 192).

Once the altar is cleared of the sacred vessels, if the Prayer after Communion is to take place at the chair, the acolyte or the deputed server removes the *Roman Missal* from the altar. If the Prayer after Communion is to take place at the altar, then the *Roman Missal* remains there. The corporal is carefully folded on the altar itself and then taken to the credence table. If the Deacon is present, and he assisted with the placement of the corporal at the Preparation of the Gifts, he may remove the corporal at this point. The corporal does not remain on the altar once the Communion Rite is concluded.

Conclusion

Every part of the Communion Rite is about communion in each of its many parts. This communion is anticipated with the "Sacrifice of our reconciliation"[33] that took place with the Eucharistic Prayer, a perfect reconciliation with our Father in Christ and with one another.[34] Therefore, if the theological meaning of the combined elements of the Communion Rite are to lead those celebrating into a more profound experience of communion, of reconciliation, and of union with God and one another, then they require that the ordained and the baptized have a clear grasp of their purpose and a practiced way to carry them out. The Our Father should be sung or spoken with the reverent affection of the children of God. The Rite of Peace should always seem personal and sincere, as the presence of Christ is acknowledged in one another. The Fraction of the Bread should call to mind in text and action the Body of the Lord broken for all. Lastly, the distribution and reception of the Body and Blood of the Lord, in its ordering in every aspect, should be the climax of communion with God and one another in Christ. This communion has already been accomplished by Christ with the Eucharistic Prayer, and now, with the Communion Rite, it is realized even more so among those assembled for the Eucharist. Such a profound experience of communion is intended by the Church with every celebration of the Eucharist. When the skills of the *ars celebrandi* are intentionally applied by the ordained and the baptized, the result is an artful and careful carrying out of the Communion Rite. Such an experience of communion is the perceived experience of the invisible reality.

The communion that occurs during the Communion Rite extends to the whole Christian life. In fact, many of the Prayers after Communion in the *Roman Missal* make this connection for those who receive Holy Communion at Mass. The whole of the Communion Rite, and especially the reception of Communion, moves the Christian from communion in worship to communion in living the Christian life. This Prayer after Communion is just one of many examples that illustrate this point:

> Renewed by this bread from the heavenly table,
> we beseech you, Lord,
> that, being the food of charity,
> it may confirm our hearts
> and stir us to serve you in our neighbor.
> Through Christ our Lord.[35]

The next and final chapter of this book looks at the Concluding Rites of the Mass, with a description of its several elements and directions for their celebration for each form of the Mass.

CHAPTER TEN

The Concluding Rites

This chapter looks at the Concluding Rites of the Mass. These rites have the straightforward purpose of bringing the celebration of the Mass to its conclusion. This typically takes place in a rather simple manner. However, despite the brevity of the Concluding Rites, each element should be conducted with the same care as the other parts of the Mass. In fact, the combination of informal elements (such as any announcements) and liturgical elements (such as the Greeting, Blessing, and Dismissal) requires attentiveness to the *ars celebrandi* so that the dignity of the celebration is not diminished at its conclusion. Following the description of each of the elements of the Concluding Rites, directions for each of the forms of the Mass are offered. Finally, the duties of the liturgical ministers for the Concluding Rites are outlined.

Description of the Elements of the Concluding Rites

The Concluding Rites of the Mass include four elements: 1) brief announcements, if any need to be made; 2) the Greeting and Blessing by the priest celebrant, which may take a solemn form or be preceded by a Prayer over the People, especially during Lent, depending on the liturgical time or occasion; 3) the Dismissal of the people by the Deacon or, in his absence, by the priest celebrant; and 4) the veneration of the altar with a kiss by the priest celebrant and the Deacon, if he assisted, which is followed by a profound bow to the altar by the priest celebrant, Deacon, if he assisted, and liturgical ministers (see GIRM 90). If the tabernacle with the Most Blessed Sacrament is in the sanctuary, the profound bow to the altar is replaced with a genuflection on the part of all (see 274).

Each of these four elements is intended to be rather brief, especially when compared to the elements of the other parts of the Mass. The Greeting and Blessing is the most significant of all four elements of the Concluding Rites. Therefore, it is important to keep a proper balance between the announcements and the other elements. The use of the Concluding Rites for announcements requires a judicious decision as to what is to be announced, and it requires that any announcements be succinct and to the point. The circumstances of a community, the solemnity of the occasion, or the need to communicate information to the assembly presumes a variety of content, style, and composition in the announcements. In every situation, the announcements should be fitting for a place in the Concluding Rites. Announcements may be made by anyone in the liturgical assembly. They are to be made from a place other than the ambo, which is reserved only for the reading of the word of God (see GIRM 309). If the priest celebrant makes the announcements, he can do so from his chair, the altar, or another suitable place, but not from the ambo. Often this soft element in the celebration of the Eucharist becomes the occasion for a great variety of other things, from the distribution of awards to a procession with a statue of the Blessed Mother during the month of May. Such things are not announcements, and they should properly take place following Mass.

The Blessing, as already indicated, can take a variety of forms, from the simple Blessing in the *Order of Mass* to the Solemn Blessings or Prayers over the People in the *Roman Missal*. The Solemn Blessings are arranged according to different liturgical times, for the celebration of the Saints, for the Dedication of a Church, and for the Dead. The Prayers over the People do not have any special designation except for the two appointed for feasts of saints. A Prayer over the People is appointed for each Sunday and weekday of Lent. Those for the weekdays of Lent are optional. Occasionally, the priest celebrant gives the Blessing, "In the name of the Father …" at the end of Mass. The Blessing that occurs during the Concluding Rites, however, is the blessing of God and should not be given in his name. In addition, the form for the Blessing is occasionally heard without the inclusion of the *and* between the Father and the Son and the Holy Spirit. Our faith informs us that the persons of the Most Blessed Trinity are three distinct divine persons and not simply modes of one another. The use of *and* as provided in the liturgical text authentically manifests the faith of the Church in the Triune God and should not be omitted from the Blessing.

In the third edition of the *Roman Missal*, four possible Dismissals may be used. Formerly, only one Dismissal was possible: *Ite, missa est*. This was the Dismissal included in the previous two typical Latin editions of the *Roman Missal* following the Second Vatican Council, and in the missals in use at the time of the Council and prior to it. In response to the Synod on the Eucharist, Pope Benedict XVI proposed additional Dismissals for the *Order of Mass* that would strengthen the understanding among the faithful of the connection between the celebration of the Mystery of Christ and the mission of Christians in the world.[1] So today, the priest or Deacon may dismiss the faithful with the words: "Go forth, the Mass is ended" or "Go and announce the Gospel of the Lord" or "Go in peace, glorifying the Lord by your Life" or "Go in peace."[2] The latter three are the new Dismissals, with the first being the translation of *Ite, missa est.* All four should be used interchangeably with some thought as to which is most fitting for a particular celebration emphasizing the link between the Mystery of Christ and the Christian life. The Dismissal for the Easter Vigil in the Holy Night and throughout the Octave of Easter and the Dismissal for Pentecost have only two of the four forms listed above. They include a double Alleluia, and the response also includes a double Alleluia. These Dismissals are found in the *Roman Missal* with the proper musical notation with the other texts for the Easter Vigil, and for the Vigil Mass and the Mass during the Day for Pentecost.[3] Once the Dismissal is given, the altar, which is the focal point of the entire celebration of the Eucharist, is venerated and reverenced. Kissing the altar and bowing profoundly before it acknowledges the altar as the sign of Christ and his saving Sacrifice. Only the priest celebrant and Deacon, if he assisted at Mass, kiss the altar then all the sacred and liturgical ministers bow to it. Still, as with the Introductory Rites, all the faithful are a part of this acknowledgment of this enduring sign of Christ and his gift of salvation and redemption. If a tabernacle with the Most Blessed Sacrament is located in the sanctuary, then the priest, Deacon, and liturgical ministers genuflect in adoration, and the profound bow to the altar is omitted (see GIRM 274).

The description of the Concluding Rites in the *General Instruction* and the *Order of Mass* ends with the veneration and reverence to the altar, and nothing more is said. Still, there is the long-standing practice of the Roman Rite that the recession of the priest celebrant, Deacon, and liturgical ministers is accompanied by singing by all, by instrumental music, or at times by silence. The music, texts, and instruments that are selected to accompany this recession, as with every other instance involving music during Mass, should be fitting to the celebration of the Eucharist. In this case, the recessional music extends the import of the Dismissal and further links the celebration of the Mystery of Christ and the Christian life.

Directions for the Concluding Rites

The directions for the Concluding Rites of the Mass as found in the *General Instruction* and the *Order of Mass* vary slightly with each of the four forms of the Mass. The *Order of Mass* outlines the Blessing for the priest celebrant and, additionally, provides for the Blessing when a bishop celebrates a Pontifical Mass. The use of this term here does not necessarily mean a Stational Mass but a Mass where the bishop celebrates with his miter and pastoral staff. Directions are given for the bishop to receive the miter prior to the greeting, "The Lord be with you," and to receive the pastoral staff prior to giving the actual Blessing. After the greeting and the response of everyone, "And with your spirit," the bishop continues, "Blessed be the name of the Lord," and all respond, "Now and forever." Then the bishop continues, "Our help is in the name of the Lord," and all respond, "Who made heaven and earth." Finally, the bishop blesses everyone with the words, "May almighty God bless you, the Father, and the Son, and the Holy Spirit," making the Sign of the Cross at each name of the Most Blessed Trinity, after which everyone responds with the "Amen." The *Roman Missal* first provides for this Blessing with musical notation and then again with the text for it. Thus, the *Roman Missal* expects this Blessing to be sung over being recited.[4] The simple tone is found in the *Order of Mass*, and the solemn tone is found in Appendix I of the *Roman Missal*, "Various Chants for the Order of Mass."

The Concluding Rites for Mass without a Deacon

The directions for the Communion Rite of the Mass allow for the Prayer after Communion to take place at the priest celebrant's chair or at the altar.[5] If the priest celebrant prays the Prayer after Communion at the priest celebrant's chair, he remains at the chair for the Concluding Rites. If the priest celebrant prays the Prayer after Communion at the altar, he remains at the altar for the Concluding Rites. Once the Communion Rite of the Mass concludes with the Prayer after Communion, then and not before the Prayer after Communion brief announcements may be made.[6] The *Order of Mass* further emphasizes that these announcements are made only if necessary.[7] It sometimes happens, most likely only because everyone is already seated, that announcements follow the distribution of Holy Communion. This practice shows a complete disregard for the purpose of this period after Holy Communion, which should be reserved for silence or a hymn of praise, leading directly to the Prayer after Communion. If the announcements that begin the Concluding Rites are truly brief, it is not necessary for everyone to be seated for them between the Prayer after Communion and the Blessing which follows them.

Once the announcements take place, if there are any, the Blessing follows. Interestingly, the *Order of Mass* speaks of the Greeting and Blessing as the Dismissal.[8] Additionally, this is also a point in the *Order of Mass* when the priest is directed to face the people. As previously mentioned, this follows from the rubrics for the Liturgy of the Eucharist which have the priest and people *ad orientem* together. Nevertheless, with every Greeting the priest celebrant extends his hands as he says, "The Lord be with you," and closes them as the faithful respond, "And with your spirit." The gestures are precise for the actual Blessing. The priest celebrant's hands are joined for the faithful's response to the Greeting. Before he gives the Blessing, he places his left hand on his breast and then raises his right hand as he says, "May Almighty God bless you," and then makes the Sign of the Cross over the faithful as he continues with the words, "the Father, and the Son, and the Holy Spirit," to which all respond, "Amen."[9] As already described, the *Roman Missal* provides an expanded form of the Blessing, such as Solemn Blessings or Prayers over the People, for certain days and occasions.[10] When the Solemn Blessing is used, after the Greeting, the priest celebrant gives the invitation, "Bow down for the blessing." Everyone except for the priest celebrant should bow until the conclusion of the blessing itself. Then, with his hands extended over the faithful, he prays the four parts of the Blessing with the faithful responding to all four parts with "Amen." During the actual blessing of the people, the priest celebrant makes the Sign of the Cross as usual at the names of the Most Blessed Trinity.[11] When the Prayers over the People are used, likewise after the Greeting, the priest celebrant gives the invitation, "Bow down for the blessing." Then with his hands extended over the faithful, he prays the Prayer over the People with the faithful responding, "Amen." With the Solemn Blessing and the Prayer over the People, the priest celebrant then adds, making the Sign of the Cross at the names of the Most Holy Trinity, "And may the blessing of almighty God, the Father, and the Son, and the Holy Spirit, come down on you and remain with you for ever," and the faithful respond, "Amen."[12] In a Ritual Mass, the priest celebrant adds, "And may almighty God bless all of you, who are gathered here/gathered for these sacred rites, the Father, and the Son, and the Holy Spirit."[13]

Once the priest celebrant has given the blessing, then with his hands joined (again the *Order of Mass* speaks of him facing the people), he announces one of the four forms of the Dismissal to send the faithful forth from Mass, to which they all respond, "Thanks be to God."[14] There is no need, nor is it permitted, to add anything to this Dismissal. For the priest celebrant to say something like "Have a great day, everyone" unnecessarily dilutes the impact of the Dismissal which seeks to link the celebration of the Eucharist as it flows into the Christian life. Such pedestrian statements should be avoided.

The *Order of Mass* itself provides the solemn tone for the Greeting, Blessing and Dismissal. The simple tone for these same for these same parts is also found in Appendix I of the *Roman Missal*, Various Chants for the Order of Mass. The *Order of Mass* itself provides the solemn and simple tones for the Greeting, Blessing, and Dismissal. The same tone, solemn or simple, should be used consistently throughout the celebration of the same Mass so there is unity with the musical genre.[15]

Once the faithful respond to the Dismissal with their "Thanks be to God," the priest celebrant goes to the altar and venerates it with a kiss, either placing his hands on the altar or with his hands joined. This veneration can take place on either side of the altar. After the veneration, the priest celebrant stands before the altar and makes a profound bow to it along with the liturgical ministers who served the Mass. After this, all recess.[16] If another liturgical action follows the celebration of Mass, such as exposition of the Most Blessed Sacrament or a procession with the Most Blessed Sacrament, then all the elements of the Concluding Rites, namely, the Greeting, Blessing, and Dismissal, are omitted.[17]

The Concluding Rites for Mass with a Deacon

The Deacon may make the announcements to the people if there are any to be made. He can do this at the side of the priest celebrant or at another suitable place other than the ambo. The priest celebrant always has the option of making the announcements himself, even when a Deacon is assisting (see GIRM 184). If the priest celebrant makes use of the Solemn Blessing or the Prayer over the People, it belongs to the Deacon to give the invitation, "Bow down for the blessing." The Deacon also bows his head for the Blessing. After the Deacon and everyone responds to the Blessing with the "Amen," the Deacon, facing the people directly and with his hands joined, announces one of the four forms of the Dismissal.[18] Once the Dismissal is announced and the faithful have responded, the priest celebrant and the Deacon venerate the altar together with a kiss and then bow profoundly to the altar. The Deacon recesses at the side of the priest celebrant (see 186). When it is fitting, the Deacon sings the invitation to the expanded Blessing and the Dismissal according to the tones provided in the Order of Mass or Appendix I of the *Roman Missal*, Various Chants for the Order of Mass.

The Concluding Rites for Concelebrated Mass

In the Concelebrated Mass, the Concluding Rites are carried out as with the Mass without a Deacon. The concelebrant remains standing at his place. The principal celebrant greets, blesses, and dismisses everyone (see 250). If a Deacon is assisting at this form of the Mass, then he gives the invitation for the Solemn Blessing or the Prayer over the People and dismisses the faithful. If a Deacon is not present, the concelebrant assumes the role of the Deacon, and gives the same invitation and dismisses the faithful from his place, or he may move to a more suitable location within the sanctuary, especially for amplification (208). Only the priest celebrant, and the Deacon if assisting, venerates the altar with a kiss in the Concelebrated Mass. The concelebrant bows profoundly to the altar from his place as the principal celebrant venerates the altar (251).

The Concluding Rites for Mass at Which only One Minister Participates

In the Mass at Which only One Minister Participates, the Concluding Rites are carried out in the same way as Mass without a Deacon. However, in this form of the Mass, when there is no assembly, the Dismissal is omitted. After the Blessing, the priest celebrant venerates the altar with a kiss. Finally, the priest celebrant and the liturgical minister bow profoundly to the altar and then recess.[19] If a Deacon assists at this form of the Mass, there is still no Dismissal, and he venerates and bows profoundly to the altar along with the priest celebrant.

Instituted and Deputed Ministers and the Concluding Rites

During the Concluding Rites, the acolyte or the deputed server can also make the announcements. If the priest celebrant needs the *Roman Missal* for the text of the expanded Blessing, the acolyte or deputed server holds it for him — that is, if the priest celebrant is not at the altar for the Concluding Rites. It makes sense that the acolyte or deputed server is in place before the priest celebrant for the whole of the expanded Blessing through to the response of the "Amen." Once again, this demonstrates the unity of a liturgical action. In this instance the acolyte or deputed server is not expected to bow or to make the Sign of the Cross. Once the Dismissal is concluded, the acolyte or deputed server bows to the altar along with the priest celebrant and the Deacon, if he assisted at the Mass. The acolyte or deputed minister recesses as well, but ahead of the priest celebrant and Deacon.[20]

Although no directions are given in either the *General Instruction* or the *Order of Mass* for the liturgical ministers as they recess except for their reverence to the altar, according to common practice whatever led the procession in the Entrance is likewise carried and leads as the liturgical ministers recess. This means that the processional cross and candles are carried by the liturgical ministers ahead of the priest celebrant and the Deacon, if he assisted at Mass. The *Book of the Gospels* is not recessed, since it has already been used for the celebration during the Liturgy of the Word.[21] Likewise, the thurible is not typically a part of the recessional, since it also has served its role during the course of the celebration of the Eucharist.

Conclusion

Oftentimes, even on solemn occasions, the Concluding Rites are carried out hastily and with little seriousness, especially when there are announcements. If the Greeting and Blessing is to stand out in each form of the Mass as the most significant element of the Concluding Rites, then the *ars celebrandi* must govern these rites as well. The Greeting once again indicates that these rites are the action of Christ the Head and his Body. The artful and careful rendering of these rites continues to evoke the liturgical participation of all as the Mass concludes, and it bridges for everyone the celebration of the Mystery of Christ in the Eucharist with the living out of this same Mystery in the Christian life.

Conclusion

The celebration of the Eucharist is an action of Christ and his Church. Christ allows, through the working of the Holy Spirit, the ordained and the baptized to be his sacramental head and body for the worship of the Father in the divine event of his saving death and resurrection. Assuming the sacramental headship of Christ and membership in his Body is not something that simply occurs on a spiritual level; rather, it includes the whole of each person — the ordained and the baptized. Everyone in the liturgical assembly participates in the Sacred Mysteries with body, mind, heart, and soul. The *ars celebrandi* directs this encounter so everyone and every part of their person can carry out their respective roles in an artful and careful manner. The use of this skill, the *ars celebrandi*, on the part of everyone is the work of constant formation and review for their authentic and full participation in the Eucharist. This book is an effort to advance this formation and review for the ordained and baptized.

The *ars celebrandi* holds the promise — when the Eucharist is indeed celebrated with renewed fidelity to its descriptions and directions in the *General Instruction of the Roman Missal* and the *Order of Mass* — to be a fruitful engagement with Christ and the Mystery of our redemption and salvation. This book seeks to promote and develop the *ars celebrandi* for the ordained and the baptized as they regularly celebrate the Eucharist. However, in truth, the baptized depend in many ways upon the ordained for the full benefit of the *ars celebrandi* — a deepening of the encounter with the Paschal Mystery of Christ in the Eucharist. When the bishop, the priest, and the Deacon are compelled by faith and humility to serve the Mystery of Christ so as to worship the Father and lead others in this same worship, then the baptized are led and encouraged to do the same.

A commitment to the *ars celebrandi* in the celebration of the Eucharist brings additional benefits, particularly a deeper participation in the Mystery of Christ. Among these benefits is a celebration marked by beauty, an objective beauty that can be recognized by all, a beauty that inspires reverence as God reveals himself through the Paschal Mystery of his Son. The celebration of the Mass intentionally guided by the *ars celebrandi* heightens the evangelical character of the Eucharist. Christ's accomplishment of our redemption in the Eucharist becomes even more apparent and so too the desire to respond with lives blessed by the immeasurable mercy of God. A focus on the *ars celebrandi* by the ordained and the baptized during the celebration of the Eucharist supports a liturgical approach to the Christian life — a liturgical spirituality. When every effort is spent in the course of the Eucharist to enter into the divine event of the death and resurrection of Christ in an artful and careful manner, everyone is better disposed to receive the abundant graces flowing from Mass and led to a deeper and more conscious communion in the dying and rising of the Savior.

The *ars celebrandi* establishes a quality of charity and justice with regard to the celebration of the Eucharist. The style and shape of the Mass is not determined by any one person or for any one circumstance. Rather, when the aim of the ordained and the baptized is to celebrate the Mystery of Christ according to the directions and descriptions of the Church, everyone is served with equal love, and right worship takes place.

Most of all, the *ars celebrandi* protects the Godwardness and givenness of the Eucharist, which is a celebration of the Mystery of Faith for the praise and glory of God, received from the Church for the holiness of all God's people.

Acknowledgments

When I was first invited to write on the *ars celebrandi*, I asked Monsignor John Miller for some of his thoughts on the topic.

Monsignor Miller gave over his entire priestly life in explicit service to the Sacred Liturgy, as a priest graduate student during the years immediately following the Second Vatican Council, as the secretary of the archdiocesan liturgical commission, as a seminary professor, and as a pastor. In all of these aspects of engaging and presenting the Sacred Liturgy, Monsignor Miller convincingly displayed the inexplicable relationship between the celebration of the Christian Mystery and living the Christian Mystery. In fact, "liturgy is life" was one of his favorite maxims.

I was privileged to know this priest, first as a seminary student and then as a brother priest for almost forty years. The artful and careful way he celebrated the Sacred Mysteries, his own surrender to the *ars celebrandi*, mentored me profoundly. Another of his frequent maxims was "the liturgy is the rehearsal for heaven." For him, the central moment of the Eucharist was the *fractio panis*. Everything in heaven and on earth came together in this moment, inside and outside of time. This was the moment of an intense encounter with the Paschal Mystery, from which we would truly eat and drink of the actual and eternal sacrifice of Christ. With every *fractio panis* in the celebration of the Liturgy and with our living it out, the more and more we were being prepared for this same event in glory.

Monsignor Miller offered me several pages of thoughts on the topic of the *ars celebrandi*. However, none of these thoughts compare to the witness of his priestly life on the topic. I dedicate this work to him.

This book has its beginnings in several presentations and conferences around the country over the past several years to clergy and the lay faithful on the significance of the *ars celebrandi*, especially as a compelling way to encounter the Saving Mystery of Christ in the celebration of the Eucharist. Along the way, many people have helped me in one way or another to bring this book to completion. I thank them so very much for their support, encouragement, and sound advice. I am especially grateful to Kevin Thorton, Deacon Mark Dillon, Sr. Marganne Drago, SSJ, and the Sister Servants of the Holy Spirit of Perpetual Adoration at Blessed Sacrament Convent, Corpus Christi, Texas. Finally, I appreciate so very much the attention and patience shown to me by Mary Beth Giltner, Senior Acquisitions Editor at OSV Books.

Notes

Preface

1. *The General Instruction of the Roman Missal* in *Roman Missal, Third Edition* (Washington, DC: United States Conference of Catholic Bishops, 2011), 21. Subsequent citations will be cited parenthetically in the text as GIRM.

2. Benedict XVI, *Sacramentum caritatis*, February 22, 2007, Vatican .va, par. 38.

Introduction

1. *Sacrosanctum concilium* (Constitution on the Sacred Liturgy), December 4, 1963, Vatican.va, par. 10.

Chapter One: A Type of Liturgical Theology

1. *Catechism of the Catholic Church*, 1101.

2. GIRM 24 and *Sacrosanctum concilium*, par. 22.

3. *Sacrosanctum concilium*, par. 7.

4. *Roman Missal*, Third Edition (Washington, DC: United States Conference of Catholic Bishops, 2011), Eucharistic Prayer I, 92.

5. *Roman Missal.*

6. *Sacrosanctum concilium*, par. 42, and *Lumen gentium*, par. 26 and 28.

7. *Lumen gentium* (Dogmatic Constitution on the Church), par. 28, and *Presbyterorum ordinis* (Decree on the Ministry and Life of Priests), par. 2.

Chapter Two: A Pathway to Authentic Liturgical Participation

1. *Sacramentum caritatis*, par. 53.

2. Ibid., par. 38.

3. GIRM 151 and Order of Mass, 91.

4. General Instruction of the Roman Missal, no. 21 (1985 edition)

5. *Lectionary for Mass*, Introduction, Chapter IV.

6. *Ceremonial of Bishops*, Part 1, chapter 1, 1–17 and Part 2, chapter 1.

7. *Musicam sacram* (Instruction on Music in the Liturgy), March 5, 1967.

8. *General Instruction of the Liturgy of the Hours*, Liturgy of the Hours, 273.

Chapter Three: Some General Considerations

1. *Order of Christian Initiation of Adults*, "Christian Initiation, General Introduction," 18.

2. Ibid., 19.

3. *Lectionary for Mass*, Introduction, Chapter I, 10.

4. *Redemptionis sacramentum*, par. 126.

5. GIRM 332 and *Redemptionis sacramentum*, par. 117.

6. *Book of the Gospels*, Introduction, 6.

7. GIRM 319 and *Code of Canon Law* can. 924§1.

8. GIRM 320, *Redemptionis sacramentum*, par. 48, and *Code of Canon Law*, can. 924§2.

9. GIRM 322, *Redemptionis sacramentum*, par. 50, and *Code of Can-*

on Law, can. 924§3.

Chapter Four: The Forms of Celebrating Mass and Preparing for Mass

1. *Ceremonial of Bishops*, Part II, Chapter I.

2. Ibid., Part I, Chapter I, 8.

3. GIRM 252 and *Code of Canon Law* can. 906.

4. *Code of Canon Law*, can. 904.

5. Ibid., can. 919§1 and §2.

6. *Roman Missal*, Preparation for Mass, "Formula of Intent."

7. *Roman Missal*, Preparation for Mass and Thanksgiving after Mass and *Code of Canon Law*, can. 909.

8. *Sacrosanctum concilium*, par. 106.

Chapter Five: The Introductory Rites

1. Order of Mass, 6.

2. Ibid., 7.

3. *Roman Missal*, "Palm Sunday of the Passion of the Lord," 11 and 15.

4. *General Instruction of the Liturgy of the Hours*, Liturgy of the Hours, 95.

5. *Roman Missal*, Appendix I: Various Chants for the Order of Mass, "Tones for the Presidential Prayers."

6. GIRM 120 and Order of Mass, 1.

7. GIRM 121 and Order of Mass, 1.

8. GIRM 122 and Order of Mass, 1.

9. *Lectionary for Mass, Second Edition*, "Introduction to the Lectionary," 4 and 10.

10. GIRM 123 and Order of Mass, 1.

11. GIRM 124, 310 and Order of Mass, 1.

12. GIRM 124 and Order of Mass, 1.

13. *Roman Missal*, Appendix I: Various Chants for the Order of Mass.

14. GIRM 124 and Order of Mass, 2.

15. Order of Mass, 2.

16. GIRM 124 and Order of Mass, 3.

17. Order of Mass, 4, 5, and 6.

18. Ibid., 4.

19. Ibid., 5.

20. *Roman Missal*, Appendix VI: Sample Invocations for the Penitential Act.

21. Order of Mass, 4, 5, and 6.

22. *Roman Missal*, Appendix I: Various Chants for the Order of Mass.

23. Ibid., Appendix II:, Rite for the Blessing and Sprinkling of Water.

24. GIRM 51 and *Roman Missal*, Appendix II: Rite for the Blessing and Sprinkling of Water.

25. GIRM 125 and Order of Mass, 7.

26. Order of Mass, 7.

27. GIRM 126 and Order of Mass, 8.

28. Order of Mass, 8.

29. GIRM 127 and Order of Mass, 9.

30. GIRM 171, 172 and *Book of the Gospels*, Introduction, 9.

31. GIRM 50 and Order of Mass, 3.

32. Order of Mass, 7.

33. *Code of Canon Law*, can. 906.

34. GIRM 256 and Order of Mass with the Participation of a Single Minister, 1.

35. GIRM 257 and Order of Mass with the Participation of a Single Minister, 1 and 2.

36. GIRM 258 and Order of Mass with the Participation of a Single Minister, 3, 4, and 6.

37. GIRM 259 and Order of Mass with the Participation of a Single Minister, 6.

38. *Book of the Gospels*, Introduction, 9.

Chapter Six: The Liturgy of the Word

1. GIRM 55-71 and Sacred Congregation for the Sacraments and Divine Worship, *General Introduction to the Lectionary* (January 21, 1981), chapter II, section I.

2. *Book of the Gospels*, Introduction, 4.

3. *Lectionary for Mass*, Introduction, 91.

4. *Book of the Gospels*, Introduction, 8.

5. *Sacrosanctum concilium*, par. 53.

6. *Roman Missal*, Appendix V.

7. GIRM 128 and Order of Mass, 10.

8. GIRM 129 and Order of Mass, 11.

9. GIRM 130 and Order of Mass, 12.

10. *Book of the Gospels*, Introduction, 10.

11. *Lectionary for Mass*, 52.

12. Order of Mass, 10 and 12.

13. GIRM 131 and Order of Mass, 13.

14. GIRM 132 and Order of Mass, 14.

15. Order of Mass, 15.

16. *Book of the Gospels*, Introduction, 18 and GIRM 134.

17. GIRM 134 and Order of Mass, 15, 16.

18. *Book of the Gospels*, Introduction, 18.

19. Ibid., 20.

20. GIRM 134 and Order of Mass, 16.

21. *Book of the Gospels*, Introduction, 19.

22. Order of Mass, 15 and 16.

23. GIRM 136 and Order of Mass, 17.

24. Order of Mass, 19.

25. GIRM 138 and Order of Mass, 20.

26. GIRM 175 and Order of Mass, 14.

27. GIRM 175 and Order of Mass, 15.

28. *Book of the Gospels*, Introduction, 10.

29. GIRM 175 and *Book of the Gospels*, Introduction, 18.

30. GIRM 175 and Order of Mass, 15.

31. *Book of the Gospels*, Introduction, 18.

32. GIRM 175 and Order of Mass, 16.

33. *Book of the Gospels*, Introduction, 20.

34. GIRM 175 and Order of Mass, 16.

35. GIRM 175 and Order of Mass, 16.

36. GIRM 175 and *Book of the Gospels*, Introduction, 21.

37. GIRM 212 and *Ceremonial of Bishops*, "Stational Mass of the Diocesan Bishop," Part II, Chapter I, 140.

38. GIRM 261 and Order of Mass with the Participation of a Single Minister, 7.

39. Order of Mass with the Participation of a Single Minister, 7.

40. GIRM 262 and Order of Mass with the Participation of a Single Minister, 8–9.

41. GIRM 263 and Order of Mass with the Participation of a Single Minister, 10.

42. GIRM 264 and Order of Mass with the Participation of a Single Minister, 11.

43. *Lectionary for Mass*, Introduction, 52.

44. *Book of the Gospels*, Introduction, 17.

Chapter Seven: The Liturgy of the Eucharist and the Preparation of the Gifts

1. GIRM 139 and Order of Mass, 20.

2. GIRM 139 and Order of Mass, 21.

3. GIRM 140 and Order of Mass, 22.

4. GIRM 140 and Order of Mass, 22.

5. GIRM 141 and Order of Mass, 23.

6. GIRM 141 and Order of Mass, 23.

7. GIRM 142 and Order of Mass, 23 and 25.

8. GIRM 142 and Order of Mass, 24.

9. GIRM 142 and Order of Mass, 25.

10. GIRM 143 and Order of Mass, 26.

11. GIRM 144, 277 and Order of Mass, 27.

12. GIRM 146 and Order of Mass, 29.

13. GIRM 146 and Order of Mass, 29.

14. GIRM 146 and Order of Mass, 30.

15. *Roman Missal*, Appendix I: Various Chants for the Order of Mass, "Tones for the Presidential Prayers."

16. GIRM 178 and Order of Mass, 27.

17. Order of Mass with the Participation of a Single Minister, 12.

18. Ibid.

Chapter Eight: The Liturgy of the Eucharist and the Eucharistic Prayer

1. *Code of Canon Law*, can. 902.

2. Order of Mass, 32.

3. *Roman Missal*, "Chants for the Eucharistic Prayers."

4. GIRM 148 and Order of Mass, 31.

5. *Ceremonial of Bishops*, Part II, Chapter I, 155.

6. Ibid.

7. For example, Order of Mass, Eucharistic Prayer I, 89.

8. GIRM 151 and Order of Mass, Eucharistic Prayer I, 98.

9. Order of Mass, 32

10. *Ceremonial of Bishops*, Part II, Chapter I, 155.

11. Order of Mass, 33 and 34.

12. See Universal Norms on the Liturgical Year and the General Roman Calendar, 39 and 42.

13. Order of Mass, 43 and 44.

14. Ibid.,45.

15. Ibid.,62.

16. *Roman Missal*, "Sacred Paschal Triduum," 18–32.

17. United States Conference of Catholic Bishops, *Eucharistic Prayers for Masses with Children* (2011), 14.

18. *Eucharistic Prayers for Masses with Children*, 22.

Chapter Nine: The Liturgy of the Eucharist and the Communion Rite

1. Order of Mass, 124.

2. Ibid., 124–125.

3. *Roman Missal*, Appendix I: Various Chants for the Order of Mass, "The Lord's Prayer."

4. Congregation for Divine Worship and the Discipline of the Sacraments, *Circular Letter: The Ritual Expression of the Gift of Peace at Mass* (2014).

5. *Roman Missal*, Appendix I: Various Chants for the Order of Mass, "Tones for the Presidential Prayers."

6. GIRM 152 and Order of Mass, 124.

7. GIRM 153 and Order of Mass, 125.

8. GIRM 154 and Order of Mass, 126, 127, and 128.

9. GIRM 155 and Order of Mass, 129 and 130.

10. GIRM 156 and Order of Mass, 131.

11. GIRM 157 and Order of Mass, 132.

12. GIRM 158 and Order of Mass, 133.

13. GIRM 159 and Order of Mass, 136.

14. GIRM 160 and Order of Mass, 134.

15. GIRM 161 and Order of Mass, 134.

16. *Redemptionis sacramentum*, par. 93.

17. *Roman Missal*, "The Sacred Paschal Triduum, Mass of the Lord's Supper," 33.

18. GIRM 163 and Order of Mass, 137.

19. GIRM 164 and Order of Mass, 138.

20. GIRM 165 and Order of Mass, 139.

21. *Roman Missal*, Appendix I: Various Chants for the Order of Mass, "Tones for the Presidential Prayers."

22. GIRM 181 and Order of Mass, 128.

23. GIRM 182 and Order of Mass, 134.

24. GIRM 183 and Order of Mass, 137.

25. Order of Mass, 137.

26. GIRM 266 and Order of Mass with the Participation of a Single Minister, 23.

27. GIRM 267 and Order of Mass with the Participation of a Single Minister, 24.

28. GIRM 268 and Order of Mass with the Participation of a Single Minister, 25, 26, and 27.

29. GIRM 269 and Order of Mass with the Participation of a Single Minister, 28 and 29.

30. GIRM 270 and Order of Mass with the Participation of a Single Minister, 30, 31, and 32.

31. United States Conference of Catholic Bishops, "Norms for the Distribution and Reception of Holy Communion under Both Kinds in the Dioceses of the United States of America," 55.

32. *Redemptionis sacramentum*, par. 105–106.

33. Order of Mass, Eucharistic Prayer III.

34. Ibid., Eucharistic Prayer for Reconciliation II.

35. *Roman Missal*, Twenty-Second Sunday in Ordinary Time, "Prayer after Communion."

Chapter Ten: The Concluding Rites

1. *Sacramentum caritatis*, par. 51.

2. Order of Mass, 144.

3. *Roman Missal*, Easter Sunday of the Resurrection of the Lord, "The Easter Vigil in the Holy Night," 69; Pentecost Sunday, "At the Vigil Mass" and "At the Mass during the Day," 13.

4. GIRM 167 and Order of Mass, 143.

5. GIRM 165 and Order of Mass, 139.

6. GIRM 166 and Order of Mass, 140.

7. Order of Mass, 140.

8. Ibid., 141.

9. GIRM 167 and Order of Mass, 141.

10. GIRM 167 and Order of Mass, 142.

11. *Roman Missal*, Blessings at the End of Mass and Prayers over the

People, "Solemn Blessings."

12. Ibid., Blessings at the End of Mass and Prayers over the People, "Prayers over the People."

13. See, for example, *Roman Missal*, Ritual Masses, "For the Conferral of Confirmation" and "For the Consecration of Virgins."

14. GIRM 168 and Order of Mass, 144.

15. *Roman Missal*, Appendix I: Various Chants for the Order of Mass.

16. GIRM 169 and Order of Mass, 145.

17. GIRM 170 and Order of Mass, 146.

18. GIRM 185, Order of Mass, 144, and *Roman Missal*, Blessings at the End of Mass and Prayers over the People, "Solemn Blessings" and "Prayers over the People."

19. GIRM 272 and Order of Mass with the Participation of a Single Minister, 33 and 34.

20. GIRM 193 and Order of Mass, 145.

21. *Book of the Gospels*, Introduction, 22.

Index

D

G

H

I

J

K

N

O

W

About the Author

Reverend Gerald Dennis Gill, ordained a priest May 21, 1983, for the Archdiocese of Philadelphia, currently serves as the Rector of the Cathedral Basilica of Saints Peter and Paul (and the Shrine of Saint Katharine Drexel) and the Director of the Office for Divine Worship. He is additionally the Parochial Administrator of Saint Agnes-Saint John Nepomucene Parish and Saint Andrew Lithuanian Parish, both in Philadelphia. He served as parochial vicar at Nativity of Our Lord Parish, Warminster, PA, and at Our Lady of Good Counsel Parish, Southampton, PA. Father Gill completed his graduate studies in the Sacred Liturgy at the Catholic University of America in Washington, DC, and the Pontifical Liturgical Institute of Sant'Anselmo in Rome. After graduate studies he served a five-year term as the Director of Liturgy at the Pontifical North American College in Vatican City State. He is presently an adjunct professor of Sacred Liturgy at Saint Charles Borromeo Seminary in Philadelphia and the Liturgical Institute in Chicago. He lectures on the Sacred Liturgy throughout the country and has published on the Sacred Liturgy.